Western Christianity
History of the Catholic Church

Richard La Belle

BROWN ROA
Publishing Media
Dubuque, Iowa

Nihil Obstat
    Rev. Michael Savelesky

Imprimatur
    ✠Lawrence H. Welsh
    Bishop of Spokane
    6 September 1987

The Imprimatur is an official declaration that a book or pamphlet is free of doctrinal or moral error. No implication is contained therein that anyone who granted the Imprimatur agrees with the contents, opinions, or statements expressed.

Scripture Sources

The New American Bible © 1970 by the Confraternity of Christian Doctrine, Washington, D.C.

Prayers have been adapted from *Prayer Book of the Saints* (Huntington, IN: Our Sunday Visitor), *The Oxford Book of Prayer* (New York: Oxford University Press), and *Short Prayers for the Long Day* (Wheaton, IL: Tyndale Press).

Book Team

Publisher—Ernest T. Nedder
Editorial Director—Sandra Hirstein
Production and Photo Editor—Mary Jo Graham
Production Manager—Marilyn Rothenberger
Art Director—Cathy Frantz
Interior and Cover Design—Cathy Frantz

Photo credits

Bob Coyle—chapter 14
Religious News Service—chapters 5, 7, 8, 27, 38
James Shaffer—chapters 3, 6, 10, 15, 18, 21, 23, 28, 29, 30, 32, 33, 34, 35, 36, 37
Three Lions—chapters 4, 9, 11, 13, 16, 19, 20, 22, 25, 31

ISBN 0–697–02648–5

10   9   8   7   6   5   4   3   2   1

Contents

Dedication

This book is dedicated to the Rev. Joseph Donovan, S.J., who taught his students that the historian's work must always be rooted in study of the primary sources.

Section I
Early Christianity

Introduction

In about the year 30 C.E., when Jesus of Nazareth died, he had scarcely any following at all. There were only his disciples, plus a few other friends, and it appears that even these few people had difficulty understanding his teachings. But by 380 C.E., Christianity was the official religion of the Roman Empire, and hundreds of thousands of people professed to be Christian. What accounts for the dramatic rise in this new faith?

Pax Romana—period of peace, 30 B.C.E. to c.a. 180 C.E., during which missionaries, such as St. Paul, spread their message.

The **Pax Romana,** the period of peace from 30 B.C.E. to ca. 180 C.E., certainly was helpful, because Christian missionaries, such as St. Paul, had a peaceful, stable world in which to spread their message. But Christianity was not the only religion with the opportunity for growth during the Pax Romana. Other religions arose at approximately the same time, and some of these new religions attracted large followings at least for short periods of time. Only the Christian religion endured, however. It is necessary to ask, then, what kind of world Jesus entered, and precisely what kind of religion the early Christians professed. Why did the Christian faith, and it alone, attract a following and continue to grow over the centuries? Why did the Christian faith fulfill the religious needs of the Graeco-Roman world more adequately than other creeds?

There is one other question that must be considered. Christianity grew as the political authority of the Roman Empire was disintegrating. The collapse of the Empire left a "vacuum" in political authority in the West, and the Church emerged as by far the healthiest and most authoritative institution, by about 600 C.E. In the centuries that followed, Christian teachings came to be part of public policies, theories of politics, and social customs. Christianity became one of the constitutive elements in what is called "Western" civilization. It is useful to ask just what kind of Christian attitudes and values were developed during the early centuries, to be passed on to later ages.

Christianity grew as the political authority of the Roman Empire was disintegrating.

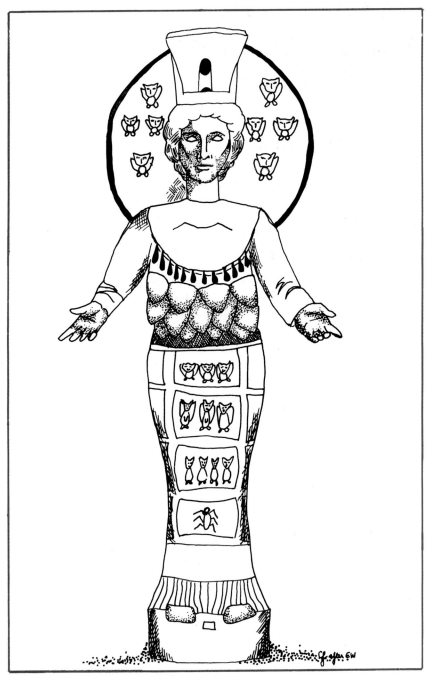

Artemis

Chapter One

The Graeco-Roman, or Pagan, World

Paganism

During the month of May, messengers were sent from the coastal city of Ephesus in Asia Minor (modern Turkey) to nearby cities and villages, to announce the coming feast of the goddess Artemis. Shortly afterward, pilgrims headed toward the city to celebrate the arrival of spring and the life-giving powers of Artemis, one of the ancient world's goddesses of fertility. Ephesus' shrine, largest of the ancient world, held up to twelve thousand people, but observers reported that as many as thirty thousand people crowded into the city each year. There, the pilgrims were treated to the spectacle of dancers, exotic animals, parading priests, and a statue of the goddess: the statue was dressed up with jewels and fine clothing. At the shrine of Artemis, priests sacrificed animals to the goddess, and many members of the crowd shared the sacrificial meal with the deity—a rare treat, as for many people it was the only time of the year when they had the opportunity to eat meat.

The rituals in honor of Artemis were duplicated, on a smaller scale, in honor of other gods and goddesses in many cities of the ancient Roman Empire. No doubt Ephesus and the other cities promoted their festivals with an eye to the money that the pilgrims would spend during their stay; but the religious sentiments of both the hosts and their guests were genuine. Many visitors went to great lengths to attend the festivals, and in moments of excitement believers in the crowds would embrace the idol (statue of the deity), or even kiss it. People paid large sums to erect shrines to their gods, leaving behind testimonials of their belief such as "I, crippled for years, make this offering to you, O Serapis, in hope that you might cure me," or "This memorial is erected to the most kind goddess Isis, through whose favor my wife has at last borne me a son."

Paganism—religions characterized by idol worship, polytheism, and the offering of sacrifices to the gods.

The religions that inspired these feelings are generally grouped together under the label **paganism.** In spite of the numerous differences between them as regards details, all the pagan religions were characterized by idol worship, polytheism, and the offering of sacrifices to the gods.

Polytheism—belief in many gods.

Polytheism, the belief in many gods, is the feature of ancient religion that might seem most surprising to a modern observer. It was not uncommon for cities, or even for small towns, to have temples for ten or more gods. All religions started locally, as each city had its own god. But many religions spread from the home city to the rest of the Empire, in one of two ways. Migration of groups of people from one city to another was common at this time, and the migrants brought their gods, and their own customs of worship, with them to the new home. Another common tendency was for Roman soldiers to serve in a faraway province, discover the frontier region's god, then bring home idols and erect shrines to the newly-found god once their tour of duty ended. The hometown people viewed any new religion with suspicion at first, but they rarely resisted the new god for long, as there was little reason to fear any new form of paganism. Generally, the pagan religions had no distinctive doctrines about the meaning of life, and no missionaries to call for a new way of living. It could be said that ancient pagans had many different gods, but only one religion: in one sense, paganism was just one religion that took dozens of different forms.

In one sense, paganism was just one religion that took dozens of different forms.

As a result, there was among the pagans an easygoing acceptance of other people's gods. A citizen of the city Rome, for example, might have devotion to Rome's patron god, Jupiter; but when making a trip to Athens to visit relatives, might still offer a sacrifice to the goddess Athena—it was the courteous thing to do. Or again, if that same traveler had a particularly strong devotion to Jupiter and there was no temple to Jupiter in the foreign city, the traveler might ask a priest of Athena to make sacrifice to Jupiter in Athena's temple.

Sacrifice

The central act of pagan worship was sacrifice, the offering of a gift to a deity. Rich people made large sacrifices, perhaps a cow or an ox, while poor people offered whatever they could afford, such as a small bird. Basic to the pagan's relationship to the god was the idea that "I give, so that you will give." I give a cow in sacrificial offering to the god, in the hope that the god will give me what I desire, such as wealth, beauty, health, children, success in politics, or a safe trip when I cross the sea.

The central act of pagan worship was sacrifice, the offering of a gift to a deity.

There was a more profound side to the sacrifice, namely the sacrificial meal. People sometimes sat down together to eat the slaughtered and roasted animal, realizing that in doing this, they were sharing the meal with their god, having communion with him. At times, the idol of the god was given a place at the banquet table alongside the guests. But if some worshippers enjoyed a sense of communion with their deity, many people's participation in the meals was on an altogether different level. At times, the banquet guests became drunk, or vomited from eating too much. The banquet with the god was considered desirable, but not necessary: during a crisis, such as a plague or an earthquake, the local priests were often instructed to sacrifice an animal, then throw it into the sea.

What was essential, in other words, was to keep the god happy. And if the god did not answer their prayers, it was not unheard of for people to spit on the idol of the god, or smash the idol to pieces. So basic was the "I give that you might give" conception that many pagans belonged to more than one religion: if it was desirable to be under the protection of one god or goddess, then protection by two or three deities was even better.

This strong emphasis upon the belief that the gods were protectors, or givers of gifts, is not surprising when one looks at the conditions under which people lived. For the great majority of people in the ancient Roman Empire, there were very few options in life, and there was the constant fear that disaster was just around the corner. Every man, for example, was expected to do what his father had done before him, and every woman was expected to do what her father planned for her. Farmers could easily be ruined by a season of bad weather, while the rare businessperson who "got ahead" could not escape the imperial tax-collectors. Everyone had his or her own "station" in life (noble, slave, merchant, plantation owner, peasant, craftsman), and it was difficult to rise to a higher station. Only the wealthy and powerful had full legal rights, such as the right to participate in city government. Those who were not blessed with riches or with noble birth were forced to turn to a powerful person for help. An influential patron could be asked for a loan, for protection from powerful enemies, or for help in legal squabbles. Many people of the ancient world viewed their relationship with a god in the same way that they understood their relationship with a patron; if asked nicely, the god could be expected to do favors. It was left to the average person, then, to care for his business or tend his farm, and pray to his favorite god so that he might escape misfortune in the future.

Philosophers

There was one other approach to dealing with the ups and downs of life. Among the few educated people of the Empire were those who followed one or another school of philosophy. **Philosophers,** such as Plato, Aristotle, Zeno, and Epicurus, speculated about the meaning of life, and raised serious questions: What is the good life? What is death? How can a person best find happiness? What is the most basic of things, from which all else comes—water or mind or spirit? From their answers to these fundamental questions, the philosophers arrived at rules for living, and each school of philosophy recommended its own characteristic way of life. In this last respect, the growth of the philosophical schools represented an important advance over the pagan religions, which had little to offer in the way of moral instruction.

Philosophers — speculated about the meaning of life.

But for all their sophistication, the schools of philosophy ultimately were not the answer to the challenges of life for the great mass of people. Philosophy appealed only to the few people who could afford an education, and could understand the philosophical concepts— perhaps less than one percent of the population. In addition, the philosophical schools shared the common pessimism of the age; they just dealt with it in a different way.

But for all their sophistication, the schools of philosophy ultimately were not the answer to the challenges of life for the great mass of people.

Many ancient religions, for example, produced myths about a golden age. In an earlier time (according to these myths), all had been good and people were happy, but as time passed, things steadily became worse. Similarly, both religious myths and philosophical writings described the passage of time as being cyclic: all things, such as the constitutions of governments, pass through a series of changes and ultimately return to their original form. There is no progress, but rather an endless cycle that produces no improvement.

One group of philosophers, called the **Stoics,** responded to this view of time by teaching that the goal of life was to seek inner calm. Given the widespread belief that every life is filled with disasters and bad luck, the Stoics taught that the key to achieving peace in one's life is to learn to accept misfortune calmly. The **Epicurean** philosophers, meanwhile, proposed that all good and evil in life takes the form of pleasure and pain. Once a person dies, he or she cannot feel either pleasure or pain; therefore, death is nothing to fear. And once a person has put aside the worst of fears, the fear of death, then he or she can be free to pursue pleasure in a reasonable way.

These and other theories of the philosophers have challenged people's minds for centuries, but most people of the Graeco-Roman world either did not understand them, or found them unsatisfactory. In fact, during the first two centuries after Jesus' death, the prevailing sense that all was not right with the world became more acute. People had long prayed to the gods to protect them from harm, but the period of the rise of Christianity was a time of almost frenzied experimentation with new religions—"I was not protected by Zeus, but perhaps I can turn to the god Mithras, or to the goddess Demeter, for the help I need." There was also an increase of belief in demons, with the hope that by appealing to a good or evil spirit, it might be possible to avert a personal disaster, or to send a disaster upon one's enemy. Practice of magic was on the rise, as was **astrology,** the study of the movements of the stars to determine what the future might hold.

Roman Leaders

If there was a single place where one might expect to find a spirit of confidence in dealing with the problems of human existence, it would be among the powerful leaders in

Rome, the capital city of the world. And in a sense there was much to admire in their approach to problems. They built an amazing network of paved roads to promote travel and commerce, they systematically drove away the pirates who had terrorized travelers on the Mediterranean Sea, and they had great success in protecting the Empire's borders against raids.

But it can hardly be said that the leaders in Rome had any greater success in coping with the challenges of personal living, or that they looked at life with a greater degree of hope. A series of emperors, for example, first promoted the practice of astrology, then outlawed it— promoted it to gain insight into what their future might be, outlawed it for fear that conspirators might gain secrets about the future and then attempt to overthrow the government. Wealthy nobles traveled the known world to visit a variety of religious shrines, with the aim of finding a deity who might favor them. There are stories about wealthy Roman nobles with chronic illnesses, who were exploited by priests who promised health in exchange for allegiance to one or another god.

Petronius, an official of the imperial government, wrote his famous work *Satyricon* about thirty years after Jesus' death, and used the book to poke fun at the powerful elite in Rome. He described a people who were so accustomed to self-indulgence and an endless round of parties that only the most extraordinary forms of entertainment could hold their attention. As one character in the book said to his party guests, "Unhappy we, man is only a breath; we shall be nothing when seized by death. So let us live while happy we may be . . . Wine lives longer than mere man, so let's get drunk."

Petronius—an official of the imperial government who wrote *Satyricon* to poke fun at the powerful elite in Rome.

Throughout the Empire there arose self-proclaimed saviors and prophets, magicians and wonder-workers who attracted large crowds, only to have people drift away from them before long, not satisfied with their teachings. The followers of Jesus of Nazareth entered into this world proclaiming beliefs which were certain to draw attention: there is only one God, who loves all persons, and calls for love in return; and true love of God takes the form of personal conversion, and right living. So distinctive a message could arise only in Palestine, home of Judaism, the only truly independent religious tradition within the Graeco-Roman world.

Summary

- Pagan religions were characterized by idol worship, polytheism, and the offering of sacrifices to the gods.

- Religions started locally and spread by either people's migrating to another town and practicing their religion there or by Roman soldiers who served in faraway provinces bringing the religions of those provinces home with them.

- People rarely resisted new religions, because there was very little to fear in any new form of paganism.

- The central act of pagan religions was sacrifice.

- People believed that the pagan gods were protectors and "givers of gifts."

- Philosophy appealed to the few people who could afford an education and could understand the philosophical concepts.

- Many people looked to Rome to find a spirit of confidence in dealing with the problems of human existence.

Prayer

Canticle of Simeon

*Now, Master, you can dismiss your servant in
peace; you have fulfilled your word.*

*For my eyes have witnessed your saving deed
displayed for all the peoples to see:*

*A revealing light to the Gentiles, the glory of your
people Israel.*

Luke 2:29–32

Discussion Questions

1. What signs suggest that the pagan
   religions of the time of Jesus were
   flourishing?

2. What three characteristics did pagan
   religions have in common, and of these
   three, which most clearly reveals the
   relationship between the pagans and their
   god?

3. What signs indicate that there was
   something "missing" in the pagan society,
   and that people were searching for
   something new?

Scale model of the ancient city of Jerusalem at the time of the second temple.

Chapter Two

Jewish Origins
of Christianity

First Christians

During the first few decades after Jesus' death,
the Christians were Jews, living mostly in
Palestine and the Jewish communities of the
eastern Mediterranean region. They
understood themselves to be Jews. They were
rarely called "Christians," and were frequently
called "Nazarenes," because their leader Jesus
had come from the Palestinian town of
Nazareth.

At that time, there was no official doctrine that
Jews were expected to follow, apart from
belief in the one God. Numerous groups
within Judaism, notably the Pharisees,
Sadducees, Essenes and Zealots, each had its
own way of understanding the religion of the
one God. Under these circumstances, the
Christians were just one Jewish group among
many, who worshipped in the synagogues and
in the Temple at Jerusalem, as did all Jews.
Like the Pharisees, they believed in the
resurrection of the dead. Like the Sadducees,
they rejected the Pharisees' interpretation of
the laws of Jewish tradition. Like the Essenes,
they looked forward to the "end times" when
God would intervene decisively in human
affairs. But unlike the Essenes, they believed
that in Jesus, God had already brought about
human salvation; for the Christians, the "end
times" were simply the culmination of God's
saving activity. And while the Essenes formed
communities in remote places of the desert to
avoid the impurity of a sinful world, the
Christians chose to live *in* the world. Like the

Christos—the Greek equivalent to the Hebrew word *Messiah.*

Zealots, the Christians emphasized belief in a "Messiah" or "Anointed One" specially sent by God. But while the Zealots believed that God would soon send a warrior-Messiah to aid His people, Christians believed that God had already sent the Messiah, namely Jesus. **Christos** (Christ), the label often given to Jesus, is the Greek equivalent to the Hebrew word *Messiah.*

Growing as it did out of the Jewish tradition, Christianity retained the fundamental characteristics of Judaism.

Monotheism—belief that there is just one God.

Growing as it did out of the Jewish tradition, Christianity retained the fundamental characteristics of Judaism. Most important was that the Christian religion, like that of the Jews, was an ethical **monotheism;** that is, both Christians and Jews believed in just one God, a God who is concerned with the way in which His people act. Twelve hundred years of experience had convinced them of God's love for them. He had sent them Moses, who led the people out of slavery and gave them a code of law; He had given them great kings, notably David and Solomon; He had given them prophets such as Isaiah and Jeremiah, who reminded the people of their obligations to God and to each other.

The teachings of Jesus came out of this tradition. Jesus taught people to follow the Ten Commandments which had been given to Israel by Moses,[1] and his great summary of how people must behave also had its roots in the literature of Israel:

Jesus' words in Mark 12:28–31
(New Testament)

A scribe asked which was the greatest commandment. Jesus replied: "Hear, O Israel! The Lord our God is Lord alone! Therefore you shall love the Lord your God, with all your heart, with all your soul, with all your mind, and with all your strength. This is the second (commandment), You shall love your neighbor as yourself."

1. Compare the original Ten Commandments, Exodus 20, with Mark 10: 17–20 and par.

Deuteronomy 6:4–6
(Old Testament)

Hear, O Israel! The Lord is our God, the
Lord alone! Therefore you shall love the
Lord, your God, with all your heart, and
with all your soul, and with all your
strength. Take to heart these words which I
enjoin on you today.

Such teachings had been revealed to the Jews
long before Jesus had begun his ministry.
Early Christianity (like the Christianity of
today) preserved the Jewish belief in
revelation. In other words, Christians believed
that God reveals Himself to His people,
especially through the words of prophets and
wise men. Certain writings, or Scriptures,
were holy because the words were inspired by
God Himself. Christians composed new
Scriptures, namely, the four Gospels, the
letters (sometimes called **epistles**), the Acts of
the Apostles, and the Apocalypse. But they
also considered the older Jewish writings to be
authoritative. The early Scriptures of the Jews
eventually came to be called the Old
Testament, while the writings after Jesus'
time were called the New Testament. From the very
beginning, the early Christians read from the
ancient Jewish Scriptures during their
religious ceremonies, and considered Israel's
written tradition to be their own.

Because of all these shared characteristics,
Christianity, like Judaism, was clearly separate
from pagan modes of thought. Nevertheless,
only a small portion of the Jewish people
converted to the Christian teachings. One
reason was that Jesus' understanding of the
Jewish Law was a threat to the ritualistic
observance with which many Jews were
comfortable. For many of the people of Israel,
being faithful to the Law was a matter of
external observances: do not work on the
Sabbath day, avoid eating the meat of unclean
animals, recite certain prayers, and so forth.
But Jesus constantly pointed toward the *spirit*

Revelation—God
reveals Himself to His
people especially
through the words of
the prophets and wise
men.

Epistle—letters
contained in the New
Testament written by
the apostles and
disciples to the early
Church.

The early Scriptures of
the Jews eventually
came to be called the
Old Testament. The
writings after Jesus'
time were called the
New Testament.

of the Law, and called for an interior change
of heart rather than an exterior observance.

Thus for Jesus, it was better to pray privately,
rather than in public as the Pharisees did; and
it was necessary to avoid not only adultery,
but also adulterous thoughts. By his own
authority, Jesus in some cases restricted the
meaning of the old Law, as when he cured
people on the Sabbath, when no "work" was
supposed to be done. And he sometimes
extended the old Law, as in the case of
divorce. To the Christians, Jesus' doctrines
represented a true fulfillment of the ancient
teachings, but to most Jews what Jesus had to
say seemed dangerous.

Who Is Jesus?

The question of the Law, then, led to the
larger question: who, or what, was Jesus? Early
Christians drew a series of titles for Jesus from
Jewish Scripture: Messiah, Prophet, the
Wisdom of God, Son of Man, even "Kyrios" or
"Lord," a title which had previously been
reserved only for God. Finally, the Christians
were entirely convinced that God had raised
Jesus from the dead. If God had raised up
Jesus, then surely these extraordinary titles
were appropriate for Jesus: he was an
authoritative figure who could modify laws,
forgive sins, and more. But if he was not all
these things, then he was only a crucified
criminal, condemned by the Jewish High
Council.

Under the circumstances of the times, the
claim that Jesus was Messiah was of particular
importance. Frustrated by Roman domination
of the Holy Land, great numbers of Jewish
people anxiously awaited a Messiah who
would liberate the Chosen People after the
fashion of David, most powerful of the ancient
Jewish kings. One religious poem from the
time shows clearly the political and military
overtones of the people's hopes:

18

> *Behold, O Lord, and raise up unto them*
> *their king, the son of David,*
> *At that time that you see, O God, that he*
> *may reign over Israel your servant.*
> *And gird him with strength, that he may*
> *shatter unrighteous rulers,*
> *And that he may purge Jerusalem from*
> *nations that trample her down to*
> *destruction.*
> *Wisely, righteously, he shall thrust out*
> *sinners from the inheritance.*
> *He shall destroy the pride of sinners as a*
> *potter's vessel.*
> *With a rod of iron he shall break into*
> *pieces all their substance.*
> *He shall destroy the godless nations with*
> *the word of his mouth; . . . (The Psalms*
> *of Solomon 17:23–27)*

It is not certain just how many of the Jews were inspired by this conception of the Messiah. But it is known that both before and after the career of Jesus, anti-Roman rebellions broke out in Palestine, and the rebel leaders were sometimes viewed as messiah-figures. One such leader even claimed, shortly before the Romans killed him, that he would part the waters of the Jordan River and lead his liberating army into the Holy Land.

Against this background, the claim that Jesus was the resurrected Messiah, the fulfillment of God's promises for the Jewish people, must have seemed incredible to many Jews. Rather than raise armies to drive out foreigners, Jesus had been a friend of lowly Gentiles[2] and women, even prostitutes and hated tax-collectors. How could he be the Deliverer who had been promised by the prophets? An even greater stumbling-block was the Cross, for in the ancient world, crucifixion was the most horrible form of capital punishment, reserved for the most lowly criminals.

2. "Gentile" was the label for any non-Jew; Jews were expected not to have any dealings with the Gentiles.

To the early Christians, the deepest issue at stake was the power of God—whether God would deliver His people in the manner which they expected, or whether salvation would come about in a strikingly new and mysterious manner. In opposition to the image of a warrior-king, the Christian writers urged that even Jesus' surprising role as suffering Savior had been foretold by the Hebrew prophets. Christians were especially fond of pointing to the prophet Isaiah, who spoke of a "servant of the Lord."

> *He was spurned and avoided by men, a man of suffering, accustomed to infirmity, one of those from whom men hide their faces; spurned, and we held him in no esteem.*
>
> *Yet it was our infirmities that he bore, our sufferings that he endured, while we thought of him as stricken, as one smitten by God and afflicted.*
>
> *But he was pierced for our offenses, crushed for our sins; upon him was the chastisement that makes us whole, by his stripes we were healed. We had all gone astray like sheep, each following his own way; but the Lord laid upon him the guilt of us all.*
>
> *Though he was harshly treated, he submitted and opened not his mouth; like a lamb led to the slaughter or a sheep before the shearers, he was silent and opened not his mouth. (Isaiah 53:3–7)*

This new understanding of the mystery of salvation showed up most clearly in St. Mark's description of Jesus' suffering and death. Mark portrayed Jesus' last hours with many references to Old Testament passages that spoke of one who was to suffer pain and insult at the hands of his people. Finally, when Jesus breathed his last, a Roman soldier—a Roman, not a Jew—was moved to declare, "Surely this man was the Son of God!"(Mark 15:39).

Such a startling change of perspective was not readily accepted by the majority of Jews. In fact, the Acts of the Apostles records several instances in which Christian leaders were seized by Jewish authorities and brought to trial (Acts 4 and 5). The Romans even had to hold St. Paul in protective custody, lest he be harmed by the crowd—one Christian, St. Stephen, had already been stoned to death by an angry mob of Jews (Acts 7; 22; 23).

Destruction of the Temple

In the meantime, continued control of the Holy Land by the Romans angered the Jewish people, who became more receptive to the ideas of the aggressively nationalistic Zealots. The period 50 to 70 C.E. saw an increase in Jewish feelings of nationalism and of resentment toward Rome. Jewish nationalism finally boiled over into open revolt, and the Romans were quick to respond. In 67 C.E., the Roman general Vespasian seized Galilee in northern Palestine, and in 70 C.E. his son Titus laid siege to Jerusalem. The impassioned inhabitants of the Holy City, along with numerous pilgrims, held out for months even though their food was running out. Finally, the Roman legions gained the city, slaughtered thousands of people, and destroyed the great Temple, a magnificent building which covered some thirty acres within the city.

The Temple had been the greatest symbol of the unity of the Jews. The Chosen People had worshipped the one God in the one Temple. Now the Temple was gone, and nonbelievers were once more firmly established in control of the land that God had promised to the Chosen. One Jewish author of the period gave expression to the feelings of his people:

Blessed is he who was not born, or he who
was born and died.
But we, the living, woe to us, because we
have seen those afflictions of Zion, and
that which has befallen Jerusalem . . .
You, priests, take the keys of the sanctuary
. . . give them to the Lord and say,
"Guard your house yourself, because,
behold,
We have been found to be false stewards."
(Baruch 10:6–7,18)

A group of learned
Pharisees assumed
leadership in the task
of forging a new form
of Judaism—a Judaism
without the Temple.
One element of the
new program was to
recommend strict
observance of the Law
as the surest way for
the Jews to maintain
identity as a separate
people in an
unfriendly world.

A group of learned Pharisees assumed leadership in the task of forging a new form of Judaism—a Judaism without the Temple. One element of the new program was to recommend strict observance of the Law as the surest way for the Jews to maintain identity as a separate people in an unfriendly world. As the Pharisees' recommendations gained acceptance, the Christians, true to Jesus' very different understanding of the Law, were viewed with increasing disfavor. In a few instances, Jewish synagogue prayers of this period included curses of those who followed Jesus of Nazareth.

The hostility, however, did not hinder the growth of Christianity. Twenty years before the fall of the Temple, the followers of Jesus had committed themselves to the task of taking their message to non-Jews. The Christian Scriptures, most of which were written during the period shortly before and after the fall of the Temple, reflected the new outlook. St. Paul made it the central point of his teaching that what saved people was not the Law, but Christ crucified. The authors of the Gospels, especially Matthew, called to mind the many times Jesus had confronted the Pharisees. And several Christian authors pointed to Old Testament prophecies which stated that because of the Chosen People's hardness of heart, the message of salvation must be carried to all nations.

Summary

• The first Christians were Jews, living mostly in Palestine and the Jewish communities of the eastern Mediterranean region.

• Christians were just one Jewish group among many, who worshipped in the synagogues and in the Temple of Jerusalem.

• Growing as it did out of the Jewish tradition, Christianity retained the fundamental characteristics of Judaism.

• Unlike many Jews, Jesus called for an interior change of heart rather than an exterior observance of the Law.

• Jewish people anxiously awaited a Messiah who would liberate them.

• Roman legions took over the city, slaughtered thousands of people, and destroyed the Temple in Jerusalem.

• Christians were received with increasing disfavor.

Prayer

Praised be the God and Father
of our Lord Jesus Christ,
He who in His great mercy
gave us new birth;
a birth unto hope which draws its life
from the resurrection of Jesus Christ from the dead;
a birth to an imperishable inheritance,
incapable of fading or defilement,
which is kept in heaven for you
who are guarded with God's power through faith;
a birth to a salvation which stands ready
to be revealed in the last days.

1 Peter 1:3–5

Discussion Questions

1. Coming out of the Jewish tradition, what beliefs did the Christians uphold that clearly set them apart from the pagans?

2. How was Jesus' approach to the Law different from that of many Jews, especially the Pharisees?

3. Chapter two states that especially as regards belief in the Messiah, the Christians were promoting a new understanding of how God operates in human affairs. What was the Christians' new understanding?

4. How did events in 70 C.E. and after hasten the split between the Christians and other Jews?

Pentecost

Chapter Three
A Catholic Church Spreads the Good News of Jesus

There were indications in the early years of Christianity that even though Jesus himself had limited his teaching activities to the area of Palestine, his followers felt called to carry his message farther. The Gospels report that at least twice, Jesus remarked about the great faith of non-Jews whom he met, and he announced that there were Gentiles who would "find a place in the banquet of God's Kingdom" (Luke 7:1–10; Matthew 8:10–12; Matthew 15:21–28). According to Matthew's Gospel, Jesus' parting words to his disciples were "Go and make disciples of all nations: baptize them in the name 'of the Father, and the Son, and the Holy Spirit.' Teach them everything I have commanded you" (Matthew 28:19–20). By the second century of the Common Era, Christians were asked to believe in "one holy catholic and apostolic Church." The word **catholic** means universal, in other words, it was a Church for all people, not just for a single race or people.

By the second century of the Common Era, Christians were asked to believe in "one holy catholic and apostolic Church," a Church for all people.

Catholic

The idea of a single faith for all people must have been difficult for the original Jewish Christians to understand. The Hebrews had believed for centuries that their God was the one true God, and that their race was God's chosen race. Non-Jews were all classified as "Gentiles," and "unclean." Jews were forbidden even to share a meal with Gentiles.

There were about four million Jews living in various cities of the Roman Empire, and there are signs that the Jewish people made efforts to bring their faith to outsiders. The maturity and sound ethical teaching of Judaism appealed to many pagans, and there are signs that pagans, sometimes called "Greek sympathizers," converted to Judaism—perhaps in fairly large numbers. Their conversion, however, did not indicate that the Jewish faith was becoming a worldwide religion; rather, it meant that converts were being made members of the Chosen People. Male converts, like all males of Israel, were set apart from other people by the physical mark of circumcision.

Not surprisingly then, the earliest Jewish Christians could not easily put aside Jewish notions of exclusiveness. But after the fall of the Temple, when the Jews were driving the Christians out of their midst, the Jewish Christians did not retire to become a little-known sect like the Essenes. In fact, Christian faith was already well rooted in Gentile communities in many parts of the eastern Mediterranean region. The original Jewish Christians, in other words, had apparently undergone a basic change of attitude before the year 70 C.E.

The Work of the Spirit

The details of this change of thinking are not known today. St. Luke, whose Acts of the Apostles in the New Testament is the most extensive record of early Christian missionary activity, portrayed the change as being the work of the Holy Spirit. Luke saw the work of the Spirit as changing the minds and hearts of people, so that they could understand what they had not understood before, and do what they had never had courage to try before. In Acts, Luke described the Spirit's powerful work in Christians' hearts by means of stories that tell about dramatic physical signs of the Spirit's presence. Most famous of these accounts is the beginning of Acts, chapter two:

*When the day of Pentecost came, it found
them gathered in one place. Suddenly,
from up in the sky there came a noise like
a strong, driving wind which was heard all
through the house where they were seated.
Tongues as of fire appeared, which parted
and came to rest on each of them. All were
filled with the Holy Spirit. They began to
express themselves in foreign tongues and
make bold proclamation as the Spirit
prompted them. Staying in Jerusalem at
the time were devout Jews of every nation
under heaven. These heard the sound, and
assembled in a large crowd. They were
much confused because each one heard
these men speaking in his own language.
The whole occurrence astonished them.
They asked in utter amazement, "Are not
all of these men who are speaking
Galileans? How is it that each of us hears
them in his native language?" . . . They
were dumbfounded and could make
nothing at all of what had happened.
"What does this mean?" they asked one
another, while a few remarked with a
sneer, "They have had too much new
wine!"*

*Peter stood up with the Eleven, raised his
voice, and addressed them: "You who are
Jews, indeed all of you staying in
Jerusalem! Listen to what I have to say.
You must realize that these men are not
drunk, as you seem to think. It is only nine
in the morning! No, it is what Joel the
prophet spoke of: 'It shall come to pass in
the last days, says the Lord, that I will
pour out a portion of my spirit on all
mankind: your sons and daughters shall
prophesy. . . .Then shall everyone be
saved who calls on the name of the Lord.' "
(Acts 2:1–8, 12–17, 21)*

The first believers' new-found ability to speak
in foreign languages symbolizes the fact that
the Christians felt called to travel out of their

homeland to spread the Gospel (a word meaning "Good News") of Jesus Christ. And all signs are that they did just that: according to tradition, the original disciples of Jesus traveled as far west as Spain, and as far east as Parthia and India with their Good News. The conclusion of the Pentecost story shows Peter, with new-found boldness, proclaiming his message to the onlookers. That boldness, too, is the work of the Spirit.

Yet at this point in Acts, Peter's speech was to fellow Jews. A second story shows the Spirit prompting Peter to be the first to take the message to the Gentiles. According to Acts 10, a Roman soldier named Cornelius had a vision in which an angel told him to send some men to a nearby town, to ask Simon Peter to come see him. Meanwhile, the angel helped prepare Peter for the visit by appearing to Peter in a vision. He instructed Peter to slaughter and eat animals that Jews considered unclean. As Peter protested, the angel responded that "What God has purified, you are not to call unclean."

"What God has purified, you are not to call unclean" (Acts 10:15).

Peter and his Jewish-Christian friends soon met Cornelius and his Gentile friends—it must have been a very uncomfortable situation. The apostle then remarked that Jews were not supposed to associate with Gentiles, but God had shown him that no person should be called impure. Peter then addressed the people with words which announced that the Christian Church was becoming more Catholic: "I begin to see how true it is that God shows no partiality. Rather, the man of any nation who fears God and acts uprightly is acceptable to him" (Acts 10:34–35). The apostle went on to preach about Jesus, and when the Holy Spirit descended upon these Gentiles, Peter took it as a sign that he should baptize them. In this way, the Christian Church began to be a Church of all people rather than a sect within Judaism.

The chief figure in the first half of Acts is
Peter, but the second half puts the spotlight
on St. Paul, who in his own letters refers to
himself as "The apostle to the Gentiles."[1] Both
the letters and Acts report that Paul had been
a Pharisee, and a persecutor of Christian Jews.
But about two years after Jesus' death, Paul
converted. He ceased persecuting the
Christians and became one of them.
Eventually, he attached himself to the
Christian community in Antioch (Asia Minor),
and along with his companion Barnabas,
began preaching.

A Crucial Decision

Having abandoned his Pharisaic beliefs, Paul
was convinced that what saved people was not
the Law, but Christ—and foremost among the
Jewish laws was the requirement of
circumcision. The Gentiles whom he
converted in Asia Minor were not circumcised,
and his new policy brought about a crisis in
the young Church. Exactly what took place is
not clear, because the two sources for the story
(Acts 15 and Paul's Galatians 2) disagree on
details. But the two sources do agree that in
the year 48 or 49 C.E., Paul and Barnabas
traveled to Jerusalem, where they met with
leaders of the Christian movement. Some
Christians, strong defenders of the Law, took
issue with Paul's refusal to circumcise his
Gentile converts; either they raised a fuss once
the meeting had started, or they had
complained earlier, and the meeting was
called specifically to deal with his complaint.
In either case, Paul's policy was upheld by the
leaders in Jerusalem.

1. Paul speaks of his mission specifically to the
Gentiles in Galatians 2:9. The word *apostle* is
derived from a Greek word meaning "one who is
sent forth." In some cases, the word is used to refer
only to the original twelve disciples of Jesus, but
Paul insisted that he, too, was called by Jesus, and
sent forth to preach the Good News.

After this important meeting, often called the "Assembly of Jerusalem," the issue did not die out completely. In fact, in spite of having been in agreement over the circumcision question, Paul and Peter later got into a squabble about whether Jewish and Gentile converts should eat meals together (Galatians 2:11–14). But a fundamental change had taken place. Some of the early Christians continued to take their message to Jews first of all, but the Church increasingly leaned toward Paul's belief that "There is neither Jew nor Greek, Scythian nor barbarian, slave or free, but Christ is in all and all are in Christ."(Colossians 3:11)

On a missionary journey in Asia Minor, Paul was "driven by the Spirit" into northeastern Greece, where he had astounding success among the Gentiles of Philippi and Thessalonika. These two cities lay along a great Roman highway that led directly to Rome itself. It is likely that Paul, moved by the ideal of preaching Christ to all, was hoping to travel to the capital of the Empire. Circumstances, however, forced him to turn south into Greece, where his greatest achievement was the establishment of a large Christian community in Corinth.

His subsequent career revealed his powerful missionary drive: he passed back and forth between Greece and Asia Minor, nearly drowned at sea, made harrowing escapes from would-be persecutors, and spent time in jail. The last reliable evidence about his life (from the later chapters of Acts) shows that he ultimately reached Rome. There, according to tradition, he and St. Peter met death at the hands of persecutors. Another less accepted tradition is that he made it safely to Spain, where he continued to preach. Regardless of how he ended his life, it is significant that in his last writing, the Letter to the Romans, he said that he was eager to visit the Romans' little Christian community before continuing west to Spain. According to Paul, all persons— Jew and Gentile alike—were sinners before

God; therefore, Jesus had died and risen to save all people, and Paul's task was to carry the message of Jesus' life, death, and resurrection to all. "I am under obligation to Greeks and non-Greeks, learned and unintelligent alike" (Romans 1:13–14; see also 15:14–33).

Paul's career is by far the best known, but there were others who were similarly active. His last letter, for example, was addressed to a little Roman community founded by an unknown missionary. While the exact details about their work are not known, the apostles Bartholomew and Simon the Zealot probably were killed while preaching the Gospel in Armenia. St. Philip preached in Phrygia, and tradition has it that St. Thomas may have gone to Parthia and even as far as India. The Age of the Apostles came to an end about the year 100, when St. John, the last of the apostles, died. By that time, there were Christian communities in Palestine, Asia Minor, Greece, Italy, Spain, the south coast of Gaul, and the north coast of Africa. The largest groups of Christians seem to have grown up in the provincial capitals of the Roman Empire, namely, Alexandria, Antioch, Jerusalem, Corinth, Ephesus and Philippi, in addition to the city of Rome itself.

As the apostles preached to the world, one other aspect of their faith showed up strongly. If indeed Christianity was the true religion and its God the only true God, then belief in other gods, such as the popular Isis and Osiris of Egypt, was wrong. Christianity soon showed itself to be a nontolerant faith. If there were but one God, then He should be revealed to all persons, not just to the Hebrews; and if He were truly the one God, then there could be room for no others. Such views ultimately put Christianity into conflict with the pagan world.

Summary

• By the second century of the Common Era, Christians believed in "one holy catholic and apostolic Church."

• Jewish Christians could not easily put aside notions of exclusiveness.

• The Christians felt called to spread the Good News of Jesus Christ beyond their homeland.

• Circumcision became an issue as Gentiles were being converted to Christianity.

• Paul was one of the first great missionaries. He preached that all people—Jew and Gentiles alike—were the same in God's eyes.

• The fact that Christians believed there was but one true God eventually put Christianity into conflict with the pagan world.

Prayer

*Give thanks to the Father for having made you
worthy to share the lot of the saints in light. He
rescued us from the power of darkness and brought
us into the kingdom of his beloved Son. Through
him we have redemption, the forgiveness of our
sins.*

*He is the image of the invisible God, the first-born
of all creatures. In him everything in heaven and on
earth was created, things visible and invisible. . . .*

*He is before all else that is. In him everything
continues in being.*

Colossians 1:12–17

Discussion Questions

1. How did the stories of the Pentecost and
   the baptism of Cornelius in Acts show the
   Spirit's work in making the Jewish
   Christians more "catholic" in their
   outlook?

2. What was the issue at stake in the famous
   meeting in 48 or 49 C.E., and what was the
   outcome?

3. Who is the most famous Christian
   missionary, and where did he go?

Peter at the house of Cornelius

Chapter Four

Community Life of the Early Christians

One of the most striking features of early Christianity was the drive to go forth and spread the Good News to others. The other remarkable feature of Christianity was that from the very first, it was a religion of a united people—a community. Acts chapter two, which begins with the story of the Spirit's empowering the apostles to spread the Gospel, ends with an account of the early Christians' community life:

Christianity was a religion of a united people—a community.

> *They devoted themselves to the apostles' instruction and the communal life, to the breaking of bread and the prayers. A reverent fear overtook them all, for many wonders and signs were performed by the apostles. Those who believed shared all things in common; they would sell their property and goods, dividing everything on the basis of each one's need. They went to the temple area together every day, while in their homes they broke bread. With exultant and sincere hearts they took their meals in common, praising God and winning the approval of all the people. Day by day the Lord added to their number those that were being saved. (Acts 2:42–47)*

All the fundamentals of Christian community life show up in this description: leadership by the apostles, shared meals, worship together, even the sharing of material things. Although it cannot be known for certain, "breaking bread together" may refer to the celebration of the Eucharist by the little community. In all these ways, the first Christians were being true to the teachings of Jesus, who said that "I pray also for those who will believe in me through their word, that all may be one as you, Father, are in me, and I in you; I pray that they may be one in us, that the world may believe that you sent me" (John 17:20–21).

Exactly how the earliest Christian communities were formed is not known, but both Paul's letters and the Acts refer to Christian "house-churches" or "households." The household was the basic unit of Graeco-Roman society. It usually consisted of a father-figure or patron, his wife and children, perhaps a few grandparents, the wives and children of married sons, even the father-figure's employees and slaves—twenty or more people in all. It appears that Paul converted the head of a household, with the result that the entire group of people were drawn to the new faith.

Members of the Christian household still maintained ties with their pagan friends and co-workers, but were encouraged to have special care for each other. Like the typical Graeco-Roman household, the Christian house-church may have retained some of its hierarchical structure—that is, there were different grades or statuses for people, from the wealthy persons of noble birth at the top, down to the poor and the slaves at the bottom. But as Paul's letters indicate, even if there were differences of status, a new sense of human dignity was crucial to life in a Christian house-church. The Greek word **ekklesia,** which is translated as "Church" in English-language Bibles, bespeaks this sense of the dignity of all believers: the word means "assembly" but specifically referred in Greek society to the assembly of those who had the privileged status of being able to vote and to shape a city's future. Paul's borrowing of this term reflected his belief that all members of the Church community were endowed with special dignity.

Ekklesia—A Greek word meaning "assembly" specifically referred in Greek society to the assembly of those who had privileged status. St. Paul's borrowing of this term reflected his belief that all members of the Church community were endowed with special dignity.

38

The same could be said about the most famous image that Paul used to describe the Church. The Church, he said, is like a human body: each part is essential to the entire body, because each has something unique to offer. The whole body suffers if one part suffers, and the whole body rejoices if one part is praised; and so it is with the Christian community (1 Corinthians 12:12–30).

The strong ties, sense of personal dignity, and mutual respect that characterized the little house-churches also existed within the entire Church as it grew throughout the Graeco-Roman world. In fact, the close ties among all the little communities that adopted the Christian faith were a unique phenomenon in society at this time. Paul spoke in 1 Thessalonians of the enthusiasm which Churches in Macedonia and Achaia expressed over the growth of the Thessalonians' little community of believers. In addition, his letters to the Christians in Greek cities contain references to a money-collection which the Greek Christians were taking up to assist the Jewish Christians in Palestine. Still further, his letters indicate that there were dozens of Christian men and women traveling from city to city, seeking refuge among the Christians of other cities, or changing residence in order to promote the growth of the faith in new Christian communities.

Shortly after the year 100 C.E., the letters of St. Ignatius of Antioch revealed the same spirit. Ignatius had been arrested for his support of the new faith, and was being escorted by guards to Rome, where he expected to be put to death. In each city where Ignatius and his persecutors stopped for rest, Christians from nearby towns came to visit and support him. Ignatius' "thank-you letters" to the towns, written during his journey to Rome, are virtually unique in ancient literature: they bespeak great warmth and a sense of personal ties, even among Christians who had never met each other face-to-face. Early Christianity

> The strong ties, sense of personal dignity, and mutual respect that characterized the little house-churches also existed within the entire Church as it grew throughout the Graeco-Roman world.

was not simply a "movement" or a new religion, but was a united people.

Eucharist

The Christians' chief means of expressing their oneness in Christ was a celebration known as the Eucharist.

Eucharist—taken from the Greek word *Eucharistia* meaning "thanksgiving."

The Christians' chief means of expressing their oneness in Christ was a celebration known as the Eucharist. At the heart of the celebration was a thanksgiving (**Eucharist** is taken from the Greek word *Eucharistia* meaning "thanksgiving") and a blessing over a community meal, the practice of which they had adopted from the Jewish tradition of solemn meal-prayers. Jesus' Last Supper had been in the setting of a Jewish meal-prayer, and the Christians made efforts to preserve Jesus' exact words, "This is my body . . . this is my blood . . . do this in remembrance of me." In addition, the early Christians apparently continued the Jewish custom of going to the synagogue on the Sabbath, where they heard readings from the Jewish Scriptures, and prayers and reflections based upon the readings.

In time, the Eucharistic prayer was separated from the regular meal, and combined with elements of synagogue worship to create a new, two-part celebration: readings and reflections, followed by a Eucharistic prayer and a sharing of the one bread and one cup of wine. One Christian's description of the ceremony about the year 150 shows that the basic elements of today's Eucharistic celebration were already present. The service, generally, began with readings from the memoirs of the apostles and from the writings of the prophets, followed by a sermon. Then all the people stood for the general intercessions, or prayers of petition.

Having ended the prayers, we salute one another with a kiss. There is then brought to the president of the brothers bread and a cup of wine mixed with water; and he, taking them, gives praise and glory to the

Father of the Universe, through the name of the Son and of the Holy Spirit. He offers thanks at considerable length for our being counted worthy to receive these things at his hands. And when he has concluded the prayers and thanksgivings, all the people present express their assent by saying "Amen." This word **Amen** *is the Hebrew for "so be it." And when the president has given thanks, and all the people have expressed their assent, those of us who are called deacons give to each of those present to partake of the bread and the wine mixed with water over which the thanksgiving was pronounced; and to those who are absent they carry away a portion.*[1]

Amen—Hebrew word for "so be it."

The places in which Christians chose to worship reflected the importance of community in their faith. Pagan worship took place in temples, which, generally, were rather small buildings, because they served only as resting-places for the gods—that is, for statues of the gods. There was scarcely any room for people, because only the priests participated in sacrifices to the gods. Christians, on the other hand, needed larger buildings because they were all "a royal priesthood, a holy people." True celebration of the Eucharist was possible only if all the people of the community came together for worship.

True celebration of the Eucharist was possible only if all the people of the community came together for worship.

Scriptures

The composition of the Scriptures was yet another sign of the communal faith. The four **Evangelists** (authors of the Gospels) drew upon the rich store of oral sayings and stories about Jesus. At first, nothing was put into writing, as the Christians expected the **Parousia,** or second coming of Christ, to take place soon. Probably the earliest writing of what is now called the New Testament was

Evangelists—authors of the four Gospels.

Parousia—second coming of Christ.

1. St. Justin Martyr, *First Apology* 65.

Paul's letter to the Thessalonians, composed in about 52 A.D. The Christians of Thessalonika were concerned that because some believers had died, they would not be able to witness Christ's second coming. Paul wrote to reassure them, and for the next ten years composed a series of letters to the communities he had founded, to explain how Christians must believe and behave. Yet even though he was a pioneer, Paul was not writing alone. His letters are filled with phrases and hymns that had been part of the people's worship services.[2] As Paul himself said, "I have handed on to you first of all what I myself received" (1 Corinthians 15:3).

In about the year 60 C.E., St. Mark realized that it was necessary to preserve the message of Jesus for later generations. To fulfill this need, he created a new type of literature, called the **Gospel** (which means "Good News"). It was not like the many biographies written in early times, but was a thematic presentation of sayings and stories designed to convey the good news of Jesus' life, death, and resurrection. Modern scholars have been amazed by the intricacy of Mark's arrangement of the story—every verse points to a lesson, as Mark draws the picture of a suffering Savior for a people who had suffered under the first anti-Christian persecutions.

In the decades that followed, Matthew and Luke built upon Mark's narrative and drew from other elements of oral tradition to offer their own insights about Jesus. But because they wrote for the people of their own separate communities, they highlighted different elements of the original message.

Gospel—means "Good News."

Mark wrote the first Gospel.

2. One of the Bible's most beautiful descriptions of Christ—the first chapter of the Letter to the Colossians, written by Paul or one of his disciples—is considered by modern scholars to have been taken from an early hymn. The same may be true of Paul's description of the Last Supper in 1 Corinthians 11:23–26.

Finally John, ca. 90, drew from his own faith and that of his community in Asia Minor to offer the story in yet another manner. In each case, the evangelist's life in the community influenced the way in which the Gospel was written.

Even though the early Christians understood themselves to be a community of believers, they wrestled with disagreement and division. The story of the early Church as it has been handed down by St. Paul, St. Luke, and others is not a Cinderella tale. The early Christians held their little communities together in the face of many difficulties, uncertainties, and even squabbles. Acts appears to suggest that the office of deacon, for example, was created in the Jerusalem community when there was a complaint that the widows of Greek-speaking Christians were being short-changed in the daily distribution of food (Acts 6:1–6).

> The early Christians held their little communities together in the face of many difficulties, uncertainties, and even squabbles.

Paul's letters, especially to the Corinthians, reveal a leader struggling against false prophets and bogus wonder-workers, as well as elitists in the community who believed they were exempt from usual laws because they possessed special gifts from the Holy Spirit. Nearly all the letters of the New Testament speak about factions,[3] and warn the faithful to avoid false teachers—there must have been many of them circulating their own beliefs.

It is true that the early Church until about 100 C.E. had the advantage of leadership by the apostles, who had known and learned from Christ himself. But in numerous ways, the early times were times of great insecurity. Christianity has never known a perfect age; the Church has always grown under circumstances of trial, internal dissension, uncertainty, and even corruption.

3. See, for example, 1 Corinthians 1:10–17 and 3 John 1:9, for examples of factions. Revelation, chapters two and three, is one example of warnings about false teachers.

Summary

- Christianity was a religion of a united people—a community.

- Acts of the Apostles chapter two gives us a good description of the early Christian communities.

- St. Paul's letters indicated that a sense of human dignity was crucial to life in a Christian house-church.

- The close ties among all the communities that adopted the Christian faith were a unique phenomenon in society at that time.

- Christians' chief means of expressing their oneness in Christ was a celebration known as the Eucharist.

- The early Christians held their communities together in the face of many difficulties, uncertainties, and even squabbles.

Prayer

I am God's wheat. May I be ground by the teeth of the wild beasts until I become the fine wheat bread that is Christ's. My passions are crucified, there is no heat in my flesh. A stream flows murmuring inside me; deep down in me it says: Come to the Father.

St. Ignatius of Antioch,
before his martyrdom in 107

Discussion Questions

1. How did Paul adapt his missionary strategy to the social structures of the ancient world?

2. What was the most important expression of community life for the early Christians?

3. In what two ways does even the composition of the Scriptures reflect the importance of the Christian community?

St. Athanasius

Chapter Five

Authority in the Early Church

According to the Gospel of Mark, Jesus' first words in beginning his public ministry were, "The kingdom of God is at hand. Repent, and hear the good news" (Mark 1:15). Among the many sayings of Jesus, this is one of the best known. It is also a saying that brings to mind serious questions. What will be the nature of this extraordinary activity of God that is about to take place? What, exactly, is the "Good News"? What is the nature of this God, and of this messenger (Jesus) who calls people to put away their old way of life and "repent," that is, have a basic change of heart?

It was said in chapter one that the other religions of the Graeco-Roman world demanded little of people beyond sacrifice to the gods, and they had little doctrinal content. But as "Repent and hear the good news" suggests, Jesus' message made serious demands upon his followers and naturally raised the question of just what this good news was that called for such tremendous personal sacrifice. From the beginning, in other words, Christianity was a religion in which the content of the teachings was of crucial importance. The early Christians developed three chief means of preserving the content of their faith: they acknowledged authoritative teachers, preserved authoritative writings, and developed short formulas called **creeds**—creed is derived from the Latin word *credo*, which means "I believe"—that summarized their most basic beliefs.

The early Christians developed three chief means of preserving the content of their faith: they acknowledged authoritative teachers, preserved authoritative writings and developed short formulas called creeds that summarized their most basic belief.

Creed-

Throughout the first centuries of the Church's existence, no one of these three foundations of authority stood by itself; each referred to the other. Thus the great teacher Paul, for instance, carried authority within the Christian communities that he founded. But when questions were raised about a fundamental issue, such as the death and resurrection of Jesus, Paul's response was to remind his hearers about a creed that he had taught them before:

> *I handed on to you first of all what I myself received, that Christ died for our sins in accordance with the Scriptures; that he was buried and, in accordance with the Scriptures, rose on the third day; that he was seen by Peter, then by the twelve. After that he was seen by five hundred brothers at once, most of whom are still alive, although some have fallen asleep. Next he was seen by James; then by all the apostles.[1]*

His argument rests on this creed, but the creed does not stand by itself. The creed includes a reminder that Jesus' death and resurrection was in accordance with the Scriptures; and it refers repeatedly to the fact that the witnesses to the resurrection were the very men, such as the twelve disciples, who were the authoritative preachers in the early Christian movement. In effect, then, the short creed supports the authoritative apostle Paul, and the Scriptures and authoritative teachers support the creed.

There were several types of teachers and authority figures in New Testament times. Traveling preachers were so important to the spread of Christianity that one document, called the Didache or The Teaching of the Twelve Apostles, even laid down guidelines

---

1. 1 Corinthians 15:3–7. The actual text states that the first to see the risen Jesus was Cephas; but "Cephas" is simply the Aramaic equivalent of the name "Peter."

for the way in which the little Christian Churches were to care for these travelers who carried the good news. There was little formal structure in the Churches, beyond the general instruction that the leaders were "first apostles, second prophets, third teachers, then miracle workers, healers, assistants, administrators, and those who speak in tongues" (1 Corinthians 12:28).

In some regions, there arose a slightly different arrangement, namely, leadership by presbyters, deacons, and bishops. The presbyters were wise elders who at the Assembly at Jerusalem (48 or 49 C.E.) apparently worked alongside some of the original twelve apostles in the young Church's crucial decision about circumcision. The deacons, like the Levites of the Jewish religion, assisted at the worship services and took responsibility for helping the needy of the Christian community. The bishop was an overseer; perhaps he was just one of the presbyters or deacons who carried the additional role of administrator at first; but later the bishop came to assume a more important role.

By about 110, the letters of Bishop Ignatius of Antioch laid down a clear order: the bishop is the authoritative leader, followed by the presbyters and deacons. The bishop leads the celebration of the Eucharist, and all actions of a Church must have the bishop's approval.[2] Part of what prompted Ignatius to emphasize the bishop's power was the existence of factions within the communities; Ignatius put forward the idea that the people should rally around their one bishop, as a sign of their unity as a people. At the same time that Ignatius was promoting his view of things, other communities were content with a concept of Church order that put less emphasis upon the bishop. But as Christianity

2. For example, Ignatius' Ephesians 4, Trallians 2, and Philadelphians 4.

headed into its second century and many communities felt their unity threatened by false teachers and internal disagreements, the idea of having a single, powerful bishop became a rule of thumb.

Development of the Canon

Even as he stressed the power of the bishop, Ignatius, like other Christian writers of his time, made extensive use of the Scriptures. The Scriptures were valued by the Christians from the very first, but by "Scriptures" the earliest Christians meant the Jewish texts that today's Christians refer to as the Old Testament. In numerous places in Paul's letters, the Gospels, and the Acts, the Christian authors made their point by quoting a passage from the ancient Jewish writings.

An important change took place about the year 100. Bishop Clement of Rome, writing a letter to the Christians of Corinth in 96, made frequent use of Scripture and quoted only Jewish sources. But Ignatius of Antioch's seven letters, written shortly after 100, quoted both Jewish and Christian authors (especially Paul) as Scripture. Virtually all of the Christian works composed after 100 made references to Christian Scriptures; what today we call the "New Testament" was coming into being. In time, those works that Christians judged to have been inspired by God were grouped together and called the **canon,** that is, the authoritative Scriptures. Most of the writings that today make up the canon of the New Testament were generally accepted as Scripture before the end of the second century C.E.

Canon—collection of books acknowledged and accepted by the Church to have been inspired.

The development of the New Testament canon, however, was a complicated process and not without conflict. The exact list of twenty-seven books that today we call the New Testament did not appear until Bishop

Athanasius of Alexandria produced it in the year 367, and it was another 150 years before this final list was officially approved by a council of bishops. Until that time, there was uncertainty about which books should be included.

Even among the works that have been preserved up to the present, there are a dozen Christian letters and treatises that Church historians still study today, but that were not included in the canon. Many are older than the latest letters of the official New Testament and some of them, especially Clement of Rome's letters, were included at first among the canonical writings, but were later dropped. In addition to the New Testament's Acts of the Apostles, there were Acts of Peter and Acts of Paul, both of which were excluded from the canon. There were numerous works of the same type as Revelation, but only Revelation became part of the New Testament. Finally, even today there exist five Gospels in addition to the four canonical Gospels. The Church, in other words, faced difficult choices.

Matthew, Mark, Luke, and John were accepted in the canon partly because their works were believed to have been written by the original apostles or their followers. But two of the noncanonical gospels, the Gospel of Thomas and the Gospel of Philip, also carried the names of the original apostles, and Thomas may even be as old as Mark. The ultimate choice for or against a work, then, was not a matter of the author's name, nor of the work's having been written in apostolic times. The content of the work was important, also. Thomas included many sayings that today's Christians would recognize, including several well-known parables and such sayings as "Blessed are the poor, for theirs is the kingdom of heaven." But this noncanonical work included other sayings that Christians would find strange:

Thomas 29: If flesh came into being because of spirit (said Jesus), it is a wonder. But if spirit came into being because of flesh, it is a wonder of wonders. Indeed, I am amazed at how this great wealth (the spirit) has made its home in this poverty (the body).

Thomas 49: Jesus said, "Blessed are the solitary and elect, for you will find the kingdom. For you are from it, and to it will you return."

Thomas 114: Simon Peter said to them, "Let Mary leave us, for women are not worthy of life." Jesus said, "I myself shall lead her in order to make her male, so that she, too, may become a living spirit resembling you males. For every woman who will make herself male will enter the kingdom of heaven."[3]

Could the Jesus of Luke's or Matthew's Gospel have said the things recorded in Thomas? The early Christians apparently thought that he did not say such things, and they would have had serious hesitations about Thomas' opening line: "These are the *secret* sayings which the living Jesus spoke. . ." Faced with such teachings, the early Christians warned against false teachers. In time, they gave their opponents the label **heretic.** The word is derived from a Greek term meaning "choice," and heretics were considered to be those who chose false teachings called heresy. Eventually, Christians differentiated between **orthodoxy,** that is, "straight teaching" or right teachings, and heresy or heterodoxy ("other teaching"). The Christians fought against movements that they considered heretical, for fear that heresy would undermine the truths which they believed had been revealed to them by God in

Heretic—a baptized person who denies or doubts a truth revealed by God or proposed for belief by the Catholic Church.

Orthodoxy—the Church's official teaching on a fundamental belief.

3. Taken from The Nag Hammadi Library, in English, ed. James M. Robinson (New York: Harper & Row, 1978).

Jesus Christ. Ignatius likened heresy to a poison covered with honey and wine, which tastes good, but brings only death.[4]

Gnostic Heresy

In the ancient world, most heresies amounted to a recasting of Christian beliefs in terms of the pagan view that the world is evil and humanity is corrupt. Both these views were prominent in the widespread movement known as Gnosticism. The word *gnosis*, which means "knowledge," was the key idea of Gnosticism, and **Gnostics** were people who claimed to have secret knowledge that would bring salvation to themselves alone.

The Gnostics, who possibly even outnumbered the Christians during the second century, taught that the material world is corrupt, as is the material part of humanity (the body, as opposed to the spirit). God, who is good, could not be the source of corruption. Many Gnostics, therefore, reasoned that there must be two gods, one of good and one of evil. Some groups among the Gnostics believed that Yahweh, the Creator-God of the Old Testament, was the evil god since He created the corrupt world, and often seemed jealous and harsh toward His people. God as described in the New Testament was the God of good, or light.

Gnosticism was an appealing doctrine, because it offered answers to many great questions in life, such as the question of where evil comes from. But to the Christians it seemed a dangerous doctrine, in part, because it was close enough to Christianity to confuse people. In the Christian Bible, for instance, good is sometimes called the light, and evil is called darkness. People are called to turn away from evil and accept Christ, who is called the "light of the world." In Gnosticism, there is the same opposition between light and

In the ancient world, most heresies amounted to a recasting of Christian beliefs in terms of the pagan view that the world is evil and humanity is corrupt.

Gnostics—people who claimed to have secret knowledge that would bring salvation to themselves alone.

4. Trallians 6:1.

darkness; but light and dark are more than images for the Gnostics; they are the two great forces of the universe.

Like Christians, the Gnostics were concerned with salvation. They taught that humanity has light, or divine spirit, trapped within their corrupt bodies. If a person has gnosis, he or she can escape from the material world to the realm of spirit. Jesus, according to the Gnostics, came to reveal the secret knowledge, the gnosis—but, as in Thomas 49, he came to reveal it only to the chosen few, called the "perfect" or the "elect." According to Christian belief, Jesus taught the twelve disciples more about God and the Kingdom of Heaven than he taught to the crowds, but he was not secretive. The Jesus of the four canonical Gospels did teach rejection of the world in favor of the Kingdom of Heaven, but he did not condemn the material world or the human body as being totally evil. Jesus did call people to salvation, but it was to be achieved through faith and right living rather than by secret knowledge. On many points, Gnosticism seemed like Christianity on the surface, and so it was able to lead people away from the Church. But it was fundamentally opposed to Christianity.

It was not apostolic and catholic, since the truth was not for all persons but only for the few who had gnosis. It called the world evil, when the Book of Genesis said that God created the earth and declared His creation good. It undermined the idea of freedom, since it taught that two powerful gods were the source of good and evil. While Christians taught that the one God is good and that humanity can do evil by free choice, Gnostics in effect could take away a sense of personal moral responsibility by suggesting that evil acts were caused or inspired by the evil god. In place of Christian ethical monotheism, then, the Gnostics offered a dualistic determinism.

The Jesus of the four canonical Gospels did teach rejection of the world in favor of the Kingdom of Heaven, but he did not condemn the material world or the human body as being totally evil.

Irenaeus

The Gnostic teacher who seemed most threatening to the orthodox Christians was a man named Marcion, who, about 140 or 150 C.E., created his own canon. Not surprisingly, Marcion's canon excluded the entire Old Testament. Of the Christian writings, Marcion accepted only a heavily edited version of Luke, plus edited versions of Paul's letters. Because the Scriptures were viewed by Christians as the crucial source of doctrine, a host of Christians wrote against Marcion. Most famous of the Christian opponents of Marcion and the other Gnostics was Irenaeus, Bishop of Lyons, France, whose work *Against Heresies* appeared shortly before the end of the second century. His attack on the Gnostics is especially important, because of what it reveals about the nature of the early Christian Church.

Because the Gnostics claimed their own set of scriptures, their own secret tradition derived from the original apostles, and their own fully developed ideas about salvation, Irenaeus had to meet the heretics on all counts. In part, he argued from Scripture. Irenaeus defended the authority of the four canonical Gospels, and in his presentation he used twenty-four of the twenty-seven books which were later to be called the New Testament. But even those who could not read the Scriptures, he said, would reject the Gnostic beliefs in favor of the Christian tradition that they had received and that had its roots in the teachings of the apostles.

> *The tradition of the apostles is manifest to the whole world. Whoever wishes to find the truth has only to examine it in every Church. We can list the bishops who have been instituted by the apostles and by their successors down to our own time.*[5]

5. *Against Heresies* III, 3, 1.

The tradition derived from the apostles, in turn, is shown to be true by the apostles' worthy behavior, behavior recommended by the Lord's words, which are found in Scripture. Like Paul's creed in 1 Corinthians 15, which was supported by the Scriptures and by the witness of the apostles, Irenaeus defended orthodox belief by means of Scripture; he defended Scripture by means of the apostolic tradition; he defended the apostles' tradition by means of behavior recommended in the Scripture, and so forth. For Irenaeus, every part of Christianity upheld the other.

In the final section of his work, Irenaeus simply opposed Gnostic ideas by restating orthodox Christian beliefs that he had learned. Against the Gnostic belief that Jesus the spiritual messenger only appeared to be human, because he could not have had a corrupt body, Irenaeus insisted upon the fully human nature of Christ-in-the-flesh; by assuming the nature of created things, the Lord redeemed created nature.

Records from early times are scarce, and it is not known whether Irenaeus' writings caused a set-back for the Gnostic religions. It is known that various forms of Gnosticism survived until the fifth century, went "underground" at that point, and reappeared in France during the twelfth century. It is certain, of course, that Christianity survived the Gnostic challenge. And Irenaeus' *Against Heresies* shows that by 200, Christianity had developed firm beliefs, a collection of sacred writings which were the chief source of those beliefs, and leaders (especially the bishops) who interpreted the writings and defended the beliefs. In the centuries that followed, this structure helped Christianity to endure further controversies within the Church, as well as attacks from outside the Church.

Summary

• The early Christians developed three chief means of preserving the content of their faith: authoritative teachers, authoritative writings, and creeds that summarized their basic beliefs.

• The order of the leaders in the Church was established.

• What today we call the "New Testament" came into being.

• Many heresies began to appear.

• Bishop Irenaeus defended orthodoxy by means of Scripture, authoritative teachers, and tradition.

Prayer

We thank you holy Father for your holy name,
which you have caused to dwell in our hearts, and
for the knowledge and faith and immorality which
you have made known to us through Jesus Christ,
your Son; to you be glory forever.

You, Lord Almighty, have created all things for
your name's sake, and have given food and drink
and eternal life through your Son. For all things we
render you thanks, because you are mighty. To you
be glory forever.

Remember, O Lord, your Church; deliver it from all
evil and make it perfect in your love, and gather it
from the four winds, sanctified for your kingdom
which you have prepared for it, for yours is the
power and the glory forever.

Let grace come and this world pass away,
"Hosanna to the God of David." If anyone is holy,
let him come; if anyone is not, let him repent.
Maranatha. Amen.

> *The Didache*
> *"Teaching of the*
> *Twelve Apostles"*

Discussion Questions

1. What were the early Christians' three chief means of protecting the content of their beliefs?

2. Why can it be said that in establishing the canon, the Christians were faced with important choices?

3. List three ways in which Gnostic beliefs were clearly different from Christian beliefs.

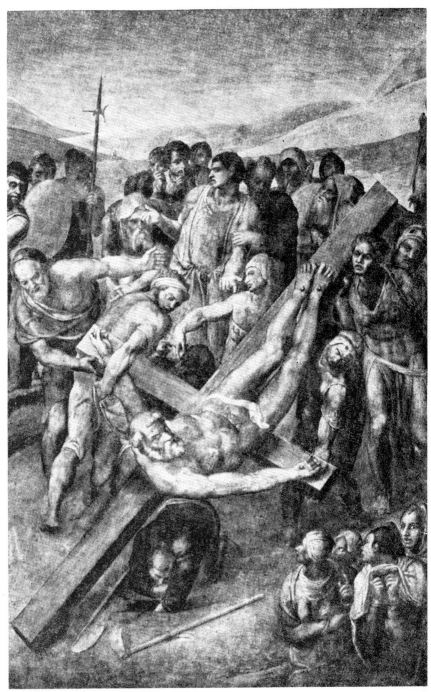

The Martyrdom of St. Peter

Chapter Six

Relations between the Christians and the Pagans

Three of the four Gospels record one dramatic incident that tells a great deal about Christianity's relationship with the world. The Jews, who had been conquered by the Romans about sixty years before Jesus' birth, had among them many members of the Zealot party, who professed strong anti-Roman views. Such views seemed dangerous to most Jewish leaders, because it was common knowledge that Rome would crush any resistance to its rule—as, in fact, happened when the Romans destroyed the Jewish Temple in 70 C.E. In an attempt to link Jesus with the radical anti-Romans, some elders asked him: "Master, should we pay taxes to the Emperor?" Jesus asked to see a Roman coin. "Whose picture is on this coin?" he asked. The answer was, "Caesar's." "Then," said Jesus, "give to Caesar what is Caesar's, and give to God what is God's" (Matthew 22:15-22; Mark 12:13-17; Luke 20:20-26).

"Give to Caesar what is Caesar's, and give to God what is God's."

Even though Christ's answer gave no satisfaction to the Zealots, his teaching on this question was more radical than anything professed by the fanatics. For Jesus was virtually alone, in all the ancient world, in suggesting that religion was clearly distinct from politics; that it was in no sense a servant of the political order. The most important political institution of the ancient world was the city, and the strong link between politics and religions was revealed in the fact that each city had its own god to watch over the people and protect them. Athens had Athena, Rome had Jupiter, Tyre and the other Phoenician cities had their baals. If the city or social group associated with the god ceased to exist (as, for the example, when the city of Carthage was destroyed in 146 B.C.E.), worship of that god ceased. Jesus' idea that the demands of God were independent of the political order, then, was a new departure.

But Jesus' directive left a great deal to the judgment of his followers. What, besides tax money, was Caesar's? What would be the Christians' position relative to society and the Roman government, if they believed they were being asked to do something that was contrary to God's law? The Christians did not have to wait long to face just such a challenge.

It was never legally required, but it was a common expectation in ancient society, that all persons would pray to their gods, and offer sacrifices, for the good of society and the Empire. It did not matter which god or goddess one chose to worship, so long as the gods, in general, were kept happy. In fact, the *Religious Syncretism*—a first two centuries C.E. were an age of **religious** downplaying of **syncretism,** when differences between differences between religions were downplayed and the very religions. general aim of keeping peace with all the gods was foremost in people's minds. At public ceremonies, for example, government officials generally began the festivities or business of the gathering by making offerings to the gods.

Jews and Christians were in an uncomfortable position because they were in an refused to take part in pagan rituals. Both uncomfortable position groups were referred to as "atheists" because because they refused of their disbelief in the gods. There had been to take part in pagan occasional outbreaks of popular violence rituals. against the Jews, but in general the pagans were conservative, willing to tolerate anyone who observed the traditions of their ancestors; Jewish religion plainly was very old, and the Jews made clear their willingness to offer their own prayers and sacrifices to their own God on behalf of the Roman emperor.

Early Persecutions

The Christians, however, could not appeal for protection on the grounds that theirs was an ancient tradition. They were clearly at odds with the Jews and to make matters worse the founder of their religion had been executed by an official of the Roman government. They frequently became victims of popular resentment for their refusal to honor the gods.

The first well known case of such resentment occurred in 64 C.E., when the city of Rome suffered a horrible fire. Emperor Nero fixed the blame for the fire on the Christians, who seemed like natural targets for blame because they were considered "criminals" known for "hatred of humanity" and guilty of "hated abominations." Tacitus, the pagan historian who recorded the incident, did not explain why the Christians deserved this reputation, but only reported that so many Christians were crucified and skinned alive for their alleged crime that even pagans began to feel that the punishments were excessive. Tradition has it that the apostles Peter and Paul were victims of this persecution.

The bloodletting in Rome in 64 was in most respects typical of the situation of the Church for the first two hundred years of its existence. Persecutions were infrequent, and local; that is, there was no general law prohibiting Christianity, but persecutions broke out in isolated places. Roman governors were given a fairly free hand in keeping order in the provinces, and because Christians did not cause trouble, the governors usually let them be. But when disasters such as earthquakes or fires befell the people, the suspicion arose that the Christians were to blame because of their disrespect for the gods. In that situation, Christians (especially bishops, presbyters, and deacons) were rounded up and required to make sacrifice to the gods. When they refused, they were executed.

All signs are that the Christians' beliefs were little known and generally misunderstood, so that when anti-Christian feelings were on the rise in a region, the populace began to accuse the Christians of disgusting "crimes against humanity." The Christians called "apologists" who wrote in defense of their religion found it necessary, for example, to insist that they were not engaging in human sacrifice during their Eucharistic celebrations. But government officials seemed uninterested in the alleged atrocities so long as the accused Christians would worship the all-protecting gods.

Martyrdom

Martyr—a person who accepts torture or death rather than give up his or her faith.

The Christians chose to be martyrs who accepted torture and death rather than betray their God by sacrificing to false gods.

The blood of martyrs is the seed of the Church.

The other feature of these episodes of persecution was that the Christians consistently refused to make people happy by sacrificing to the gods. They chose, instead, to be **martyrs** who accepted torture and death rather than betray their God by sacrificing to false gods. Proclaiming confidence in eternal life, they even ran to the support of fellow Christians who were in trouble with the authorities, putting themselves at great risk. This behavior was so unlike the pagans' rather easy-going allegiance to their gods, that many people simply dismissed the Christians as strange misfits. But as one Christian writer put it, "the blood of martyrs is the seed of the Church"; in other words, the persecutions contributed to the growth of the Christian Church, as some people began to ask questions about this religion that gave rise to such strong convictions. Far more people were converting to Christianity than were being executed by the authorities, and the Church was growing rapidly.

The situation changed dramatically in the year 250, when the Emperor Decius began the first general persecution of Christians throughout the Empire. Decius died in 251, but Valerian, Emperor from 253 to 259, renewed the anti-Christian policy. Forty years of toleration followed, until the Emperor Diocletian unleashed a deadly attack against Christianity in 303. The exact reason behind these actions is not known, but one possibility is that the emperors were applying the same reasoning that earlier pagans had used against the Christians in the face of local disasters: with barbarian armies threatening the Empire at its border, they may have wished to eliminate the Christians who resisted the sacrifices to the protecting gods.

Decius' law called for citizens to obtain a paper which certified that they had sacrificed to the gods. Terrified by the threat of the death penalty, some Christians performed the required religious acts, and a larger number bribed officials to obtain falsified certificates. But once again, the spirit of martyrdom was strong. The example of St. Cyprian, Bishop of Carthage, typified the attitude of the martyrs. After Decius' persecution came to an end, many who had denied their faith were asking to be reinstated in the Church. Cyprian insisted upon a policy of firmness, saying that they needed to undergo severe penalties for their weakness. Then when Valerian's persecution singled out bishops as prime targets, Cyprian was arrested, and he confessed his faith. A Roman document recorded Cyprian's final meeting with the officials at which the bishop was given a last chance to save his life:

> *Decius' Law*—called for citizens of the Roman Empire to obtain a paper which certified that they had sacrificed to the gods.

> *"The most holy emperors have ordained that you are to offer sacrifice to a statue of the Emperor."*

> *"I will not do it."*

> *"Take care."*

> *"Do what you have been commanded to do. In so clear a matter there is no need to deliberate."*

After short consultation the judge announced, *"We ordain that Cyprian is to be put to death by the sword."*

65

Cyprian's reply was,

"Thanks be to God."

Courageous statements such as these by Cyprian were multiplied throughout the Empire. Much blood was shed, as by this time the Christians were far too numerous and too prominent in society to be easily hidden. But a turning-point had been reached. The records of the persecutions show that in spite of the emperors' policies, many governors in the provinces often were carrying out their instructions without enthusiasm. Two hundred years of experience had shown that the Christians were not dangerous, were religious people (in their own, nonpagan way), and were not going to be eliminated by threats of death. Diocletian's persecution was called off in 313, but in the western half of the Empire it was given up in 306. Candidates for the imperial throne even began to seek support of the Christians, because the Church was clearly the healthiest institution within a declining Empire. Legend has it that in 312, on the eve of a battle that would bring him to imperial power, General Constantine had a vision in which he saw a symbol of Christ with the message, "By this sign you will conquer." He proclaimed Christ as his protector, won the battle and issued the **Edict of Milan** in 313, that granted Christians the right to practice their religion.

Edict of Milan—edict issued by Constantine that recognized Christianity as a religion and granted Christians the right to practice their religion.

Favoritism for the Church

Constantine himself was baptized shortly before his death in 335. But before taking this personal step, he established a new policy such as the ancient world had never seen before: he became the first emperor to promote one religion over others. He promoted Christians in imperial office, treated bishops as dignitaries worthy of honor, and used public funds to build magnificent buildings for Christian worship.

The Christians, of course, had always insisted that all other gods were false gods, and now the most powerful man on earth was championing their cause. Another Christian emperor, Theodosius, took the final step in 380, by proclaiming Christianity to be the official religion of the Roman Empire. Until 313, the very existence of the Christian religion was threatened, but Theodosius' policy in 380 brought about a situation that has continued for 1600 years. Christianity became the dominant religion of the Western world.

Summary

- Jesus suggests that religion was distinct from politics.

- Each city had its own god to protect it.

- Jews and Christians refused to take part in pagan rituals.

- Christians' beliefs were little known and generally misunderstood.

- Christians suffered persecution to such an extreme that even pagans felt that the punishments were excessive.

- Constantine issued the *Edict of Milan* in 313 that granted Christians the right to practice their religion.

- Christianity became the dominant religion of the Western world.

Prayer

*Lord, God, Almighty Father of your beloved and
blessed Son Jesus Christ . . . I bless you because I
may have a part, along with the martyrs, in the
chalice of your Christ. . . . May I be received
today as a rich and acceptable sacrifice, among
those who are in your presence. . . . For these and
for all benefits I praise you. I bless you, I glorify
you, through the eternal and heavenly High Priest,
Jesus Christ.*

> *Prayer Said by St. Polycarp
> at His Martyrdom*

Discussion Questions

1. In what sense does Jesus' "Give to
   Caesar . . ." represent a new way of
   looking at things?

2. It could be said that there were two stages
   in the history of anti-Christian
   persecution: before and after 250. What
   was the nature of the persecutions at each
   stage?

3. What does it mean to say, "the blood of
   martyrs is the seed of the Church"?

4. Why was the year 313 an important
   turning point for Christianity?

Council of Nicea

Chapter Seven
The Christological Controversies

Constantine began his policy of supporting the Christian Church shortly after he became emperor, and almost immediately he faced a great embarrassment; this Church, which he was endorsing in the face of the pagans' criticisms, seemed on the verge of splitting. Nor were the Church's leaders squabbling over a minor matter; the issue was serious disagreement over who, or what, they understood Jesus to be. To protect his "investment" in this religion, Constantine took firm action, by calling three hundred of the Church's bishops to meet at the first general, worldwide council in the history of Christianity.

Constantine's council was held in 325 in Nicea, a town near the Empire's new capital city of Constantinople, where Europe meets Asia. By means of long and often complicated arguments, the bishops at Nicea did arrive at a landmark decision concerning the most basic of Christian beliefs. But the Council of Nicea turned out to be just one important stage in a controversy that had begun long before Constantine's time, and that continued through a series of councils until the year 451.

Divine or Human

In simpler form, the controversy and speculations about Jesus had begun even before the New Testament was written. The resurrection of Jesus, an event that had transformed Jesus' confused and timid followers into a band of men totally devoted

71

to spreading God's word even at the risk of their lives, had also raised questions: just what was Jesus, who had been raised up by God? Of course, he was a man; the disciples, who had walked with him, shared meals with him, and witnessed his death had no questions about that. But had God's raising of Jesus indicated that Jesus was something more than an ordinary man?

Apparently, the very first generation of Christians addressed such questions, and soon they began making bold assertions about Jesus. An early hymn, for example, recorded later by Paul in his Letter to the Philippians, stated that:

> *Though he was in the form of God, he did not deem equality with God something to be grasped at. Rather, he emptied himself and took the form of a slave, being born in the likeness of men.*
>
> *He was known to be of human estate, and it was thus that he humbled himself, obediently accepting even death, death on a cross!*
>
> *Because of this, God highly exalted him and bestowed on him the name above every other name.*
>
> *So that at Jesus' name every knee must bend in the heavens, on the earth, and under the earth, and every tongue proclaim to the glory of God the Father: JESUS CHRIST IS LORD![1] (Philippians 2:6–11)*

This hymn appears to suggest that even before his birth, Jesus was God—or at least god-like—and that his way of living and dying justifies our calling him Lord. *Lord* is a translation of the Greek word *Kyrios,* which in Greek translations of the Old Testament had been used as a label for only God Himself.

1. Philippians 2:6–11. Also very old and also characterized by bold assertions about Jesus is Colossians 1:15–20.

Other evidence pointed to a similar conclusion. Writing sometime after the year 60, Mark recalled specific events from well before the death and resurrection that suggested that Jesus was divine, or at least endowed with divine powers. Near the beginning of his Gospel, for example, Mark reported that Jesus had offended Jewish observers by forgiving a man's sins— something that the people of Israel believed only God had the power to do. But Jesus' response was a firm assurance that "the Son of Man has the power to forgive sins" (Mark 2:1–12).

To make essentially the same point, Matthew and Luke pointed to the extraordinary circumstances of Jesus' birth, and John went so far as to assert that "In the beginning," Jesus, the "Word" of God, was God and was with God.[2] These and other lines from the New Testament pointed to the conclusion that Jesus was divine. Such ideas were so prominent that by the second century, some of the Gnostics established the doctrine called **Docetism,** which proposed that Jesus was God, and only appeared to be human. But Docetism, like many ideas from Gnosticism, was rejected as heresy; Docetism did not square with the apostles' experience of Jesus' humanity.

Docetism—doctrine proposing that Jesus was God, and only appeared to be human. It was rejected as heresy.

Christology

The two hundred years of discussion from New Testament times to the Council of Nicea reflected the fact that early **Christology**—the study of the nature of Christ—was influenced strongly by Christianity's Jewish heritage as well as by the Church's exposure to Greek ways of thinking. The evidence that suggested Jesus' divinity was viewed as unsettling because, true to the message of the Old Testament, the Christians believed that there is only one God; and to call Jesus divine

Christology—the study of the nature of Christ.

2. Matthew 1 & 2; Luke 1 & 2; John 1:1–17 (the Prologue to the Gospel).

seemed to lead to "bi-theism" (or to "tri-theism," because the question of the Holy Spirit's nature was also under discussion). Great thinkers in the Church, then, struggled to find ways of expressing the divinity and humanity of Christ in such a way as to preserve the fundamental belief in the oneness of God.

But as a large number of people converting to the Church were highly educated persons trained in the tradition of Greek thought, it was also necessary to express belief in the oneness of God, the humanity of Jesus, and the divinity of Jesus in a manner that would be intelligible to them. Greek educational tradition had long been characterized by concern over questions about *being, nature, oneness, sameness* and *difference*—questions that had not been raised by the people of Jewish background. Part of the challenge, then, was to apply Greek philosophical terms and questions to data drawn from Jewish Scriptures. Further, the confrontation with the Gnostics had shown the Christians that unless they could express their convictions with complete precision, the way would be open for misunderstandings and distortions of Christian belief.

Theories

Adoptionism—heretical theory that Jesus had so thoroughly identified himself with God's will that God raised him up to divine status, presumably at the time of Jesus' resurrection.

Sabellianism—heretical theory that Father, Son, and Spirit were just different "energies" or "modes" of one God.

Theories advanced during the second and third centuries were designed to preserve the belief in the oneness of God. One such theory was **Adoptionism:** the man Jesus had so thoroughly identified himself with God's will that God raised him up to divine status, presumably at the time of Jesus' resurrection. Another theory, **Sabellianism,** held that Father, Son and Spirit were just different "energies," or "modes," of one God; insofar as God creates and gives life, God is Father; in those actions pertaining to humankind's redemption, God is Son; when making each person holy, God is the Spirit. Both

74

Adoptionism and Sabellianism were rejected as heresy, largely on the grounds that the theories could not be reconciled with data from the Scriptures. The passages from Philippians 2 and John 1, in particular, clearly indicate that Jesus existed before he became man. Sabellianism faced the further objection that it claimed, in effect, that God the Father and Spirit equally died with the Son at Calvary, in which case it is hard to explain how the Father raised Jesus from the dead, or to explain how God was truly united to the human Jesus who died on the cross.

Various thinkers continued to offer theories, but it was the Egyptian priest Arius who sparked the controversy which led Constantine to call the Council of Nicea. His teaching (called **Arianism**) was that the opening words of the Gospel of John, "In the beginning was the Word," indicated that Jesus was created by God in the beginning; all other things were created after the Word, so that Jesus, in effect, was an exalted being who was neither fully divine nor fully human.

Arianism—heretical theory that claimed that the opening words of the Gospel of John, "In the beginning was the Word," indicated that Jesus was created by God in the beginning; all other things were created after the Word, so that Jesus, in effect, was an exalted being who was neither fully divine nor fully human.

A large majority of bishops at Nicea rejected Arius' theory as inconsistent with both Scripture and traditional teaching, but they were uncertain about how best to express Christian convictions about the nature of Jesus. As the bishops struggled over the wording of a definitive creed, Athanasius of Alexandria proposed two lines for the creed that would rule out Arius' beliefs altogether; Jesus, true God, is "begotten not made, of the same substance with the Father." The Greek word *homoousios,* meaning "of the same substance," caused hesitations because it had never been used in the Scriptures. But Athanasius argued successfully that even though that exact philosophical term had not appeared in the Scriptures, it was a true reflection of the *sense* of the Scriptures. Athanasius' reasoning prevailed, and the Council of Nicea made two decisive steps; it put forth a creed that provided an authoritative statement of belief about Jesus, namely that he is truly God and truly man; and it effectively opened the door to the possibility that philosophical language could be used to express beliefs drawn from Scripture.

Councils at Constantinople and Chalcedon

Council at Constantinople— reaffirmed the teaching from Nicea, refined the wording of the Creed to eliminate possible Arian interpretations, and added several lines about the Holy Spirit, to advance the Christian belief in God as Trinity.

Council of Chalcedon— established the present definition of the Creed.

A decade later, Constantine's son became emperor, and for political reasons he withdrew his support of the Nicene Creed. Athanasius found himself exiled for his beliefs five different times after the council. Then in 381, a **Council at Constantinople** reaffirmed the teaching from Nicea, refined the wording of the Creed to eliminate possible Arian interpretations, and added several lines about the Holy Spirit, to advance the Christian belief in God as Trinity: one God, three Persons in God.[3]

The definitive proclamations at Constantinople set off another flurry of debate, until at last a **Council at Chalcedon** in 451 established the definition that Christians have accepted up to the present. Even a short excerpt shows how intricately worded the credal statements about Jesus had become. The council, affirming Jesus' divinity and humanity once again, attributed to Jesus

> . . . *two natures without confusion, without change, without division, without separation, the difference of the natures being by no means removed because of the union, but the property of each nature preserved, coalescing into one person.* . . .

3. The Creed that Catholics recite today during Mass is the one developed at Constantinople, but it is sometimes called the Nicene Creed because most of the ideas were first developed at Nicea.

A small number of people left the Church over these statements, but the great majority of Christians accepted the Council of Chalcedon's teachings as orthodoxy.

The history of the Councils of Nicea, Constantinople, and Chalcedon reveals a number of things. The first is that the Church rarely defined its teachings unless a challenging new doctrine was brought forth. Then, when a creed or definition was proclaimed, it set forth only a few essentials for belief. For the most part, each council defined the limits for Christians' speculation, and identified certain paths as being unacceptable.

The declaration at Chalcedon, for example, eliminated three types of speculation about Jesus, all of which had been raised during the century following the Council of Nicea. The theory of Nestorius—**Nestorianism**—that Jesus' humanity and divinity were not united within a single person, was not accepted. Also rejected was the theory of Apollinarius, that God's "Word" was the spiritual principle that gave life to Jesus' body. **Apollinarianism** denied that Jesus was truly human, in that he did not have a human mind and human will. Further, the council's definitions eliminated **Monophysitism,** the doctrine that Jesus' divine nature overshadowed his human nature. The bishops at Chalcedon insisted that all speculations about Jesus had to keep in mind that Jesus was one person, "fully like us as regards his humanity, fully like God as regards his divinity."[4]

Another important feature of the centuries of debate about Jesus was that no matter how complex and concerned with technicalities the discussion became, the leaders of the Church remained aware of the way that the theoretical questions had bearing on the Christian life.

4. This phrase is drawn from a letter by Pope Leo I. Leo could not attend the council, but his letter was used extensively by the bishops at Chalcedon.

Nestorianism—heretical theory that Jesus' humanity and divinity were not united within a single person.

Apollinarianism— heretical theory that denied Jesus was truly human, in that he did not have a human mind and human will.

Monophysitism— heretical doctrine that Jesus' divine nature overshadowed his human nature.

This was particularly the case with Athanasius, who insisted that the arguments over "natures" and "being" ultimately influenced Christians' understanding of God and of salvation.

The councils' assertion that Jesus is God said a great deal about God's love: that it is unconditional, not dependent upon people's goodness; that it is offered to the poor, the outcast, the sick, and especially the sinners. Such had been the character of Jesus' work as reported by the Gospels, and so it also revealed the nature of God. The councils' assertion that Jesus is fully human made it clear what "being human" can mean, such as caring for others, and putting one's trust entirely in the will of the Father, as the human Jesus had done. In the centuries that followed, only a handful of scholars recalled the details of the councils' Christological debates. But those beliefs about God and salvation, which the councils' debates were meant to protect, continued to exercise profound influence upon Christian living.

Summary

- Early Christology was influenced strongly by Christianity's Jewish heritage as well as by the Church's exposure to Greek ways of thinking.

- Many theories were advanced during the second and third centuries, regarding belief in the oneness of God.

- Constantine called the Council of Nicea in 325.

- The Council decreed that Jesus is truly God and truly human.

- The teaching from Nicea is reaffirmed, and the wording of the Creed is refined at the Council of Constantinople; several lines are added to the Creed regarding the Holy Spirit.

- The Council of Chalcedon eliminated several types of speculation about Jesus.

Prayer

We acknowledge the Trinity, holy and perfect, to consist of the Father, the Son, and the Holy Spirit.

In this Trinity, there is no intrusion of any alien element or of anything from outside, nor is the Trinity a blend of creative and created being.

St. Athanasius

Discussion Questions

1. After years of controversy, what did the Church insist upon as basic Christian belief about God, and especially about the nature of Christ?

2. Pick any of the Christological or Trinitarian heresies, and explain why the Church judged that particular theory to be inadequate.

3. What are the practical effects of the Church's belief about the two natures of Christ?

St. Augustine by Fra Filippino Lippi

Chapter Eight

Christianity vs. Paganism: The Ideals of St. Augustine

Age of the Fathers

The period in the Church's history from ca. 200 to ca. 600 is sometimes called the Age of the Fathers. The title is in honor of certain men whose reflections upon Christ's teachings were so carefully thought out, so in touch with the Spirit, that they have provided insights to Christians ever since. They are the spiritual "fathers" of later Christians who have built upon the firm foundation of their thought. Most of them have been honored with the title of *saint,* that is, "holy person."

There were several great fathers who lived in the eastern half of the Roman Empire, such as St. Athanasius who vigorously opposed the Arian heresy. They are usually called the "Greek Fathers" because they wrote in Greek. The fathers from the western half of the Empire wrote in Latin, and are called the "Latin Fathers." Of the Latin Fathers (whose ideas had the greatest influence upon later generations of Christians in Europe), St. Ambrose and St. Gregory the Great are remembered primarily for their reflections upon Christian worship. St. Jerome is remembered for his translation of the Bible into Latin. The **Vulgate,** as Jerome's Latin translation is called, was widely used by Catholic Christians for fifteen centuries. St. Augustine was the Latin Father who wrote on

St. Jerome is remembered for his translation of the Bible into Latin.

Vulgate—St. Jerome's Latin translation of the Bible.

81

the widest variety of subjects, and whose fertile ideas had the greatest effect upon later thought.

It was Augustine, a bishop who lived from 354 to 430, who most clearly recognized the differences between the Christian and pagan understandings of reality. People who still believed strongly in the pagan gods argued against Christianity when the Christians began to be promoted in the imperial government, and Augustine was the leading spokesman for the Church during this controversy. He was the best possible spokesman, because he had grown up as a pagan himself. In a famous book about his life, called the *Confessions,* he described his own progress toward becoming a Christian.

A successful student, he had left his home in northern Africa to teach rhetoric in Rome. Through the writings of Cicero, he was attracted to the great Greek and Roman thinkers. But his keen mind saw weaknesses in all he read, and though he examined all the great works of pagan wisdom, he was never completely satisfied by what they taught. For a while, he even joined a Gnostic cult called the Manichees. Of all the pagan writers, only Plato drew Augustine's admiration.

Augustine finally concluded that Christianity best answered all his questions about life. He decided to become a Christian, but still could not take the final step, especially as he was living a life of sin. As St. Augustine explained in *Confessions,* God finally gave him the necessary strength, and he was baptized into the Church at the age of thirty-three.

Among the Christians, no one understood paganism so well as he. But his contribution to Christian thought was not limited to arguments against non-Christian attitudes. Even the story of his life as told in *Confessions* revealed a deep Christian insight that was new to the ancient world: time is not cyclic, and it does not always have destructive effects; God uses time for His own good purposes. Augustine believed strongly in God's "grace," or "gift"; because of God's love working within him, Augustine was able to progress, to become a better man.

The Fall of Rome

God's use of time and history was a major theme in another of Bishop Augustine's famous books, called *City of God*. In the year 410, Alaric and the Goths defeated a Roman army and spent three days looting and destroying the city of Rome, while the Romans looked on helplessly. It was a terrible event that made a deep psychological impression upon all citizens of the Empire. Rome, which had been the most powerful city in the world for the past 600 years, was the symbol of the everlasting Empire. Its fall symbolized the end of the Empire itself.

Followers of the pagan religion saw the fall of Rome as a sign the gods were angry. Rome had risen to greatness when its people were worshipping the pagan gods, but now that its people worshipped the Christian God, the Empire was collapsing. From this pattern, the pagans reasoned that the Christian God did not listen to prayers, and that paganism ought to be brought back as the official religion of the Empire.

Christians responded by writing pamphlets and books in defense of their faith. Augustine's *City of God* was the most important book of this sort. Hundreds of pages long, the book took thirteen years to write. Augustine defended Christian belief and criticized pagan attitudes on all points, and in this respect *City of God* was the final stage of Christianity's replacement of paganism as the worldview that was shaping the lives of men.

Most important, Augustine argued against the non-Christians that God is, indeed, listening to prayers and watching over the events of the

Augustine believed strongly in God's "grace," or "gift"; because of God's love within him, Augustine was able to progress, to become a better man.

Providence—the idea that a loving God watches over the events of people's lives.

world. The bishop believed strongly in God's **providence,** God's quality of overseeing all activities of humanity with a concern for humanity's betterment. Like the great Old Testament prophets, Augustine urged that God might as easily send defeats or suffering as send victory to His people, depending upon their deepest needs.

> *If they had sense, the pagans would see that the hardships and cruelties which they suffered from the enemy (in 410) came from that Divine Providence who makes use of war to reform the corrupt lives of men. . . . The tide of trouble will test, purify, and improve the good men, but beat, crush and wash away the wicked. So it is that, under the weight of the same affliction, the wicked deny and blaspheme God, and the good pray to Him and praise Him. The difference is not in what people suffer but in the way they suffer.[1]*

Augustine's thinking was rooted in the idea of ethical monotheism, a God who is concerned with leading His people to a better way of living. His Christian theory is far removed from the pagan view of a protector-god who exists to ensure victories and prosperity for his people. In *City of God*, the bishop explained there are two kinds of people, two "cities," in the world. The earthly city, or City of Man, consists of people who view life on earth as the only life; they are concerned with power, and with building empires to last forever, because those are the only values they know. The heavenly city, or City of God, consists of the people who see God as the highest reality and eternal life as the goal. The ups and downs of earthly life are important only as indications of God's will. These two "cities" naturally have very different understandings of the purpose of religion.

1. *City of God,* Book 1, chapters 1 and 9.

Here we have the very heart of the earthly city. Its God (or gods) is He or they who will help the city to victory after victory, and to a reign of earthly peace; and this city worships, not because it has any love for service, but because its passion is for domination. This, in fact, is the difference between the good men and the bad men, that the former make use of the world in order to enjoy God, while the latter would like to make use of God in order to enjoy the world—if, of course, they believe in God and His providence over man, and are not so bad as those who deny even this.[2]

With these words, Augustine was developing Jesus' idea that religion is not the servant of politics. In fact, if anything, politics should be the servant of religion. The responsibility of Christians (citizens of the City of God), said Augustine, is to reshape the City of Man in the image of the City of God. They must try to develop society's attitudes, laws, and institutions in terms of Christian ideals so that humanity can be led toward eternal life. Jesus had said, "Give to Caesar what is Caesar's, give to God what is God's." In effect, Augustine was teaching that *Caesar is God's.*

Augustine was developing the idea that religion is not the servant of politics.

For about one thousand years after his death, Augustine was admired as the greatest of all the Fathers. Many of his concepts, including his view of the relation of religion and politics, were put into practice in European society. Europe during the Middle Ages was a distinctly new kind of society largely because it was built upon Christian principles rather than the older pagan principles.

Europe during the Middle Ages was a distinctly new kind of society largely because it was built upon Christian principles rather than the older pagan principles.

Pagan Writers

There remained another serious question for Christians to deal with, and Augustine addressed this problem, too. Christians recognized that their beliefs were far removed

2. *City of God*, Book 15, chapter 7.

from the pagan view of things, but they also admired the wisdom of the ancient non-Christian writers. In many Christians' opinions, great thinkers such as Plato and Aristotle had gone as far toward a perfect understanding of the world as they could go without the aid of God's revelation. Most educated Christians had learned how to read, to write, and to reason by studying works by Homer, Vergil, Cicero, and many other pagan writers. Yet many of these works contained ideas that by Christian standards were false and harmful. What, they wondered, is the proper attitude to take toward pagan literature?

A few Christian intellectuals, especially those living in Alexandria, the "heartland" of Greek culture, were enthusiastic about the study of pagan works. They recommended liberal use of these works, especially of Platonic philosophy. Others, like the African writer Tertullian, rejected the non-Christian literature entirely. For them, everything a person might need to know was in sacred Scripture. Pagan ideas were dangerous.

St. Augustine took a middle road between the two opinions by calling for a careful, critical use of pagan literature. He explained his approach by means of an image. The Egyptians, he said, had gold and silver ornaments which the Hebrews, during their escape from slavery in Egypt, claimed for themselves. By God's command, they took possession of these riches, even as they were turning away from Egypt's oppression.

> *In the same way, all the teachings of the pagans have counterfeit and superstitious notions and oppressive burdens of useless labor. Any one of us Christians, following Christ and rejecting paganism, ought to reject these. However, the pagan works also contain very useful principles about morals; even some truths about the service*

*of the one God Himself are discovered
among their writings. These are, in a sense,
their gold and silver.*[3]

It was Augustine's idea of critical borrowing
from the wealth of pagan wisdom that was
most popular during the Middle Ages. Thus in
a sense, the transition from a world guided by
pagan beliefs to one guided by Christianity
was complete. Not only did Christians see that
their views were distinct from those of their
predecessors; but also they were so sure of
their basic Christian principles that they could
borrow freely but carefully from their
predecessors' store of wisdom.

Summary

• The period in the Church's history from ca.
200 to ca. 600 is sometimes called the "Age of
the Fathers."

• It was Augustine who most clearly
recognized the differences between the
Christian and pagan understandings of reality.

• Augustine understood his own and the
empire's progress in terms of the ideas of
grace and providence.

• Augustine developed Jesus' idea that
religion is not the servant of politics.

• It was Augustine's idea of critical borrowing
from the wealth of pagan wisdom that was
most popular during the Middle Ages.

3. *On Christian Doctrine,* Book II, chapter 39.

Prayer

Lord Jesus, let me know myself and know you,
And desire nothing save only you.
Let me deny myself and love you.
Let me do everything for your sake.
Let me humble myself and exalt you.
Let me think of nothing except of you.
Let me die to myself and live in you.
Let me accept whatever happens as from you.
Let me banish self and follow you,
And ever desire to follow you.
Let me fly from myself and take refuge in you,
That I may deserve to be defended by you.
Let me fear for myself, let me fear you,
And let me be among those who are chosen by you.
Let me distrust myself and put my trust in you.
Let me be willing to obey for your sake.
Let me cling to nothing save only you,
And let me be poor because of you.
Look upon me that I may love you,
And forever enjoy you. Amen.

St. Augustine
From his biography
Confessions

Discussion Questions

1. Explain why it can be said that Augustine's personal experience shaped his own belief about grace.

2. Sum up, as well as you can, Augustine's "providential" explanation of the events in the year 410.

3. What approach to non-Christian writings is Augustine recommending in his book *On Christian Doctrine?*

Introduction of Christianity into Britain

Chapter Nine

Early Christian Beliefs about How Humanity Is Saved: Conversion and Baptism

Matthew, Mark, and Luke all relate the story of a young man who asked Jesus what he needed to do to share in everlasting life. Jesus explained that he must follow the commandments, and the young man responded that he had done this ever since his childhood. "There is one further thing," Jesus added. "You must sell all you have and give to the poor. . . .Then come follow me." Because the young man was wealthy, he was dismayed by these instructions and he went away. Jesus went on to say that it was easier for a camel to pass through the eye of a needle than for a rich man to enter the Kingdom of Heaven.

The disciples were, as Mark and Matthew put it, "completely overwhelmed" by this teaching. The young man followed the law, as did the disciples themselves. But now Jesus was saying that this was not sufficient, which made his doctrine sound hard indeed. The disciples exclaimed to one another, "Then who can be saved?"—because it seemed nearly impossible. "Jesus fixed his gaze on them and said, 'For man it is impossible but not for God. With God all things are possible'."[1]

1. Matthew 19:16–26; Mark 10:17–27; Luke 18:18–30.

In this story, a pattern emerges that is to be repeated throughout the history of the early Church: it is God who saves; in response to God's initiative, the believer follows the law, and far more important, undergoes a fundamental change of heart. The outward sign of the change is baptism. Such was the basic pattern of belief and practice that was repeated through the centuries. But as the Church faced changing circumstances and as it reflected upon the meaning of the message, the belief and practice assumed new shapes.

At the very first, the chief emphasis was upon the change of heart. When some of the Jews of Jerusalem accepted Peter's preaching, they asked what they needed to do, and Peter simply said, "Reform and be baptized." Some three thousand people were baptized that same day.[2] Baptism had to be accompanied by true change of heart to be effective in cleansing a person of sin, as is shown in the story of Simon the Magician in Acts (Acts 8:9–24). Also, there does not appear to have been a set ritual for baptism—one time, a ship's captain was baptized by sliding down a rope into the sea.

Baptism had to be accompanied by true change of heart to be effective in cleansing a person of sin.

By the year 110, there was a shift of emphasis. One document called the *Didache* listed a long series of moral teachings that Christians had to accept before baptism could take place. Probably the Church could no longer assume that all converts were Jews who were already familiar with the Jewish law, and so now the teachings received more emphasis. After instructions, the prospective Christian fasted, prayed, and professed belief in the moral teachings, and was baptized. The rite was flexible: baptism should be in running water, but if that was not possible cold water was better than hot. If a pool or similar source was

2. Acts 2:36–41, the process is similarly brief with the conversions of Cornelius, Acts 10, and the Ethiopian eunuch, Acts 8:26–39.

not available, it was sufficient to pour water three times upon the head. Even at this early date, it was believed that baptism brought rebirth, and remission from sin; it was like a "spiritual circumcision," a mark of belonging to God's people.[3]

The Catechumenate

By the year 210, the Church still recognized the importance of baptism and change of heart, but there was even greater emphasis upon instruction in the doctrines of the Church. The experience of the persecutions was teaching the Christians some painful lessons: nearly all converts by this time were pagans who may have had difficulty grasping Judeo-Christian modes of thinking; and in the face of persecution many lost heart and abandoned the faith.

To combat these problems, the Church eliminated applicants whose means of employment seemed inappropriate to the Christian life (such as gladiators and prostitutes) and accepted only those candidates who were "sponsored" by Church members in good standing. Once accepted, the candidates were enrolled in a three-year program called the catechumenate, during which they received extensive instruction. Equally important, they had plenty of time to examine their own commitment to Christ. The **catechumens,** as these students were called, finished their three years with a period of fast, then were baptized, confirmed, and given holy Eucharist at the **Easter Vigil.** Easter Vigil, the night preceding Easter morning, became the Church's most elaborate and joyful celebration of the year.

Catechumen—a person accepted into a three-year program of instruction before becoming a Christian.

Easter Vigil—the night before Easter morning during which the joyous Christian catechumens were initiated into the Church.

The practice of baptizing the convert only after a long period of trial and instruction was a workable one that remained in use for

3. These ideas show up in several writings by St. Irenaeus.

93

several hundred years. Eventually, most of the population was Christian, and the practice arose of baptizing infants. The elaborate, three-year process of preparation died out after there were scarcely any non-Christian adults left to convert. Noticing changes in the society, the Church recently restored the long catechumenate as the norm for initiating adults into the Christian community.

Summary

- Baptism had to be accompanied by a true change of heart to be effective in cleansing a person of sin.

- The catechumenate—a three-year program of instruction—was established for persons wanting to become Christians.

- The Church recently restored the catechumenate as the norm for initiating adults into the Christian community.

Prayer

No one can serve two masters. He will either hate one and love the other or be attentive to one and despise the other. You cannot give yourself to God and money.

Matthew 6:24

Discussion Questions

1. In Matthew 19, what *two* things does Jesus recommend as being necessary for salvation?

2. After all variations are taken into account, what one thing appears to have been necessary in the early ritual of baptism?

3. In third-century practice, how long did people spend in preparation for baptism and why did the Church require this process?

Constantine the Great Embraces Christianity

Chapter Ten

Early Christian Beliefs about How Humanity Is Saved: The Life of the Baptized Christian

The opening words of Jesus' public ministry, "Repent and hear the Good News," assume that human beings sin, and need to be reformed. According to early Christian belief, baptism offered a person forgiveness for sins. But what was to be said or done about sins committed after baptism?

The Christian community understood itself to be continuing the work of the risen Christ. As Jesus had forgiven people's sins, so also the Church had the authority to release people from their sins. In fact, Jesus had specifically bestowed this power on his apostles:

> Whatsoever you declare loosed on earth shall be held loosed in heaven. (Matthew 18:18)

> Receive the Holy Spirit. If you forgive men's sins, they are forgiven them; if you hold them bound, they are held bound. (John 20:22–23)

Two other considerations, however, influenced the early Church's belief about its own mission of forgiveness. One was that, if the Christian community was to be the visible representative of Christ on earth, then the Church had the responsibility of protecting its own holiness, that is, the holiness to which

God was calling people. Thus, for example, Paul in one instance counseled the Christians of Corinth to cast out a member who was engaging in a scandalous sexual relationship (1 Corinthians 5:1–5). The other consideration was every bit as fundamental: if a person's decision to be baptized reflected conversion, or basic change of heart, then what did serious sin after baptism indicate? Should serious sin be viewed as another change of heart, an anti-God choice? That seems to be the sense of the following passage from the Letter to the Hebrews:

> If we willfully sin after receiving the truth, there remains for us no further sacrifice for sin—only a fearful expectation of judgment. . . . (Hebrews 10:26–27)

From the earliest times, then, the Christian community found itself wrestling with the question of what to do when its members broke God's laws. Records are scarce, but it appears that the Christian Church developed a ritual for forgiving its members' sins. A bishop would announce the community's forgiveness of the sinner, and he would "lay hands" on the repentant person—place his hands on the forgiven one's shoulders or head. The ritual of laying on hands was symbolically equivalent to an embrace, a sign that the forgiven person was once again reconciled with the community. This act gave expression to ancient Jewish and Christian belief that sin harms the community. The first thing that an offender had to do was to be sorry for all sins, and then the first action was to reestablish ties to the Church, that was, after all, the representative of God on earth.

In various regions where Christianity was flourishing, there appeared lists of the most serious sins. Opinions varied but, generally, all the lists started with biblical guidelines such as the Ten Commandments, and virtually all the lists included murder, adultery, and **apostasy** (a Christian's denial of belief in Jesus). All three of these sins, besides being

Apostasy—a Christian's denial of belief in Jesus.

terribly harmful to the community, were consciously willed sins—a person does not murder another by accident, for example.

The **rigorists,** who preferred to preserve the purity of the Church at all costs, judged that a serious sin such as apostasy should be considered beyond forgiveness. But it appears that, in general, the Church valued reconciliation as highly as purity, and allowed an extremely serious sin to be forgiven just once in a lifetime.

Rigorists—those who preferred to preserve the purity of the Church at all costs.

A Three-stage Process

Writing about the year 200, the famous African Christian, Tertullian, described forgiveness as a three-stage process. First, the sinner identified himself or herself as a penitent, seeking the once-in-a-lifetime forgiveness. Other sources give the impression that this was accomplished by making confession to a bishop. Second, the penitent undertook a harsh penitential discipline, which might include surviving on a simple bread-and-water diet, wearing course, rough clothing, and publicly begging the faithful to pray for the penitent's pardon. Finally, there was the ritual of absolution or forgiveness, and a return to Communion.

It is a sign of how deeply the Church was split over the question of forgiveness that Tertullian himself later abandoned the Church to join a Christian rigorist sect. The question whether the Church should forgive grave sins became most heated during the latter half of the third century, when the persecutions reached their peak. Apostasy was common, and when the persecutions temporarily eased, many apostates even attempted to exert pressure so that they could be readmitted to the Church. Leaders such as St. Cyprian took care to follow a middle path between extreme rigorism and extreme laxness: reconciliation was possible for the sinners, but only by means of the harsh, once-in-a-lifetime process.

Eventually, the rigorist groups went their own way, and the three-stage process of penitence became the law of the Church.

Constantine's Edict of Milan, which made Christianity one of the recognized religions, effectively ended the problem of apostasy in 313, because people were no longer tempted to leave the Church to avoid punishments. But the Emperor's policies ultimately created far greater problems for the Church's use of its emerging sacrament of forgiveness. After Constantine ended the persecutions and endorsed the Church, the number of new Christians increased dramatically. In spite of the efforts to prepare catechumens well, there were many converts, raised in pagan ways, whose behavior fell far short of Christian ideals. All such people could have been considered prime candidates for entry into the penitential process.

But it was not just historical circumstances that created the difficulties. It could be said that the Church's penitential practice was not well adapted to the weaknesses in human nature: temptation and falls into sin are always part of the human condition, but forgiveness was a one-time event.

Soon many people delayed confession/ reconciliation, just as others (including Constantine himself) delayed baptism; their hope was to receive forgiveness late in life, so that they could die pure. To make matters worse, as Church leaders reflected on human behavior, they added other sins to the list of those that required special forgiveness. Thus nearly everybody *needed* to confess, but hardly anyone *did* confess. One council of bishops even discouraged young people from confession, because with years of life remaining, young people were too likely to sin again.

A few people who were especially devout partook of confession/reconciliation, out of a desire to face penitential discipline and improve themselves. It appears, then, that the Church's rite of forgiveness was being used mostly by the people in the community who least needed it.

Obviously, the Christian people were not entirely clear about how the element of sin and forgiveness should be considered in their quest for salvation. In addition, there were difficulties of a more abstract, theoretical sort. One group of people, following a man named Pelagius, rejected the idea that Adam's Original Sin was inherited by all of humankind. They emphasized the importance of a person's own self-discipline and pious practices in bringing about salvation. Another group, following St. Augustine (who built upon St. Paul's teaching[1]), accepted the doctrine of Original Sin. They contended that people's ability to avoid sin and perform good works is the result of grace, that is, God's love working within the person. **Pelagianism** was officially condemned as a heresy, but some of Pelagius' ideas continued to be widespread.

Pelagianism—rejected the idea that Adam's Original Sin was inherited by all of humankind.

While Pelagian controversy involved mostly the intellectuals of the Christian Church, the practices concerning sin and forgiveness involved nearly everyone. Christianity had challenged humankind to a new type of moral behavior, and many had answered the challenge. But the Christian faith had also raised new issues and new problems. The central problem of how to be saved in a world filled with sin and temptation prompted many different responses during the long history of the Church. One response, which arose during the fourth century, changed the lives of thousands of people over the centuries. The monastic movement, as it was called, will be treated in the next chapter.

1. Romans 5:12.

Summary

• Jesus gave his apostles, the early Church, the power to forgive sins.

• The Church was deeply split over the issue of forgiveness.

• Constantine's Edict of Milan effectively ended the problem of apostasy—denying belief in Jesus to avoid punishment.

• Because the Church granted forgiveness only once in a lifetime, many people delayed confession/reconciliation until late in life so they could die pure.

Prayer

Have mercy on me, O God, in your goodness;
in the greatness of your compassion wipe out my
offense.
Thoroughly wash me from my guilt
and of my sin cleanse me.

Psalm 51:3–4

Discussion Questions

1. Why did it ever occur to Christians that perhaps some sins were beyond forgiveness?

2. What was the issue separating the "rigorists" from the rest of the Christians?

3. What was Pelagius proposing, and what was Augustine's argument against Pelagius' view?

The Hermitage on the Mountains above Assisi

Chapter Eleven

Early Christian Beliefs about How Humanity Is Saved: The Monastic Movement

Almost all of the religions of the ancient world made similar demands upon their followers, and offered the same reward. They asked their people to avoid such serious offenses as theft, murder, and adultery, and to make regular sacrifices to the gods. People who fulfilled these requirements could expect to be rewarded with prosperity and comforts throughout their lives. Judaism made greater demands, such as the requirement of justice toward the poor, and strict rules concerning proper worship of Yahweh; but the Jews, too, subscribed to the belief that if people worshipped God and avoided grave wrongs, God would reward them with long life and prosperity.

Jesus' followers, on the contrary, were never told to expect comfort or riches as a reward for a good life. Riches could even be an obstacle to salvation. Instead, Christians were urged to put their hope in heaven, since life on earth could be filled with hardships. The kind of moral behavior expected of Christians was like that of other faiths, but the *quality* of their personal goodness was supposed to achieve a new greatness; they were asked to love one another even as Jesus had loved them, when Jesus' love had led him even to the Cross.

During the first three centuries of Christianity, the faithful were constantly aware of how much they were sacrificing to be followers of Christ. Simply to be a Christian called for great devotion, because to be a Christian was a crime punishable by death. But by the time that Emperor Diocletian halted the last of the persecutions and Emperor-to-be Constantine decreed that Christian faith was legal, Christians of deep faith began to search for new ways to express their devotion to Christ and ensure salvation.

They already had one powerful example of devotion. In the year 271, a man named Anthony gave up all that he owned and moved out of his home in Alexandria to build a crude hut in the desert. There he lived on bread and water, and devoted all of his time to prayer. Anthony's holiness was a source of excitement to people who heard about him, and soon Anthony had people coming from Alexandria to seek his advice. His life also carried a message: there existed another, more direct path to heaven than the path of everyday Christian living in the city.

Hermits

Soon Anthony had his imitators. Many men were taking quarters next to Anthony's in the desert. While he could not deny that it was good to see so many people devoted to a life of prayer, Anthony himself was frustrated because he had been seeking total solitude. And so, after his life had attracted a following, he moved away to build another hut deeper in the desert. Again he sought utter simplicity, lack of comfort and a life of prayer. Again, however, people moved deeper into the desert to join him and, ultimately, Anthony moved even farther into the desert. The life of **St. Anthony,** the father of **monasticism,** demonstrated two things: the monastic life, the life of single-minded dedication to prayer, held an enormous attraction for Christians

During the first three centuries of Christianity, Christians were constantly aware of how much they were sacrificing to be followers of Christ.

St. Anthony—father of monasticism.

Monasticism—a way of life in community characterized by prayer and self-denial.

seeking a meaningful commitment to God; and even when men like Anthony sought to live the life of a **hermit,** they could never entirely ignore the community aspect of the Christian life. Men famous for their holiness were constantly sought out for their advice; it was reassuring to people to hear the opinions of a man who seemed to be in direct contact with God.

Hermit—a particular type of monk, who lived in solitude.

Both these facts showed up dramatically in the life of Simeon Stylites, the most unusual and most famous of all hermit-monks. Simeon lived in Syria during the fifth century, and is called "Stylites" because he lived on top of a *stylos* or pillar. He chose to live on top of the pillar to achieve total solitude, but like Anthony he found that his advice was constantly being sought. The common people had such tremendous respect for Simeon that he found himself performing healings, judging lawsuits, prophesying for the people, and handing out advice to the ruling nobility of the area near Antioch. Strange as he may sound, Simeon was not the only of his kind. Other Syrian holy men built pillars in imitation of him, and the arid mountains of Asia Minor were the home of many hermit-monks, some of whom even dressed in the skins of wild animals. Daily life in the cities of the crumbling Empire seemed so corrupt that some persons hoped to find a totally new pathway to heaven.

The hermit's life, though, seemed much too harsh for most people, even though they were attracted by the monastic ideal of total dedication to prayer. Pachomius, an Egyptian soldier who was impressed by the example of St. Anthony, decided to imitate Anthony's life of prayer. But he chose to build a community of monks, whose life of prayer would be assisted by a group discipline. He began his experiment in 320, and within seventy-five years St. Pachomius' followers included more than seventy-five hundred men who prayed in little desert communities. The communities were organized according to a set rule of life, and by A.D. 400 "rule-monasticism" had become a distinct movement alongside the original "hermit-monasticism."

Benedict's Rule

In the West, the most famous rule was that of St. Benedict, an Italian. All of Benedict's monks constituted a family, with the abbot, their leader, taking the role of a father who imposed discipline in a loving way. The purpose of the discipline was clear: to help men gain salvation. As Benedict wrote in the prologue to his rule,

> And if, fleeing the pains of hell, we wish to attain eternal life, then we must—while there is still time, while we are in this body—hasten to do now what will profit us for eternity. Therefore, we must establish a school for the service of the Lord, . . .

Benedict's style of "school for the service of the Lord" became the model for thousands of monasteries throughout the Middle Ages. According to the *Rule of Benedict*, no one owned anything and everything was held in common, so that no one could become proud or possessive. Praise to the Lord was emphasized, and at set times the monks would gather (several times per day, even before dawn) to pray and sing the psalms, the hymns of praise from the Old Testament. Manual labor was required for all but the very aged, as well as periods of silent prayer and silent work. The silent work usually consisted in copying, line by line, ancient writings. The monks played a key role in keeping alive the civilization in the West, by means of their copying.

In the increasingly chaotic world of the crumbling Empire, the monastic communities under their rules were outstanding for their organization. With Benedict's requirement of

Benedict's style of "school for the service of the Lord" became the model for thousands of monasteries throughout the Middle Ages.

manual labor for all, the monasteries became efficient economic units providing for the material needs of their members. Thanks to the atmosphere of silence and provision for group prayer, the monasteries were ideally suited to meet the spiritual needs of their members as well. In short, the monastic life was eminently successful.

For the majority of Christians, the path to heaven was not nearly so clear, and the Church's difficulties concerning sin and forgiveness remained unresolved. But monastic practices began to "spill over" into the life of the Church as a whole; the monks' conception of penance and of prayer were particularly influential. Monasticism was a constitutive element in the new society which grew up during the Middle Ages, and will be an important topic in subsequent chapters.

Summary

- During the first three centuries of Christianity, Christians were constantly aware of how much they were sacrificing to be followers of Christ.

- After Constantine declared Christianity to be legal, people sought new ways to express their devotion to Christ.

- Monasticism became a way of life for Christians who wanted to make a more meaningful commitment to God.

- Many followed St. Anthony's example and became hermits.

- St. Benedict started the first "school for the service of the Lord."

- Monastic practices began to "spill over" into the life of the Church as a whole.

Prayer

O Lord, I place myself in your hands and dedicate myself to you. I pledge myself to do your will in all things—to love the Lord God with all my heart, all my soul, all my strength.

St. Benedict of Nursia

Discussion Questions

1. Why, according to the chapter, did monasticism become popular when the persecutions were coming to an end?

2. How did the career of even the hermits demonstrate the importance of community to Christianity?

3. What was the stated purpose of life under the *Rule* of Benedict?

Section II

Christian Society during the Middle Ages

Introduction

In the preceding chapters, most of the description of early Christianity could be applied to the Church wherever it existed. From about the year 600, however, the history of the Church in the eastern Mediterranean region became different from that of the western Mediterranean and the European lands. This text focuses primarily upon the Western tradition, to show the roots of modern Roman Catholicism and Protestantism.

Christians in the West took care to further the traditions of early Christianity, and the Christians in the Greek-speaking (Mediterranean) lands did also. Yet while the two traditions are substantially in agreement today, in many ways they are different: their theologies, their art, their music, their Church discipline, their concepts of authority differ on some points. The dissimilarities can be explained by the fact that each branch of the Church has grown under different circumstances, and each has been in close contact with a particular culture.

Christianity leaves its imprint upon the peoples who accept Christ's message, but at the same time, the various peoples leave their imprint upon Christianity. The Greeks certainly were affected by Jesus' message, for example; they were "Christianized." And in contact with these people, Christianity became "Graecified." The heresies described in chapter seven, for instance, reflect Greek concerns about rational categories and definitions. The ancient Jews most likely would not have asked whether Christ is "one in *being* with the Father," but for Greek intellectuals, concepts such as "being," "sameness," and "difference" had crucial importance. Similarly, the Romans converted to Christianity while the Church acquired the typically "Roman" characteristics of order and uniformity and emphasis upon law.

The contact between the Church and the
Germanic peoples of the north—the
"barbarians," as the Mediterranean peoples
called them—gave rise to new qualities in the
same way. The chapters that follow will treat
the barbarians themselves; then the focus will
be upon the new problems, the new
civilization, and the new style of Christianity
that arose through the meeting of the
Christian faith and the Germanic races.

Christ the King and Lawgiver

Chapter Twelve
The Conversion of the Germanic Tribes

Throughout the history of the ancient world, Germanic peoples came from the north into the friendlier climate and the more settled civilization of the Mediterranean basin. Germanic invasions of Greece, for example, took place ca. 1100 B.C.E. It was not until C.E. 300 to 500 that the Roman Empire, itself in a state of near-collapse, proved unable to absorb or repulse the barbarians any longer.

As the barbarian peoples were violently seizing power in the West during the fifth and sixth centuries, some Christians saw the barbarians as people who needed to hear the Word of God. Christianity had always had missionaries such as St. Paul to spread the Gospel, and the missionary spirit was still strong when the Lombards, Franks, and other Germanic tribes were establishing control over Europe.

The conversion of these peoples, however, presented a new challenge to the Church. Christianity had grown up in the civilized urban centers of the ancient world; but the barbarians were far from civilized, and the lands of Europe were so disrupted by decades of warfare that organized political and economic life were all but nonexistent. The Germanic tribes that contributed to the downfall of the Empire in the West—the Vandals, Goths, Lombards, and Franks—all stood out as warlike peoples, who grouped themselves into clans under the leadership of a fighting chief, or lord. The Church's efforts to spread the Gospel among these peoples were both aided and hindered by the tribes' fighting spirit and loyalty to the chief.

Methods of missionary work that had proved workable in the past now seemed inappropriate. There could be no three-year catechumenate for adults, for example, when none of those adults could read and when frequent wars were disrupting the countryside. The Christians focused instead upon drawing people immediately into the Church, in the hope that they could eventually grow in faith. In some instances, as in the case of Clovis, greatest of the Merovingian kings of the Franks, conversion was a relatively simple matter. But the nature of the man's commitment to Christ was something very different from what the Church had seen before.

The turning point of Clovis' conversion was a battle against the Alamanni tribe in the year 496, when his Franks faced sure defeat. Clovis called upon Christ for help because his wife had told him Christ was powerful, and in Jesus' name he turned the tide and routed the Alamanni. Not long afterward he was baptized, and loyalty to the chief was so strong that three thousand of his soldiers came into the Church with him (although it would be fair to wonder whether the soldiers understood the meaning of their baptism).

Shortly after his baptism, Clovis made war upon the Goths of southwestern France, on the grounds that the Goths were Arian heretics who ought to be punished as enemies of true faith. No doubt the fact that the Goths also had rich lands was a factor in Clovis' thinking, although it is true that the Goths were Arians. When Bishop Gregory of Tours recounted the story of Clovis in his *History of the Franks,* he attributed the following words to Clovis: "It irks me sore that these Arians hold a part of Gaul (France). Let us go forth, then, and with God's aid bring the land under our control." In the eyes of a warrior-king, any neighboring territory is fit to be seized, and if the plan is to pick on someone, who better than a heretic?

The same rough-and-ready approach to Christian living showed up in the career of Charlemagne, greatest of the Frankish conquerors. After two particularly fierce and bloody campaigns against the Saxons of Germany, Charlemagne ordered his defeated enemies onto their knees and had them all accept Christian baptism or face death by the sword. Great numbers, then, were accepting Christianity, but it was a Christianity characterized by a violence unknown in the early history of the Church.

Great numbers were accepting Christianity, but it was a Christianity characterized by a violence unknown in the early history of the Church.

Before the arrival of Christianity, the cult of the hero, or chief, had powerful religious significance. Kings of northern Europe, for example, were respected as having ancestors fathered by the god Wodin, and they were believed to be specially protected by the god Thor. To oppose such beliefs, the Church consciously promoted the cult of the saints to supplant the cult of the chiefs. Holy men like St. Martin of Tours were depicted in **hagiographies** (biographies of the saints) as having amazing powers over the forces of evil. Pope St. Gregory the Great recommended building churches with relics of the saints upon the sites of pagan shrines, so that the common people could easily make the transition from their pagan worship to Christian worship. The strategy, apparently, was a success because when Clovis marched his army against the Arian Goths, for example, he attempted to detour around Tours; and when they passed through the edge of the region of Tours, they were careful not to plunder lest they offend St. Martin. In this account, Gregory spoke of Martin as a force to be dealt with, even though Martin had been dead for a century at the time of Clovis' march.

Before the arrival of Christianity, the cult of the hero, or chief, had powerful religious significance.

Hagiography—a biography of saints.

At the same time, the Germanic reverence for the lord of chief facilitated the growth of a Christian concept of kingship. Particularly with Charlemagne in the latter half of the eighth century, the Christian king emerged as a special servant of God, charged with a holy mission. The Old Testament books of 1 and 2 Samuel and 1 and 2 Kings were carefully read to find models of perfect kingship. Charlemagne saw himself as a new David, and Charles' son was to be a new Solomon. The Christian monarch's kingdom on earth was parallel to God's kingdom in heaven. Especially in the art of the early Middle Ages, Christ was pictured as a lawgiver or a king wearing a crown, more often than he was portrayed as the baby Jesus or the suffering Savior.

Missionary Monks

The Church's contact with the barbarian culture, then, was yielding some results. For better or worse, the warrior-peoples were being drawn into the Church with their leaders, and Germanic Christianity was giving birth to new religious images that were meaningful to the people. At the same time, slow and patient missionary work was being carried out by Christian monks in all corners of Europe. There were no wandering missionaries on the model of St. Paul, because travel was dangerous and a solitary traveler might have starved to death—agriculture was at a bare, subsistence level, and food was scarce. But monasteries were self-contained communities that could provide for the spiritual and material needs of their members, so that a few of the monks could go forth and preach the message of Christ.

The earliest instance of missionary activity by monks was in Ireland in the fifth century. Little is known about the origins of Irish monasticism, although the man credited with bringing Christianity to Ireland is St. Patrick.

Ireland had no tradition of Roman culture, and the Celtic tribes of the island were even more rough and uncivilized than the barbarians of the Continent. Irish monks were strongly motivated by the ideal of **asceticism;** that is, they were willing to deprive themselves of pleasures and hone themselves to a kind of spiritual perfection after the manner of St. Anthony. The fierce barbarism of the Celts was more than matched by the fierce asceticism of the monks, and soon there were converts.

Asceticism —life without physical pleasures.

The fierce barbarism of the Celts was more than matched by the fierce asceticism of the monks.

Interestingly, the converts all seem to have been not simply Christians, but Christian *monks;* further, in accepting the Christian monastic life they also accepted the Latin language and culture, for the Irish monks were dedicated students and master copyists, whose beautiful manuscripts are still admired today. It is surprising that a crude and uncivilized people could be attracted by such a radical change in their lives. But there were surprising parallels between the Celtic barbarians and the monks. The Celts were sworn to loyalty to their chief, and the monks were sworn to obedience to their abbot; the Celts followed a code of bravery in battle, and the monks had their own "code" in their monastic rule; the Celts told tales of their fighting heroes, and the monks told tales about their spiritual heroes, the saints. There were just enough parallels between the barbarians' and the monks' lives that the transition from one life to another was possible.

The new combination of Christian faith and personal loyalty soon yielded fruit in the form of missionary activity. One group of Irish monks led by St. Columba spread out to the north and founded new monasteries in Scotland and northern England, while another led by St. Columban traveled to the Continent, about the year 590.

Even as the Irish monks were spreading the Word of God in Europe, European monks were doing the same in England. It was Pope Gregory the Great, a monk himself and the author of a biography of St. Benedict, who decided to send the monks to England. Legend has it that Gregory went for a walk in the city of Rome and came upon a slave market. Impressed by the handsome appearance of the blonde-haired slaves, he inquired about what kind of people they might be. "Angles," came the response. "These are not Angles," said Gregory, "they are angels." He put together a monastic mission to Angleland (England), under the leadership of a man named Augustine. After the monks had won a number of converts, Augustine was named Archbishop of the new diocese of Canterbury, England. (He is usually called Augustine of Canterbury, not to be confused with Augustine of Hippo, the great Father of the Church.)

Like the Irish monks before them, the English monks both converted the pagan population and maintained little centers of advanced learning. And as had happened in Ireland before, the English monastic movement outgrew its homeland. The missionary urge of the English monks was symbolized by St. Boniface, who left England about the year 710 to preach the message of Christ in Germany. The advanced learning of the English monks was symbolized by Alcuin of York, who ultimately studied in the court of Charlemagne about the year 790. Alcuin led a revival of learning after years of virtual "darkness" in France.

But the one clear difference between the efforts of the Irish monks and those of the English monks was that by the time of the English monastic movement, the papacy[1] had risen to a position of leadership in the West.

1. *Papacy* refers to the office of pope. For an explanation of the origins of the word *pope* and *papacy*, see chapter thirteen, note 1.

The mission to England was sponsored by the papacy, and its "children," Boniface and Alcuin, were loyal to Rome. St. Boniface was made an archbishop by the orders of the pope, and he regularly wrote to Rome for advice in the direction of the new German Church. When Pope Zacharias endorsed Pepin as new king of the Franks, it was St. Boniface who anointed Pepin as king. Slightly later, Alcuin attempted to reform and standardize religious ritual in France, using the practices of Rome as his guide to proper forms. The influence of the papacy was growing.

Alcuin was the leader of a group of scholars from all over the Christian world who gathered in the court of Charlemagne. Europe was coming to be **Christendom,** Christ's kingdom or domain, an international society strongly influenced by Christian beliefs. The Frankish monarchy, the papacy, and monasticism were the three forces which gave shape to the society.

Christendom —Christ's domain, as Europe came to be called.

By the ninth century, almost the entire population of Europe was Christian. (The lone exception was a small number of Jews, who at times received rough treatment at the hands of the Christians.) The conversion and civilization of an entire society was a remarkable achievement, but the achievement was accompanied by certain dangers. Because all people, saints and sinners alike, were Christians, the Church often fell prey to corruption and loss of spiritual vigor. The Middle Ages witnessed a series of ups and downs, reform movements, and periods of decay.

Because all people, saints and sinners alike, were Christians, the Church often fell prey to corruption and loss of spiritual vigor.

Summary

- The conversion of the Germanic peoples presented a new challenge to the Church.

- Before the arrival of Christianity, the cult of the hero had powerful religious significance, and the Church consciously promoted the cult of the saints to replace it.

- Slow and patient missionary work was being carried out in all corners of Europe.

- The papacy rose to a position of leadership.

- By the ninth century, almost the entire population of Europe was Christian.

- Because all people, saints and sinners alike, were Christians, the Church often fell prey to corruption.

Prayer

*This is what is written: the Messiah must suffer and
must rise from death three days later, and in his
name the message about repentance and the
forgiveness of sins must be preached to all nations.*

Luke 24:46–47

Discussion Questions

1. List three characteristics of the Germanic
   peoples who were accepting Christianity
   during the early Middle Ages.

2. Give examples to show why Clovis' and
   Charlemagne's Christian faith was
   different from anything seen before.

3. Why were monks the most important
   missionaries of the early Middle Ages?

4. Which groups worked together to
   Christianize European society?

Peter receives the keys to the kingdom

Chapter Thirteen

The Rise of the Papacy

One of the distinctive features of Roman Catholic Christianity during the Middle Ages was the acknowledgment of the special authority of the bishop of Rome, otherwise known as the pope.[1] The papacy was a powerful force in the medieval[2] world, interpreting the teachings of Christ and casting them into laws to govern the Church and all of the people of God. As the supreme authority in the Christian society, the papacy in its times of good health could reinvigorate the entire Body of Christ. But when the papacy was in need of reform, its own sickness spread like a disease throughout the society. Thus it is impossible to understand the Middle Ages without some knowledge of the history of the medieval papacy.

As has been the case with so many of the Church's institutions, doctrines, and practices, the papacy had its roots in the teachings of Christ himself, but the specific forms which the institutions assumed were conditioned by historical circumstances. According to the Gospel of St. Matthew, Jesus gave his disciples the power to bind and loose sins, and he assured them that "Wherever two or more of

As has been the case with so many of the Church's institutions, doctrines, and practices, the papacy had its roots in the teaching of Christ himself.

1. The word *pope* comes from "papa" or father; the pope's institution is often called the "papacy" from which the adjective "papal" also is derived.

2. *Medieval* is a commonly-used adjective referring to anything associated with the Middle Ages; the word comes from the Latin for "middle age."

you are together, there I am in your midst" (Matthew 18:15-20). At the same time, he granted special authority to Peter alone:

> I for my part declare to you, you are "Rock," and on this rock I will build my church, and the jaws of death shall not prevail against it. I will entrust to you the keys of the kingdom of heaven; whatever you declare loosed on earth shall be loosed in heaven. (Matthew 16:18-19)

The granting of authority to Peter ("Rock") was similar to the granting of authority to the other apostles, but the terms were even more explicit: Jesus gave Peter the "keys of the Kingdom of Heaven." He also was named the "Rock" upon which the Church would be built up—at the very least, Jesus had chosen to use a potent image. The Gospels of John and Luke also included incidents in which Christ seemed to have singled out Peter for special power (John 21:15-17; Luke 22:31). In the Acts of the Apostles, Peter did emerge as the leader of the apostles. After the descent of the Holy Spirit, Peter was the chief spokesman for the Christians in Jerusalem (Acts 2:14-41), and during the controversy at the Council of Jerusalem it was his testimony that led to acceptance of a new policy toward the Gentiles (Acts 15).

Doctrinally, the roots of the papacy lie in identifying later bishops of Rome with St. Peter. It is known that Peter journeyed to Rome, where presumably he served as leader of the Christian community until both he and St. Paul were martyred during Nero's persecution. In those early days, the office of bishop was not so clearly defined, and there is no early record that Peter held that title. But if Peter's position in Rome was at all like that which he held in the Jerusalem community, then he was a bishop and more than a bishop.

Shortly after Peter's death, the bishop in Rome was acknowledged to have special dignity. Bishop St. Clement of Rome, third successor of

After the descent of the Holy Spirit, Peter was the chief spokesman for the Christians in Jerusalem.

Peter, wrote a letter to the Christians in Corinth in C.E. 96, chiding them for their disunity and giving them instructions. In making recommendations, Clement warned that "Should anyone disobey what has been said by Him (God) through us, let them understand that they will entangle themselves in transgression and no small danger."[3] He was writing authoritatively to the Corinthians, and the question can be raised why was the Bishop of Rome writing to Christians in faraway Corinth at all. Clement's letter reflected detailed knowledge of conditions in Corinth, so it can be presumed that some of the Corinthian Christians, at a time of local crisis, wrote to Rome because they believed that they ought to turn to the Bishop of Rome for a judgment.

Bishop St. Ignatius of Antioch, in a letter to the Roman Christians in 110, wrote in reverent terms about the Church in Rome, attributing special dignity and honor to it.[4] Near the end of the second century, Bishop St. Irenaeus of Lyons wrote his praises of "the greatest, most ancient and well-known Church, founded by the two most glorious apostles, Peter and Paul, at Rome."[5] The importance of Rome and its bishop stood out perhaps because of the centrality of Rome in the Empire, and it is not clear to what extent the bishop's relation to St. Peter was an important factor.

By the year 375, the references to Peter became more clear. St. Jerome, one of the great Latin Fathers, was concerned about a doctrinal issue; and seeing that there was confusion and dissension among the leaders in the East, he decided that "I ought to consult the chair of Peter, and the faith praised by the mouth of

3. Clement, Letter to the Corinthians, article 59.

4. Ignatius of Antioch, Letter to the Romans.

5. Irenaeus of Lyons, *Against the Heretics III*, chapter 3, part 2.

the Apostle, asking now for food for my soul. . . ."[6] The fourth century was the age of the great heresies, most of which originated in the cities of the eastern half of the Empire. The bishop of Rome never attended the councils in the East, but always sent a representative or a letter to state his position; and he always upheld the orthodox view.[7]

The fifth century witnessed the clearest development of a doctrine of the papacy. In 445, Emperor Valentinian III issued an edict that upheld the power of Rome's bishop (by this time called the "pope") in a controversy. The Emperor acknowledged the primacy of the pope, that is, the first place in authority which the pope was to have in relation to other bishops:

> . . . We decree by this eternal law that it shall not be lawful for the bishops of Gaul or of the other provinces, contrary to ancient custom, to do aught without the authority of the venerable pope of the eternal city (Rome). And whatever the authority of the apostolic see has sanctioned, or may sanction, shall be the law for all. . . .[8]

Peter's Successors

Several years after Valentinian's edict, Pope St. Leo I composed a sermon that very explicitly interpreted the gospel account of Peter the "Rock" as an offer of special authority to St. Peter. Leo then proclaimed that the popes acted in the name of Peter and were his successors, carrying out his work as chief of

6. Jerome, Letter 15, to Pope Damasus II.

7. Pope Honorius wrote a letter praising the views of the Bishop of Constantinople in 625, and those views were later condemned by the Council of Constantinople; Protestant scholars have pointed to Honorius' letter as proof that the popes were not always orthodox in their views.

8. The edict *Certum Est.*, July 8, 445.

the apostles.[9] At the end of the fifth century, another pope, Gelasius I, composed a letter to the Emperor Anastasius explaining the relationship between royal and priestly authority. Gelasius did not speak about papal power explicitly, but he laid down a principle that was to be crucial to the teachings of the medieval popes: royal power and priestly power are clearly separate, and each is supreme within its own sphere; because the sphere of priestly authority pertains to salvation of the soul, even the emperor should obey the priestly authority in spiritual matters.[10]

City of Rome

At the same time that the theory of papal supremacy was being developed, the city of Rome was prominent as a shrine for pilgrims. Christians of the ancient and medieval centuries attributed tremendous importance to physical objects as signs of divine power. Rome attracted numerous pilgrims because the bodies of Peter and Paul, the greatest apostles, were buried there. The pope's seat of authority was upon the very ground which was made holy by the presence of Peter himself.

Christians of the ancient and medieval centuries attributed tremendous importance to physical objects as signs of divine power.

The importance of the city of Rome and the development of theories of papal primacy would have meant little, however, if the early medieval popes had not shone forth as true leaders of the Christian people. Rome, in fact, was badly damaged and depopulated by the end of the sixth century. And the emperors, descendants of the Emperor Valentinian who upheld papal power, had ceased to be a factor in the politics of the West. They were in no position to offer support. The papacy made good its theoretical claims to power when gifted men like St. Gregory the Great (who ruled 590–604) emerged as spiritual and even

9. Pope Leo I, Sermon No. 3.

10. Pope Gelasius I, Letter to Emperor Anastasius.

political leaders. The Roman Senate was never heard of after 579, and probably had ceased to be a power much earlier. Papal officials were taking over all the tasks that had belonged to the Roman government, and for a while the popes even fed the masses in Rome as the emperors had done before. When the Lombards conquered northern Italy and made thrusts toward the central portion of the Italian Peninsula, the pope was the natural leader of Rome against the invaders. Gregory the Great and other popes were political leaders, engaging in diplomacy to protect their people.

Many of the popes were political leaders.

Papal Allies

To counterbalance the strength of the Lombard kings during the eighth century, the papacy allied itself with the Frankish monarchy, which was becoming the most vital force in European politics. The line of Merovingian kings in France (Clovis' descendants) had all but died out, and the true leader of the Franks was Pepin, mayor of the king's palace. Pepin sent a representative to Pope Zacharias for endorsement in 749, and the pope answered that the man who truly held power should be declared king. Pepin was anointed king by an archbishop shortly afterward. Several years later, when Rome was being threatened by Lombard armies again, Zacharias' successor Stephen appealed to Pepin for help. Pepin not only vanquished the Lombards, but also donated the conquered lands of northern Italy to the pope. Pepin's son Charlemagne likewise was asked to protect Rome, and he conquered the Lombards once and for all. Charles traveled to Rome in the year 800, to aid Pope Leo III in a dispute. At Mass on Christmas Day, Leo placed a crown on Charles' head while the congregation hailed him as "pious Augustus," that is, the new Roman Emperor. Experts disagree about whether Charlemagne even wanted to be called Emperor, but the title of Holy Roman Emperor continued to have great importance during the Middle Ages.

Donation of Constantine

At about the same time, the power of the papacy and the close relationship between pope and emperor were enhanced by the "discovery" of a document known as the **Donation of Constantine.** Forgeries were very common at this time in history, and it appears that someone forged a document that was alleged to have been written by Emperor Constantine. The emperor, busy in faraway Constantinople and motivated by love for the Church, was supposed to have given the pope power to rule Rome as a kind of imperial deputy. The Donation of Constantine contained mistakes that revealed it to be a forgery, but it was not until the fifteenth century that two scholars were able to detect the errors. In the meantime, the Donation of Constantine strengthened the popes' claims to be political as well as spiritual rulers in Rome.

Donation of Constantine—a forged document, supposedly written by Emperor Constantine, that strengthened the popes' claims to be political as well as spiritual rulers in Rome.

By a combination of well-articulated theory and bold political maneuvering, the papacy was growing to be one of the most powerful institutions in the Latin West. The papacy fell upon hard times during the two hundred years after the coronation of Charlemagne. After a reform during the eleventh century, however, the ancient tradition of papal primacy and the habit of bold action were pressed into action once more. The popes became the leaders of the medieval world, spearheading an attempt to reform society in terms of Christian beliefs.

The popes became the leaders of the medieval world, spearheading an attempt to reform society in terms of Christian beliefs.

Summary

- The papacy was a powerful force in the medieval world.

- Peter was named the "Rock" upon which the Church would be built.

- The roots of the papacy lie in identifying later bishops of Rome with St. Peter.

- The early medieval popes stood out as true spiritual and political leaders of the Christian people.

Prayer

And so I tell you, Peter: you are a rock, and on this rock foundation I will build my Church, and not even death will be able to overcome it. I will give you the keys of the kingdom of heaven; what you prohibit on earth will be prohibited in heaven, and what you permit on earth will be permitted in heaven.

Matthew 16:18–19

Discussion Questions

1. According to Roman Catholic belief, how did the bishops of Rome inherit extraordinary powers?

2. In what ways do Clement's letter to the Corinthians reveal the special status of Rome's bishop?

3. List any three of the historical factors that contributed to the growth of papal power.

Chapter Fourteen

New Forms of Christian Worship

The Christian faith of the Germanic peoples of the West was being expressed in ways that were entirely new. You have already seen how the missionary spirit of the early Church continued during the early Middle Ages, but under a different form. The medieval Church also shared the early Church's reverence for the Jewish heritage. But while the early Church had focused upon the messianic prophecies and the Jewish prayer customs, the medieval Church was attracted to the Hebrew lawgivers, especially Moses and Solomon. The community spirit of early Christianity also lived on, but under radically different forms. While the Eucharist had been the center of early Christian community life, in the medieval world the drive for community found clearest expression in the monasteries; and of course the monasteries had numerous ties with the society as a whole.

Similarly, the forms of worship, like the other elements of Christian life, underwent changes during the early Middle Ages. The practices of initiation into the community, forgiveness of sins against the community, and Eucharistic worship were all transformed during the fifth through ninth centuries.

The concept of initiation was subject to changes that reflected new social conditions and new understandings of Christian doctrine. During the third and fourth centuries, initiation into the community had followed upon the several-year-long process known as the catechumenate. As time went on, the lengthy catechumenate fell into disuse. The period of preparation was shifted to the priesthood: while in many cases priests received little or no training, the ideal was to have extensive preparation for every candidate for ordination.

It became the general practice in the Middle Ages to baptize infants rather than adults. As the doctrine of Original Sin became more widely accepted, many Christians preferred infant baptism because they believed that an unbaptized person would be deprived of full union with God in heaven. In fact, the Church found it necessary to discourage the popular belief that an unbaptized baby could be condemned to eternal separation from God. The earlier practice of delaying baptism until old age had few adherents in the Middle Ages, especially because medical procedures were primitive and infant death was a common phenomenon.

Frequent Penance

Concupiscence—a general inclination of humans toward sin.

The reasoning that influenced people's thinking about baptism also contributed to a new view of penance. According to the reasoning of St. Augustine, Adam's original fall had done more than just put people in immediate need of divine forgiveness. A related effect of the fall was **concupiscence,** a general inclination of humans toward sin. If indeed an inclination toward sin was part of people's fallen nature, then the impracticality of the early Christians' once-in-a-lifetime confession and reconciliation would soon become apparent. That insight into humanity's sinfulness and humanity's need of Christ's healing power is credited to St. Patrick, founder of the Church in Ireland. He originated an entirely new penitential practice: frequent individual confession.

Among the Irish monks, it was common for a young monk to speak with his abbot or another prominent holy man of the community. The monk would speak about his progress in the spiritual life and seek out the wisdom of an elder. In time, it came about that the young man confessed his sins to the elder, and the elder laid hands on him as a sign of Christ's healing of the wounds of sin. But this was not the end of the innovations. In the frontier environment of the Irish missions, far from the homeland of Christian tradition, the confession and reconciliation were not a one-time thing, but an oft-repeated experience. The process bespoke a concept of general spiritual growth throughout one's life.

Further, the old custom of a long period of penance before absolution was replaced by an immediate laying on of hands, followed by the performance of penitential acts *after* the forgiveness of sins. Finally, the healing power of Christ was not reserved for people guilty of just the major sins, but was extended to all people regardless of whether their transgressions were great or small. The penances assigned to the confessed sinner were mild or severe, depending upon the gravity of the sins that were confessed. Handbooks even appeared, prescribing set penances for each type of sin, so that the penances would suit the offenses according to a consistent rule of thumb.

The old custom of a long period of penance before absolution was replaced by an immediate laying on of hands, followed by the performance of penitential acts after the forgiveness of sins.

When St. Columban and his followers landed on the Continent to begin their missionary efforts, they brought the new type of penance with them. Councils of bishops initially condemned the Irish form of penance because it was contrary to tradition. But before long the private confession was widespread and the bishops' councils were endorsing the new form. They recommended that a person confess at least three times per year. The new form of penance gained wide acceptance for three reasons: it was based upon a realistic view of human nature, it was consistent with the prevalent understanding of human sinfulness, and it was readily incorporated into the life of the Christian community.

Even though the acts of confession and absolution were private in the new Irish form of penance, the community still played an important role. Loyal in one respect to the older tradition, the new type of penance was characterized by generally harsh penances. Long pilgrimages or forty-day fasts on just bread and water were common, even for offenses that a modern-day Catholic might consider to be minor. As many people had difficulty performing these acts of satisfaction, there arose a system whereby a penance could be commuted into an act of charity within the community—the requirement of a long fast, for example, could be dropped if the penitent made a contribution to the poor.

Changes in the Mass

The changes in the Mass during the early Middle Ages were equally as great as the changes in baptism and penance. Here, too, the spread of monasticism contributed to the transformation. But the roots of the changes in Eucharistic worship grew out of new theories about the Eucharist that had their origin in the early Church. The early Christians had emphasized the idea that the Eucharist was a prayer of thanksgiving to God, and a memorial of Jesus' Last Supper with the disciples. They understood their type of worship to be utterly different from pagan worship, in which animals were sacrificed on altars to please the gods. As some early Christian thinkers expressed it, "Our sacrifice to God is the offering of our own good lives and pure hearts." They were being careful to avoid the pagan notion that a ritual sacrifice, performed perfectly, could help them to get what they wanted from the gods.

At the same time, Christians believed that Christ himself was a sin-offering. He was sometimes described by the image of the "Lamb of God," whose death and resurrection were an offering to God for humanity's sins, so that humanity could share in everlasting life. Because Jesus' body had been offered up for humanity's sins and his blood had been shed for the same end, the Eucharistic words "This is my Body; this is my Blood" could be understood to suggest the idea of sacrifice. By the fourth century, the differences between Christianity and paganism were unmistakable, and Christianity was legally established as the official religion of the formerly pagan Empire. Under these circumstances, great thinkers such as St. Ambrose and St. Augustine developed the idea of the sacrificial character of the Mass. By the time of St. Gregory the Great, it was commonly believed that each time the Mass was celebrated, the death and resurrection of Jesus were reenacted. People became more convinced of the importance of God's power at work in the Mass. The idea of Mass-as-memorial and Mass-as-community-celebration did not disappear, but they received less emphasis.

By the time of St. Gregory the Great, it was commonly believed that each time the Mass was celebrated, the death and resurrection of Jesus were reenacted.

When the popes sent the monks to preach the Gospel in distant lands during the sixth through eighth centuries, it became common practice for many monks to be ordained as priests. The aim was to allow the monk-priests to fulfill more roles—such as saying Mass or hearing confessions or baptizing converts—in the outlying territories. Monk-priests soon became common even within monastic communities which were not in remote areas. In keeping with the well established practice of delegating responsibility for prayer to the monks in society, many monasteries encouraged their monk-priests to celebrate Masses for individuals. These came to be known as **"votive" Masses,** that is, Masses said for a person's special intentions. A rich noble, for example, might donate a piece of land to the monastery in exchange for having a Mass said every day for the protection of his soul.

Votive Masses—Masses said for a person's special intentions.

A few intellectuals challenged this practice on the grounds that the good performed by Christ on the Cross and by Christ in the celebration of the Eucharist was for all people, so that a multiplication of the number of Masses said by monk-priests was totally unnecessary. But to the mind of the everyday Christian, the special Mass said daily for his or her special intentions offered tremendous reassurance that spiritual powers were being called up for his or her own protection and that of loved ones. The votive Mass continues to be popular up to the present day.

The votive Mass continues to be popular today.

Another objection to the multiplication of Masses said by individual monk-priests was that the Masses were said in private. The old practice of gathering the community of Christians to praise God together over a meal was being lost. In addition to the rise of the private votive Masses by solitary priests, other factors worked toward making the Eucharist less a community affair. Latin was evolving into new, local languages for the common people of the West during the Middle Ages, but Latin continued to be the language used in the Mass. Before long, the congregations did not know what was being said in the Mass, because their own language was far removed from Latin. Physical acts, such as the raising of the consecrated **Host** (Body and Blood of Christ) by the priest, assumed even greater importance. The priest offered the sacrifice of the Mass to God, and turned his back to the community. Altar rails were erected to separate the common people from the holy activities of the priest's ritual. Most people received Holy Communion rarely, if at all; but their devotion was so strong that they would often stay for several Masses on Sunday. They believed that each time the Body and Blood of the Lord were elevated, if they saw the Lord each time, even from a distance, they would benefit from the effects of God's power. The people received Holy Communion so rarely that bishops' councils decreed that the faithful

Host—the consecrated Body of Christ.

must partake of Communion at least three times a year, and hear Mass once a week if possible.

Even though traditional Christian values such as emphasis upon community were very much alive during the early Middle Ages, the forms which these values assumed were radically altered. In the case of Eucharistic worship, the forms were almost the complete opposite of what they had been centuries earlier.

Related to these changes was a growth in the importance of the priesthood in medieval society. The long process of preparation was shifted out of the sphere of baptism and into ordination; priests were assuming new roles as private confessors; and they were the ordained few who handled the holy objects in the Mass. Medieval society was coming to be a **sacerdotal** society, that is, one in which priests held a prominent place. This was one of the most important features of medieval society, as you shall see in chapter sixteen. While the Protestant churches later rejected this sacerdotal character of the Church, it has continued to be an important factor in the Roman Catholic community up to the present.

Sacerdotal—dominated by priests.

Summary

• It became general practice to baptize infants rather than adults.

• The custom of long periods of penance before absolution was replaced by an immediate laying on of hands, followed by penitential acts.

• Frequent confession was encouraged.

• Votive Masses came into being and are still said today.

• Latin became the language of the Mass and the priest celebrated Mass with his back to the people.

• The old practice of gathering the community of Christians to praise God together over a meal was being lost.

• A growth in the importance of priesthood was seen.

Prayer

*Merciful God, good Lord. . . .You are our all: our
life and our light, our food and our drink, our
salvation and our God.*

> *St. Columban*
> *Irish Monk and*
> *Scholar*

Discussion Questions

1. How did the emphasis upon Original Sin
   affect popular beliefs concerning baptism?

2. What are the most obvious differences
   between the early and medieval (Irish)
   forms of the Sacrament of Penance?

3. What was the basic difference in emphasis
   between early Christian and medieval
   Christian understandings of the Eucharist?

4. What does it mean to say that medieval
   society was becoming "sacerdotal," and
   how did this change come about?

The Bishop of Augsburg administers Eucharist to Otto I on the battlefield.

Chapter Fifteen

Reform and Renewal during the Tenth and Eleventh Centuries

Spiritual and Secular

The ancient Church had grown in a hostile pagan world, and the early Christians were acutely aware of the fact that their Church was a separate community within the empire. That attitude began to change when the Christian faith was first tolerated, then legally established as the official religion of the empire. During the early Middle Ages, the involvement of the Church in the Germanic society was intimate: popes were negotiating treaties, bishops were serving as regional administrators, lesser clergy were assistants to kings, monks were maintaining frontier outposts and performing a host of social and spiritual tasks for the people of their local communities.

The two basic "realms" within society, then, were being united in many ways: the *secular* (that is, worldly) realm was not clearly distinguished from the *spiritual* realm (the Church). In some cases, this situation arose quite by accident, but in other instances the leaders of the Church consciously chose to assume secular tasks. Would the pope have been a good pastor for his people if he had not organized resistance to the Lombard invasions in the sixth century? Could Boniface's mission to the Germans have continued if his

The two basic realms within society were being united in many ways: the secular realm was not clearly distinguished from the spiritual realm (the Church).

147

monasteries had not become like little cities? Could not a bishop bring Christian values to the community more effectively if he were also the local lord of a region, passing laws and administering justice? The man who wrote the biography of one tenth-century bishop had these questions in mind when he defended his bishop's involvement in worldly affairs:

> If anyone who is ignorant of the divine dispensation objects to a bishop ruling the people and facing the dangers of war, and argues that he is responsible only for their souls, the answer is obvious: it is by doing these things that the guardian and teacher of the faithful brings to them the rare gift of peace and saves them from the darkness in which there is no light.[1]

Most likely, the bishop's actions were being defended because some objection had been raised. As a matter of fact, the intimate involvement of bishops and other Churchmen in the secular world often led to abuses during the early Middle Ages, as the pursuit of worldly responsibilities led them to neglect their higher responsibilities as Christians. It might be said that the Church became involved in the world, so that it might spiritualize the secular realm; but a frequent result was that the spiritual realm itself became secularized.

Invasions

Worldliness was a constant temptation for the medieval Church, and a new set of problems confronted the Church during the ninth century. At that time, Europe was subjected to new barbarian invasions, nearly as horrible and as shattering as the invasions several

1. Ruotger, *Life of Bruno, Archbishop of Cologne,* chapter 23; cited in R. W. Southern, *Western Society and the Church in the Middle Ages,* Pelican, p. 174.

centuries earlier. Saracen (Moslem) pirates raided the Mediterranean coast of Italy and France; Hungarian tribes terrorized Germany and northern Italy; Vikings swept out of the north into continental Europe. One Viking tribe, the Danes, conquered Britain. While most of the Vikings came to raid rather than to conquer, the political structures of the young Germanic kingdoms were so fragile that they all but collapsed under the pressures.

Under these circumstances, the Church suffered in many ways. Monasteries were plundered, and episcopal[2] administrations broke down, which meant that essential tasks, such as the education and discipline of priests, were not being adequately carried out. Many priests were keeping women in their households, and engaging in **simony,** the selling of religious offices and services. Kings and dukes, meanwhile, were passing out episcopal offices to their relatives, with little concern about the spiritual qualities required of a bishop; and the bishops, too, often promoted their own family members to offices in the Church. (The practice of giving employment to one's relatives is called **nepotism.**)

Simony—the buying or selling of religious offices or services.

Nepotism—the practice of giving employment to one's relatives.

Reform

These ills had many causes that were not easily cured, and the result was a general decline in the quality of religious devotion. Unspiritual bishops were not as responsible as they could have been in maintaining the discipline of their priests, and undisciplined priests were not as solicitous as they might have been in the care of their flock. Similarly, uninspired abbots were not effective in maintaining discipline in their monasteries.

2. The Latin word for "bishop" is episcopus," from which the English adjective "episcopal" is derived. The bishop's office sometimes is called an "episcopacy" or a "bishopric."

Out of this dismal situation arose the spirit of reform. Early in the tenth century, councils of bishops met to discuss the problems and call for reform in society and in the Church. Their proclamations about the poor state of the Church leveled criticisms even against themselves. They called for a renewal of discipline for their priests and spoke up against the most obvious cases of abuse. Some bishops, for example, ruled more than one diocese and did not even maintain residence in the dioceses that they ruled; they just collected the taxes. There were abbots, too, who had concubines living with them in the monasteries. Unfortunately, modern research has not yet determined how effective the bishops' reform programs were.

A great deal is known about the tremendous successes that were achieved by monastic reformers, however. The monasteries had long served as the spiritual "leaven" in early medieval society, and they were restored to that role when a number of monastic houses returned to the invigorating discipline of St. Benedict's Rule. By far, the most famous of the success stories was the new monastery of Cluny, which was founded in Burgundy (eastern France) in 910. Its foundation charter gave the monks the right to elect their own abbot, so that the office of abbot could never become a political "prize" for an unscrupulous noble to hand out to relatives. The foundation charter also specified that bishops, kings and nobles were to have absolutely no control over the business of the monastery—again, the aim was to free Cluny from all sources of corruption. At the same time, Cluny was placed under the authority of the pope. The papacy was no pillar of reform in the tenth century, but it probably seemed more attractive to be under the jurisdiction of a distant pope rather than a local bishop.

Cluny adhered closely to the Benedictine Rule and became a model of discipline for all of Europe. So renowned were the Cluniac monks

Cluny adhered closely to the Benedictine Rule and became a model of discipline for all of Europe.

that other monasteries asked to be placed under the jurisdiction of the Abbot of Cluny. On this point, the new monastery departed from Benedict's program: Benedict envisioned a single monastery under a powerful abbot, but Cluny placed all monasteries under the jurisdiction of its own abbot. The list of the abbots of Cluny from 910 to about 1100 is full of names preceded by the title of "saint": a remarkable succession of gifted, spiritual men ruled Cluny and her daughter houses, which eventually numbered in the hundreds. Cluny's reform, along with parallel monastic movements in England, northern Italy, and the Rhine Valley of Germany embraced nearly all of Christendom.

The new plan of having many monasteries under the Abbot of Cluny gave rise to the Church's first highly organized religious **order;** in other words, the monks in the various monasteries all lived under the same rule as interpreted by Cluny's abbot, and so all of the monks lived the same sort of spiritual life. Cluny's interpretation of the Benedictine Rule placed strong emphasis upon praying the **Divine Office,** the cycle of prayers based upon the Psalms. The monks composed beautiful, poetic prayers for every feast day of the year, and set the prayers to a special form of music known as **Gregorian Chant.** Chant has no "beat" of rhythm in the modern sense of the term, and can convey a sense of timelessness and presence of God—the exact opposite of the busy life in the secular realm. Because of improvements in agricultural technology, the Cluniac monks were free to downplay St. Benedict's emphasis upon manual labor in favor of more prayer. They may have spent up to six hours a day chanting their praises of the Lord.

Order—a group of monks, nuns, or priests all living the same kind of life under the same rule.

Divine Office—a cycle of prayers based on the Psalms.

Gregorian Chant—a special form of music used by the monks to recite their poetic prayers.

Cluniac spirituality was the dominant force in European monasticism for nearly two centuries. But by the end of the eleventh century, the reform spirit was turned against Cluny itself. A young man named Stephen

Harding, dissatisfied with the discipline at his monastery, set out with a few friends to build a new monastic house deep in the forest of Citeaux (northern France). The more simple lifestyle at Citeaux attracted so many followers that it became necessary to build another monastery in a forest called Clairvaux. The Abbot of Clairvaux was St. Bernard, who became the spokesman for a return to the letter of the Benedictine Rule: silence throughout most of the day, manual labor for all monks, and a simple lifestyle in contrast to Cluny's richness and elaborate prayers. The conservative reaction of Bernard and the Cistercian Order[3] was matched by that of the Carthusians, yet another order that arose in Italy at the same time. Even today, the Carthusian Order is renowned for its somber asceticism.

Reform of the Papacy

The reform and renewal of monasticism had effects throughout society, but ultimately it was the reform of the papacy that revolutionized Western Christianity. Europe in the tenth and eleventh centuries was rapidly changing: technology was improving, population was growing, wilderness areas were being cleared out and settled, trade was increasing. The monks had been the chief agents of growth in the early Middle Ages, when their monasteries served as outposts of civilization in a land sparsely populated by barbarians. But even Western monasticism, with its relatively close ties to society, was founded upon the notion of retirement from the secular world; while it continued to be a factor in the spiritual lives of many Christians, it could never serve in a directive role in the aggressive new society that was emerging. Leadership passed to the reinvigorated papacy.

3. *Cistercian* is an adjective derived from "Citeaux."

There had been a few men of exceptional talent on the papal throne during the ninth and tenth centuries but, generally, the papacy had become just another prize for secular rules to pass out to their friends and relatives. To make matters worse, several noble families in Rome were engaged in constant competition for power. The pope would usually belong to whichever family maneuvered most skillfully among the competitors. Rome continued to attract pilgrims, but the power lay in the tomb of St. Peter, not in the hands of the successor of Peter.

After Charlemagne's dynasty fell, the kings in Germany assumed the title "Holy Roman Emperor" for themselves, and in some instances, they sought to have themselves crowned by the popes. Such was the case in 1046, when King Henry III traveled to Rome to be crowned emperor. What he found there was not one pope but three candidates, each representing a family and each claiming to be pope. Henry was disgusted. He dismissed the three would-be popes and installed a German candidate of his own—a bishop who was interested in reform. Unfortunately this reformer died after several months, probably the victim of poison. Henry appointed a second pope, whom the local nobles poisoned after just a few weeks. A third appointee to the papal throne, who took the name Leo IX,[4] survived six years (1048-1054). He was a bishop from the Rhine Valley, where monastic reform had encouraged a strong spirit of reform and renewal.

Leo IX brought that spirit to the papacy. He assembled **synods,** or councils, in Rome to denounce simony and to promote **celibacy** among priests. His next step changed the papacy from a Roman office to a position of leadership for the entire Church: not content to call for reform from Rome alone, he

Synod—synonym for "council."

Celibacy—a life of abstention from sexual relationships.

4. Whenever a man is elected pope, he assumes a new name as a symbol of his new status. Thus Karol Wojtyla, for example, took the name John Paul II.

traveled personally to France and Germany to put the authority of St. Peter behind a general reform of the Church. At Rheims (France) and Mainz (Germany) he brought local bishops into councils. Both councils condemned simony, concubinage and clerical marriage; both discouraged clerics (Churchmen) from bearing arms or following worldly occupations; both promoted the idea that a bishop should be elected by the clergy and the people.

In a remarkably bold move, Leo demanded that the bishops at Rheims make a confession if they had purchased their offices. Those bishops who confessed to simony, Leo forgave and restored to their offices. The one bishop who resisted was summoned to Rome to be dealt with later. From that moment, there was no doubt that the successor of Peter had assumed leadership of the Church.

Two other things done by Leo IX set the stage for future popes. His councils included condemnations of divorce and incest, and they called for protection of the poor from fraud and theft. Thus Leo began the process by which the papacy expanded the reform of the Church into a general reform of the entire Christian society. Also, he initiated the practice of sending **legates** (representatives) in his name, carrying his authority throughout Christendom to see that his reforms were being carried out. In just five years, Leo IX transformed the papacy from a weak office, badly in need of reform, to a powerful office in charge of reform.

Legate—a representative sent out by the pope.

His career ended sadly. Norman knights had left their homes in northern France to seek their fortunes in southern Italy. Their raids were disrupting the lives of Italian people, and Pope Leo led an army to stop them. Unfortunately the Normans defeated and captured the pope, who died soon afterward.

Leo's successors ultimately made alliances with the Norman conquerors in southern Italy. They hoped that the strength of the Normans might serve as a counterbalance to the strength of the German emperors. For under the leadership of a theorist named Humbert, the popes began calling for reforms that would surely offend the emperors. In 1059, Pope Nicholas II decreed at a synod that bishops should never be invested with their powers by lay leaders—thus opposing a long tradition of royal appointment of bishops. In the same year, the pope decreed that the emperor could not select a pope; all popes from that time forward were to be elected only by **cardinals,** the men (most often bishops) who were appointed as special assistants to the popes.

Cardinal—a special assistant to the pope.

In the general reform of the Church during the tenth and eleventh centuries, laymen played key roles. A layman, Count William of Aquitaine, donated lands for the monastery of Cluny and drafted the foundation charter that freed Cluny from common sources of corruption. A layman, Henry III, used his imperial powers to break the nobles in Rome and liberate the papacy to become the leader of the reform movement. But with the theorists who affected Rome's policies after the pontificate[5] of Leo IX came a new vision: lay involvement was to be shunned in order to purify the Church of secular influence. The full meaning of this momentous change of policy was not evident until a fiery monk named Hildebrand became Pope Gregory VII in 1073.

5. *Pontificate* means "papal region," or the period of time when a particular person served as pope. In ancient pagan Rome, *pontifex* was the Latin word meaning "priest." "Pontifex Maximus" or "High Priest" was the title assumed by the Roman emperor. As another kind of high priest, the pope came to be called the "Roman pontiff," and his decrees were sometimes referred to as "pontifical" decrees.

Summary

- The spiritual and secular realms of society were being united in many ways.

- Worldliness was a constant temptation for the medieval Church.

- Councils of bishops met to discuss the problems of the Church and called for reform in both society and the Church.

- The monastery of Cluny placed all monasteries under the rule of the Abbot of Cluny.

- Cluniac spirituality was the dominant force in European monasticism for nearly two centuries.

- The reform of the papacy revolutionized Western Christianity.

Prayer

A church leader must be without fault; he must be sober, self-controlled, and orderly. . . .He must be mature in the faith, so that he will not swell up with pride and be condemned. . . .He should be a man who is respected by the people outside the Church, so that he will not be disgraced and fall into the devil's trap.

1 Timothy 3:2,6–7

Discussion Questions

1. What in medieval belief were the two "realms," and how did medieval Christians see the relationship between these two realms?

2. List the foremost examples of Church corruption in the Middle Ages.

3. What is a religious "order," and what were some prominent features of the Order of Cluny?

4. What things did the papal reformers promote and what did they condemn in their efforts to overcome corruption?

Henry IV, in the garb of a penitent, waits at Canossa to see Pope Gregory VII.

Chapter Sixteen

Papal vs. Imperial Authority in Christendom

Feudal System

The papal theorists' rejection of secular influences upon the Church between 1050 and 1075 was certain to be poorly received by the kings in Christendom, who considered a close alliance between themselves and their bishops to be essential to good order within their kingdoms. To understand the kings' viewpoint, it is necessary to examine the feudal system of political organization that existed in medieval Europe.

Because the technology of transportation and communication was limited during the Middle Ages, a king could not maintain firm control over a large, integrated national state such as exists today. Instead he had to delegate his authority to powerful noblemen, usually called magnates or barons or dukes, who controlled large regions in the name of the king. Similar limitations forced the dukes to subdivide their own territories among lesser nobles, often called counts or knights. The noble was the king's "vassal," the king was the vassal's "lord"; the same terminology governed the relationship between a duke and his counts. The lord in a feudal relationship provided protection and justice for his vassal, and he granted the vassal a "fief," or piece of land, so that the vassal could support himself comfortably. The vassal in turn performed services for the lord (such as military duty) or, in the late Middle Ages, made money payments to the lord as a form of rent. Bonds between men were very strong in medieval society, as the vassal knelt down and performed an act of "homage" to the lord; on oath he swore fidelity to his lord, and swore to be his lord's "man."[1]

The feudal system had so many practical advantages that it endured under a variety of forms throughout the Middle Ages. But for the king there was the one great disadvantage that it diminished his power. Lords became attached to their lands, and succeeded in passing on their lands and privileges to their sons. The noble family became entrenched, an independent power. Here lay the advantage of a close relationship between king and bishop: a bishop, being celibate, had no children to inherit rights and lands. When a bishop died, the king could simply appoint another bishop of his own choice to rule an important region within the kingdom. Kings were pleased because they gained well-educated lords who had no families that might become attached to the land. The Church was happy because the medieval economy was not a money economy, and the grant of a fief provided the bishop with the income necessary to carry out his **ecclesiastical** functions.

Eccelsiastical—an English word derived from the Greek word *ecclesia* meaning Church.

It would not be fair to the kings to portray the bishop-king relationship as one of mere economic and political convenience. A large proportion of the medieval kings saw themselves as servants of the Lord God, exercising authority on behalf of God and administering God's laws. They were well schooled in the Old Testament texts which proclaimed that kingship was a holy office, and they were anointed with consecrated oil in a ceremony parallel to the ordination of bishops. French kings from Charlemagne to King St. Louis IX, English kings such as Alfred

1. *Homage* today refers to any act of reverence; but it is derived from the Latin *homo,* meaning "man."

(Charlemagne's contemporary) and St. Edward the Confessor, German emperors such as Otto I, II, and III and Henry III, who worked to support a healthy papacy all provide clear examples of royal sanctity.

Nevertheless, abuse of royal power in the appointment of bishops was quite common, and the papal reformers of the late-eleventh century were determined to assert the Church's complete independence in choosing its own leaders and formulating its own policies. Their determination was sure to lead to problems, because they were threatening one of the foundations of the feudal system. The conflict shows up quite clearly in the clash of England's King Henry I with the Archbishop of Canterbury, named Anselm; and in the famous dispute between Henry II and Archbishop Thomas Becket in the same country. But the most serious conflict arose between the popes and the Holy Roman emperors of Germany. The emperors could claim to be the rightful secular leaders of all Christendom (at least in theory), and they had claims to jurisdiction over Italy, which claims they often supported by means of armed might.

Abuse of royal power in the appointment of bishops was quite common.

Investiture

The original issue at stake was lay investiture. When a bishopric became vacant, the king would choose a new man as bishop and "invest him" with a symbolic ring and a pastoral staff, called a **crozier.** The new bishop would perform an act of homage to the king and become the vassal in charge of a large parcel of land. Often the candidate for bishop, a rich man from an aristocratic family, paid the king a fee for the privilege of becoming the master of a valuable fief. The reformers immediately perceived that the episcopal candidates who paid fees for their appointments were guilty of simony. Wealthy bishops who were facing the wrath of the

Crozier—a bishop's pastoral staff, which is still used today during ceremonies.

reformers contended that the fee was only for the right to receive the lands, not for the right to become bishop. But that line of argumentation only brought the reformers to the heart of the matter: why, then, did the king invest the bishop with the pastoral staff, symbol of the bishop's role as spiritual shepherd over the flock?

Leo IX had brought many reformers with him from Germany to aid him at Rome. Among them was a man named Humbert, who was made Cardinal-Archbishop of Silva Candida. Humbert was a fiery-tempered man, inclined to express his views in extreme terms, and in this period of controversy he helped to bring matters to a head. Like most reformers in most ages of the Church's history, he argued that his apparently "new" conclusions actually represented a return to the early Church's way of doing things. In early times, he said, a bishop was chosen by the people of the Church, and then consecrated by the other bishops of the area. The current practice of having the king choose the bishop was entirely improper, and people chosen in this manner were not true bishops—especially because they have gained their positions by committing the sin of simony. (In fact, the book in which he presented this opinion had the title, *Against the Simoniacs*.)

Obviously, this line of reasoning was going to cause a clash with Europe's kings. If the kings and the pope were opposed, whose wishes should prevail? In a treatise written during the 1050s, Humbert addressed that very problem. He adopted Pope Gelasius II's old theory of the priestly and royal powers. Priestly power pertains to higher values, and ought to be higher than royal power. Or—to use Humbert's analogy, which was adopted by papal theorists for the next two centuries:

> *Just as the soul excells the body and*
> *commands it, so, too, the priestly dignity*
> *excells the royal or, we may say, the*

heavenly dignity, the earthly. Thus, that
all things may be in due order and not in
disarray, the priesthood, like a soul, may
advise what is to be done.[2]

What Humbert and the reform party were
proposing, ultimately, was a revolution in
outlook. Europe was a united Christendom,
directed by Christian teachings. Granted the
principle that spiritual matters have greater
dignity than the secular, and that priesthood
pertains to the higher spiritual affairs, then it
followed that the pope—first among all
priests—was the supreme authority of
Christendom. It is no accident that the
eleventh-century reform popes took names in
honor of earlier popes who had been powerful
leaders; "Leo" was one such choice, "Gregory"
was another. The conflict over investitures was
not, to the reformers' way of thinking, merely
a squabble over a procedural matter. It was
part of a serious effort to establish right order
in Christendom.

Prominent among the reform cardinals was a
monk named Hildebrand, who had been a
"power behind the throne" since Leo IX's day.
When Pope Alexander II died in 1073, the
Roman crowds cheered for Hildebrand (a
native Roman) to be their new pontiff. When a
vote by the cardinals confirmed the people's
choice, Hildebrand became Pope Gregory VII.
Shortly after his election. Pope Gregory strove
to enforce the papal decrees against lay
investiture. He was opposed by Henry IV, the
new King of Germany. Gregory's decree
against lay investiture was issued in February
of 1075, and just one month later he issued a
document called *Dictatus Papae.* Among the
revolutionary statements in *Dictatus Papae*
were the assertions that the pope had the
power to depose an emperor, and the pope
had the power to release subjects from loyalty
to an unjust king.

Prominent among the
reform cardinals was a
monk named
Hildebrand.

2. Humbert, *Priesthood and Kingship.*

To Henry IV, these were the words of a madman. Late in 1075 he tested Hildebrand's resolve by supporting his own candidate for the bishopric of Milan, against the bishop chosen by the pope. Gregory wrote a letter to Henry to criticize this action, and Henry's response was to summon a council of German bishops and pressure them into denouncing Gregory. Finally, in February of 1076, the pope unleashed his most potent weapon: he declared Henry IV to be **excommunicated,** that is, cut off entirely from the Christian community and unable to receive the sacraments. He also deprived Henry of all royal authority and forbade Germans to recognize him as king.

Excommunication—the act of excluding a person from the Christian community, and depriving the person of the sacraments.

Papal Supremacy

Here, at last, the reformers' extreme view of papal power was being put to the test. The result was an extraordinary victory for papal supremacy. The bishops who had denounced Gregory VII wrote to him seeking pardon, and the German subjects abandoned the king. There were always rival claimants to the throne in Germany, and soon a faction arose in support of another prominent noble as king. Henry, clearly beaten, arranged for a council to be presided over by the pope himself, in Germany, to decide Henry's fate. Then, as Gregory traveled northward to attend the council, Henry IV slipped away privately to meet him at Canossa, a small Italian outpost. Henry came on his knees through the January snows, confessing his sins and begging forgiveness.

Clearly, this was the pope's ultimate victory—but it was also his undoing. He left Henry waiting three days in the snow; finally, he felt that he could no longer deny a confessed sinner his rights, and he granted Henry absolution from his sins. Although he did not restore him to the kingship, he lifted the ban of excommunication. This may have been the best course for him to take as a priest, but politically the absolution amounted to a fatal blunder. Henry's opponents in Germany were left in a weakened position without papal support, as Henry began patching up his old political alliances. Their election of Rudolf of Swabia as king touched off three years of civil war against Henry's followers. In 1080, Gregory finally declared Rudolf to be the true king, and he excommunicated Henry IV once more; but this time the excommunication had little political impact. An embittered Henry slew Rudolf in 1080, then manipulated the election of a rival pope to challenge Gregory VII's authority. The emperor's armies besieged Rome in 1081 and 1084, and Gregory finally died in exile in 1085.

Similar ups and downs characterized the papacy's efforts against the German emperors over the next seventy-five years. Emperor Henry V showed himself to be his father's son when he laid siege to Rome in 1111, made Pope Paschal II his prisoner, and tried to coerce the pope into endorsing an imperialist policy concerning lay investiture. The Synod of Worms, in 1122, finally formulated a compromise between the papacy and the German ruler on the question of lay investiture: each bishop was to be elected by the clergy according to Church laws; the king had the right to be present at the election; the king was not to invest the bishop with the staff and ring, since they were symbols of the bishop's spiritual authority; but the bishop could perform homage to the king for any fief that he might receive from the king. The new arrangement worked to the king's advantage, because the ruler could refuse to accept a new bishop's act of homage, and effectively exercise a veto against the Church's choice.

The popes and emperors continued their struggle through the twelfth century, but the issues became less clear-cut. When Emperor Frederick Barbarossa sent his armies into Italy, for example, his motive was conquest of Italy.

Documents espousing imperialist, antipapal theories appeared at about the same time, but they were primarily a smokescreen for the emperor's ambitions. The papacy, meanwhile, struggled to maintain its leadership in opposition to **"anti-popes"** whom the emperors promoted to undermine the real popes' credibility. Popes became supporters of a league of northern Italian cities that resisted the emperor by force; the papacy even contributed material support to the resistance, since it was developing its own political base in central Italy, called the Papal States. During the conflict, excommunication was occasionally used against the emperors, but its effect was not so great as it had been under Gregory VII.

Anti-popes—false claimants to the Holy See.

The series of incidents between the popes and the kings could be interpreted as a defeat for the papacy. The compromise solution in the investiture controversy actually worked out to the king's advantage, overuse of excommunication dulled its effectiveness as a tool, and the popes' involvement in Italian politics established a precedent which was the undermine of the papacy's credibility in spiritual leadership during later centuries.

Overuse of excommunication dulled its effectiveness.

But the twelfth and thirteenth centuries actually turned out to be the time when the popes rose to the pinnacle of authority in Christendom. On a theoretical level, the only papal claim that was not generally accepted was Gregory VII's assertion of the right to depose a king. Even the men who wrote pamphlets on behalf of the emperors cited Gelasius' arguments about the two spheres of authority; and like all the learned men of Christendom, they accepted the notions that spiritual values were higher than secular values, and that the pope was the undisputed guardian of the spiritual values. Before the eleventh century, the pope claimed the title of "Vicar of Peter" (representative of Peter), and bishops throughout the European world operated relatively independently. By the twelfth century, however, the pope was addressed by the lofty title of "Vicar of Christ," and was master of a highly centralized Church organization.

By the twelfth century, the pope was addressed by the lofty title of "Vicar of Christ," and was master of a highly centralized Church organization.

The theoretical supremacy of the pope was born out in practice as well. Within the Church itself, numerous monasteries placed themselves directly under papal rather that episcopal jurisdiction. Papal legates gave authoritative instructions to bishops, and met little opposition. The clergy established the right to be judged only in Church courts, never in secular courts, and the pope was the highest judge in the ecclesiastical court system.

Dispensing Justice

The power of dispensing justice was the key to the pope's predominance over the secular realm, too. The power of kingship lay in the investing of bishops, it is true, as well as in levying taxes and raising armies. But in medieval society, the greatest single power was that of dispensing justice. Local lords judged cases for their vassals during the early Middle Ages, and by the twelfth century, the kings' chief method of increasing their own power was to establish appellate courts; the kings encouraged their subjects to make appeals from local courts to the royal courts, where they could receive a decision from the highest possible authority. The triumph of the papacy lay in the fact that in the eyes of Europe's Christians, the pope was a higher judge than any king. Case after case was appealed to Rome, to such an extent that the best-known popes of the 1100s and 1200s were lawyers in charge of an ever-growing judiciary machine.

In the eyes of Europe's Christians, the pope was a higher judge than any king.

Disputes over legal rights occupied a very large portion of people's attention during the Middle Ages. Contracts were not so carefully worded as they could have been, because legal expertise was not yet well developed. Property lines were not so easily determined, and records of ownership were often incomplete. By the very nature of feudalism, there were numerous overlapping jurisdictions. As a result of these weaknesses, there were many opportunities for disagreement, and the pursuit of justice was an all-consuming preoccupation for medieval people. Records still exist which indicate that occasionally a single case would be bounced around from court to court for fifty years or more.

Rome was the ideal final court of appeals, because the most highly educated jurists resided there, and because—this is the crucial consideration—there could be no appeal beyond the judgment of the supreme lord of Christendom. A judgment from Rome was final as no other judgment could be. Kings themselves appealed to the pope.

The popes' prestige as the final arbiters in Christendom lent credence to their efforts to be leaders in other endeavors. The Roman pontiffs directed a variety of efforts which aimed at giving a distinctly Christian character to Western society. A summary of their successes and failures will be the subject matter of chapter eighteen.

Summary

- The feudal system existed in medieval Europe.

- To protect his power, a king would appoint a bishop to rule over an important region.

- Medieval kings saw themselves as servants of God, exercising authority on behalf of God and administering God's laws.

- Pope Gregory VII called for reform and strove to enforce the papal decrees against lay investiture.

- The papacy struggled to maintain its leadership in opposition to "anti-popes."

- The pursuit of justice was an all-consuming preoccupation for the medieval people, and the pope's court became the final court of appeals.

Prayer

We love you, O God, and desire to love you more and more. Grant that we may love you as we wish to love you and as we should love you. O dearest Friend who has loved us so deeply and redeemed us, come and take your place in our hearts . . . and we need no longer fear for soul and body.

St. Anselm of Canterbury

Discussion Questions

1. Why did kings find it to their advantage to hold onto the power of appointing bishops?

2. What were some ways in which Gregory VII attempted to apply Humbert's theory of papal supremacy in his struggle against Henry IV?

3. Explain the claims that no matter how the dramatic clashes turned out, on a day-to-day basis the popes exercised supreme power, especially through the courts.

Icon of Blessed Mother of Perpetual Help

Chapter Seventeen

The East-West Split

In one sense, the conflict between royal and papal power took place because the papacy insisted upon asserting its leadership in Western society, against kingship which had long been the dominant institution. The break between the Eastern and Western halves of the Church was similar: the pope (bishop of Rome) asserted his primacy over the **patriarch** (bishop of Constantinople), and the latter refused to acknowledge the claims. The two sides each pursued an independent course after the critical year 1054, and they have remained separate up to the present day. The pope is the supreme leader in the Western, or Roman Catholic, portion of the Church, while the patriarch exercises varying degrees of authority over the different branches of the Eastern Orthodox portion of the Church.

Patriarch—the bishop, or father-figure, of a great Christian city.

You have already read about how the bishop of Rome rose to a position of unmatched authority in the Latin West. Among the Greek-speaking Christians Rome had long been considered an important See, but because of historical circumstances they were quite surprised by the papacy's assertiveness during the eleventh century, and they were not at all receptive to the papacy's claims of special authority.

In the early Church, four cities were prominent: Rome, Alexandria, Antioch, and Jerusalem. The bishops of those cities were honored as "patriarchs." Jerusalem was important because it was the place of the Church's origins, and the other three cities stood out for their political and economic importance. After the fourth century, the bishop of Constantinople also came to be called a patriarch.

Islam

Early in the seventh century, the prophet Mohammed founded the new religion Islam.

Jihad—the "holy war" of the Moslems, to bring new territories under Islam.

Early in the seventh century, the prophet Mohammed founded the new religion Islam, and his followers launched the **jihad,** or "holy war," which brought most of the lands of the Mediterranean Basin under their control. By the year 700, three of the five patriarchal Churches, Jerusalem, Antioch, and Alexandria, lay under the control of the Moslems. Of the two remaining churches of special dignity, Rome clearly was the more ancient of the two, and of course only Rome could claim to be the resting-place of St. Peter.

Constantinople was important as the capital of the Roman Empire, but in Constantinople it was the emperor who ruled, not the patriarch. In Rome, meanwhile, the pope was serving the important role of deputy for the emperor. The Byzantine (Eastern Roman) emperors repeatedly sent expeditions against the barbarian chieftains in a desperate attempt to keep Italy within the Empire, and the popes ruled on their behalf in Italy. (The claims that were made in the Donation of Constantine were not entirely far-fetched: the pope was ruling at the emperor's request.)

But by the eighth century, the Eastern Empire was reeling under the blows of the Moslems, and it was no longer feasible to maintain dreams of empire in the West. As Constantinople's influence ceased to be felt in Italy, Rome's influence grew. The popes followed an independent course in their leadership of the Church, as they directed missionaries, such as St. Boniface. At the same time they followed an independent course in their political activities. The turning-point was

As Constantinople's influence ceased to be felt in Italy, Rome's influence grew.

Pope Stephen II's decision to ally with the Frankish monarchy after 750. Rome saw the new alliance as a political necessity, while Constantinople saw it as an insult.

Cultural Differences

Because the Eastern and Western Christians shared a common faith and a common tradition, the new political developments did not appear to threaten the unity of the Church. When Church leaders fled the East to escape the Moslems after 650, for example, many chose Rome as a natural refuge, and some of them even were elected pope between 650 and 750. But as the years wore on, the cultural differences between the Greeks of the East and the Latin and Germanic peoples of the West grew steadily. The more the Germanic peoples developed their own distinctive culture, the less they had in common with the people who lived in the old heartland of Christianity. Some historians contend that the rupture between Constantinople and Rome in 1054 only made "official" a decision that had been growing for three centuries.

When the final break came about, there were no serious differences East and West, but there were many small sources of irritation. Oddly enough, the two sides divided at a time when political developments seemed to favor East–West unity. Leo IX, first of the reform popes of that era, found himself caught up in a struggle against Norman warlords who were attempting to conquer southern Italy. That region was officially under the jurisdiction of the Byzantine Empire. Thus in 1053, when Leo was captured by the Normans, he wrote letters to Constantinople seeking an alliance against his captors.

The response he received, though, indicated that the Patriarch Michael Cerularius and others in the East were critical of Western

173

practices on many counts: Western Christians, he complained, were using unleavened bread in the Mass, singing the Alleluia during Lent, fasting on Saturdays, and so forth. In 1053, Cerularius ordered that the Latin churches in Constantinople be closed.

Papal Authority

While none of these complaints touched the fundamentals of the faith, Leo recognized in them a denial of papal authority. He composed letters stating very carefully the theory of papal supremacy, and he sent the letters to Cerularius in the hands of legates who had instructions to take a firm stance in negotiations with Patriarch Cerularius. One of these legates was Cardinal Humbert, the most outspoken of all the defenders of papal authority. Humbert delivered a very diplomatic letter to the emperor, but a very strong letter to the Patriarch. The negotiations ended abruptly when Humbert excommunicated Michael Cerularius, and Cerularius excommunicated the Latin delegation.

Final Division

The year of the excommunications, 1054, is the date traditionally given for the rupture between the Greek and Latin Churches. But the divisions had been growing for centuries, and as the Westerners developed their own distinctive culture under papal leadership after 1054, they made only half-hearted attempts to heal the wounds. It is a sign of the lack of real kinship between Greek and Latin Christians that in 1204, during the Fourth Crusade, the soldiers on their way to fight the Moslems got side-tracked, and raided and looted Constantinople instead. One council of the Western Church actually proposed offering friendship to the Greeks in 1274, and the Byzantine Emperor was willing to accept—the

Moslem threat was growing, and he desperately needed allies. But the people of the Greek Church, both clergy and laymen, had not forgotten 1204 and other wounds. They rejected the offers of friendship.

The end of the story of East–West negotiations during the Middle Ages is nothing less than tragic. After 1400 the Byzantine Empire, the last remnant of the empire created by the Romans some fifteen hundred years earlier, was finally collapsing. The Moslems were literally at the gates of Constantinople. There were a few unenthusiastic discussions of another Latin crusade against the Moslems, but nothing materialized. Constantinople fell to the Moslem army of Mahomet II in 1453. Greek Church leaders and intellectuals fled to the West, especially to Italy, bringing with them treasured texts from the ancient pagan writers. The Greek teachers and the new-found works of Plato and others stimulated tremendous growth in thought among the Westerners, and contributed to the movement known as the **Renaissance.** But the renewed friendship between all types of Christians came too late. Constantinople was reduced to a shadow-Church beneath the hot sun of Islam.

The end of the story of East–West negotiations during the Middle Ages is nothing less than tragic.

Renaissance—a period of radical changes in the intellectual, artistic, political, social, and even geographical structure of Christian civilization.

175

Summary

- The Eastern and Western Churches each pursued an independent course after 1054.

- The pope is the leader of the Western (Roman Catholic) portion of the Church, and the patriarch exercises varying degrees of authority over the Eastern (Orthodox) portion of the Church.

- The prophet Mohammed founded the new religion, Islam.

- Constantinople collapsed and fell to the Moslems in 1453.

Prayer

I do not pray for them alone. I pray also for those who will believe in me through their word, that all may be one as you, Father, are in me, and I in you; I pray that they may be one in us, that the world may believe that you sent me. I have given them the glory you gave me that they may be one, as we are one—I living in them, you living in me—that their unity may be complete. So shall the world know that you sent me, and that you loved them as you loved me.

John 17:20–23

Discussion Questions

1. How did historical circumstances create a rivalry between the bishops of Rome and the bishops of Constantinople?

2. Show two things other than doctrinal differences that contributed to the breakdown of communication between East and West.

Medieval Merchants

Chapter Eighteen

Papal Leadership in the Attempt to Create a Christian Society

Church Leadership

Chapter sixteen showed how the popes achieved leadership in medieval society by means of promoting the papal court as the highest court of appeals in Christendom. This work fit into a larger pattern of promoting the rule of law. The Church's law, known as canon law, became influential not only in the operations of the Church, but even in judging tendencies within society at large.

Canon law became influential not only in the operations of the Church, but even in judging tendencies within society at large.

The medieval papacy has often been criticized by historians for promoting its own power and laws. In the four Gospels, many of Jesus' clashes with Jewish authorities arose when Jesus challenged their excessive emphasis upon law. And certainly, Jesus had no desire to exercise authority himself: when put on trial, for instance, he insisted that "My kingdom is not of this world" (John 18:36).

By one reading of the Bible, then, the papacy's methods of establishing leadership are open to criticism as being inconsistent with Jesus' teachings. Rome's policies, however, were not entirely unbiblical: the Old Testament provides numerous examples of powerful men and lawgivers, such as Moses, who were men of God. These Old Testament figures could have been cited as justification for what the popes did, but the real explanation for the papacy's policies was that the popes were responding to a serious problem within medieval society.

To evaluate the popes' desire to reform society by means of laws, it is necessary to understand the conditions which existed at the time. Europe during the early Middle Ages was plagued by political disorganization, and law was no exception to this pattern. "Law" was just the collection of customs in a region, and because each region had its own customs, there was frequent confusion. Merchants, in particular, were often frustrated by the primitive state of early medieval law.

Roman Law

Corpus Iuris Civili — compilation of ancient Roman law, plus commentaries upon the law.

In Italy, the need for refinement of the law was most evident, because the seaport cities engaged in extensive trade throughout the Mediterranean region. And it was in Italy that attention was first focused upon an ancient collection called the **Corpus Iuris Civili** (The Body, or Collection, of Civil Law). It was a compilation of ancient Roman law, plus commentaries upon the law, which had been put together around the year 525 at the request of Justinian, greatest of the eastern Roman emperors. It was a monumental work that summarized all the centuries of Roman practice and theorizing about law. Of the scholars who first attempted to adapt Justinian's law to medieval usage, the first who stood out was a man named Irnerius, who lectured and wrote at the Italian city of Bologna during the eleventh century. Irnerius' commentaries upon the rediscovered Roman law were widely studied, and law students soon were in great demand in Europe's governments. They alone were familiar with the Roman law, the greatest organizational tool that the world had ever known. The men who had this training revolutionized the art of government during the twelfth and thirteenth centuries.

Ecclesiastical Law

Meanwhile, prominent thinkers within the Church surveyed ecclesiastical law and found it to be even more in need of order than the laws of governments. Popes and councils had been passing laws for centuries, and no one was able to sift through the mass of decrees to find any consistent patterns in canon law. Finally, during the twelfth century, an Italian monk named Gratian used his training in Roman law to impose some order upon canon law: the result was his great work, *The Concordance of Discordant Canons,* which came to be called *The Decretum.* As the long version of the title suggests, Gratian categorized the Church's laws, then attempted to reason out the disagreements (discordance) between laws and arrive at consistent principles. Gratian's work had no authority except its own value, yet it came to be universally accepted within the Church. His commentaries upon the law were placed at the beginning of a new, official compilation called the *Corpus Iuris Canonici* (Body of Canon Law).

Natural Law

The newly organized canon law was a fine tool for the Church to use, but of equal value was speculation about "natural law" by Gratian and later commentators. The ancient Roman experts in law had developed the notion of a "law of nature," from which they derived the idea that Rome's laws ought to be applied equally to all of the Empire's millions of citizens. These men likened the natural law to instinct, which people shared with the animals. Gratian and his contemporaries, influenced by the ideas of the Fathers of the Church, transformed the old Roman concept of natural law: the law of nature, they urged, corresponds with *reason* rather than with instinct. Humans, by their nature as rational creatures, are able to distinguish right from wrong.

The following set of principles, developed by the canon lawyers, dominated medieval thought and has played an important role in Catholic Christian thought up to the present. Positive law, as the canon lawyers called the written laws of the governments, is derived from the natural law. Natural law is not actually written down; it is the theoretical basis of the written laws. Natural law, in turn, is derived from God's law. Since God is rational, divine law is reasonable, too; and humans, creatures with the power of reason, can understand the divine law. But sin has weakened humans, and because of their weakened state they do not always use reason properly. God has given humankind the Ten Commandments and the Gospel so that God's law can be known by all. All authority comes from God, and so does the authority of law. Therefore, if a positive (written) law commands something contrary to the law of nature and the divine law, then the written law is not really law—it has not the force of true law, and people do not have to obey it.

This conception of law was a tremendous aid to the Church and society. Take away the natural law, and all that is left is force: a law is to be obeyed simply because the king who made the law is strong enough to enforce it. But with the concept of natural law comes the idea that any written law can be rejected if it is unreasonable. At the same time, with the idea of divine law came the idea that a written law can be rejected if it is against the principles of Christian morality. This conception influenced the many men who received legal training and then went to work for the kings of Europe. Such a conception also supported the Church's claim to be the dominant force in society, for it was clearly the Church's role to interpret the law of God.

Lawyer-Popes

The development of canon law and of the theory of natural law might have had only a limited effect upon the life of the Church, except for one thing: canon lawyers began to be elected to the papal throne. First of the lawyer-popes was Alexander III (1159–1181), an aggressive, talented man whose pontificate could even be described as the high point of papal power. The man traditionally considered the most powerful of all the popes was Innocent III (1198–1215), who was also a lawyer. Alexander, Innocent, and others produced many new laws, so that it became necessary to revise the collection of canon law. Legal experts soon began writing commentaries on the new papal law. One such commentator was the lawyer-pope Innocent IV (1243–1254), who legislated new laws while also serving as commentator upon the law—he even wrote learned opinions about his own new decrees. Gregory IX (1227–1241) was yet another lawyer-pope who wielded tremendous power in Christendom. The power of popes was summarized in one legal opinion written by Innocent IV: the pope's power of making new canons, he said, comes from Christ himself; but the emperor's authority as legislator is drawn from the Roman people; the pope, therefore, is the spokesman for the highest authority of all.

General Councils

The concept of natural law was an undercurrent in all the official proclamations and policies of these popes. To promote their understanding of society, however, the lawyer-popes made use of another new tool, the general council. After the general councils, which dealt with the heresies in the early Church, there were very few councils for several hundred years. Then between 1123 and 1215, there were four councils, which all had in common the fact that they were convoked, and directed, by the popes. The meetings were held in the Lateran Palace in Rome, and the agenda for each session was prepared by the pope and his cardinals.

At the First Lateran Council, convoked by Pope Calixtus II in 1123, the pattern emerged that was to be repeated at the next three councils. There were about three hundred bishops present from all over Europe, and nearly twice that many abbots. The agenda for the meeting was prepared by Calixtus, and the laws passed by the council were of two sorts: decrees concerning Church discipline and religious affairs, and decrees aimed at reforming society at large. The latter had never been a prominent feature at earlier councils, and they are a clear sign that to the leaders of the medieval Church, there was no distinction between "religious" matters and "secular" matters. In the integrated society of the Middle Ages, all things were related to the life of faith.

Lateran I's decrees concerning Church discipline included a renewal of the law of celibacy for priests, and a renewal of the warnings against simony. According to another decree, bishops alone had the power to appoint parish priests—this was just another step in the Church's efforts to free itself from the control of lay lords.

Then, going beyond strictly "Church" matters, the council voted to excommunicate any thieves who molested pilgrims on their way to religious shrines. Finally, involving itself in the affairs of society, the council passed a decree of excommunication upon counterfeiters, who apparently were a threat to the stability of the economy. They also renewed Pope Urban II's earlier decrees concerning the **Truce of God:** warfare was unlawful except on Mondays, Tuesdays and Wednesdays, and fighting was absolutely forbidden every day during the seasons of Advent, Lent and Easter. Bishops were reminded of their duty to excommunicate anyone who might violate the Truce of God.

Truce of God—Pope Urban II's decree that warfare was unlawful except on Mondays, Tuesdays, and Wednesdays, and fighting was forbidden every day during Advent, Lent, and Easter.

Lateran Council II, under Pope Innocent II in the year 1139, followed an identical pattern. There were more decrees that made the old laws against clerical marriage more explicit. There was an instruction for bishops to teach the faithful that the outward acts of penance, associated with confession of sins, must be accompanied by an inward change of heart. This appears to be an attempt to foster greater spiritual maturity among the people of God.

Then, at Lateran II as at Lateran I, there were decrees that were not of a strictly religious nature. The law against molesting pilgrims was extended to protect merchants. Laws were written against **usury,** as well. Usury, the practice of loaning money for a fee (interest), was condemned by the Church on the grounds that it amounted to taking advantage of poor people who needed money—it was a denial of the Christian ideal of charity.

Usury—loaning money for a fee; this practice was condemned as a denial of Christian charity.

Lateran II continued the struggle against the constant warfare in medieval society. Bishops, for example, were warned of the dire consequences if they failed to excommunicate people who violated the Truce of God. Apparently the earlier law was proving difficult to enforce. But there were new laws, too. A new weapon, the catapult, was being used to hurl large rocks and batter down walls and men. The bishops showed their willingness to resist the twelfth century's version of the "arms race" by threatening to excommunicate anyone who used the new weapon against Christians. Finally, according to the council fathers any knight who was killed in a jousting tournament was to be denied a Christian burial.

The Third and Fourth Lateran Councils, summoned by Alexander III and Innocent III, respectively, were very similar to the first two, although Innocent's council must have seemed unnecessary to some observers, as he himself had issued six thousand official proclamations during his pontificate. The four councils established an important precedent by placing the Church in the role of judge over all the affairs of society. St. Augustine's ideal was being put into practice: Christians were attempting to remake the City of Man in the image of the City of God. Whether they were very successful is hard to determine. Several of the laws decreed at one council had to be restated at a later council, which would suggest that there was difficulty in enforcing the decrees. Warfare does not appear to have abated during the latter Middle Ages, and within the Church simony and clerical immorality continued to be sore points. But even if the Church's laws were not followed, it may have been useful for lawbreakers to realize that they were transgressing a moral code. Further, some of the decrees—for example, the law against usury—at least established the principle that social, political, and economic activities ought to be governed by a higher law.

> The four Lateran Councils established an important precedent by placing the Church in the role of judge over all the affairs of society.

Innocent III

Like the decrees of the four councils, the day-to-day policies of the popes are not easy to assess. In their dealings with the kings and nobles of Christendom, the pontiffs often were thwarted. But Innocent III, perhaps the most powerful of all the successors of Peter, faced several situations in which he managed to impose his view of the natural moral law upon unwilling kings. When he was a student at Paris, Lothario di Segni (the future Innocent III) journeyed to England to visit the spot where St. Thomas Becket, the archbishop who had defied King Henry II, had been murdered. When he became pope at the age of thirty-seven, Lothario did not hesitate to confront any king.

Philip II of France, probably the most powerful monarch in Christendom at the end of the twelfth century, married a woman named Ingeborg, from a Danish noble family. No sooner was Philip married to her than he set her aside and openly kept a mistress. While the King's behavior was certainly unkind, it was not uncommon. Royal families often arranged marriages for political advantages, and kings often went outside the marriage to seek pleasure. But when Ingeborg petitioned to Innocent, the pope took this transgression of the natural moral law so seriously that he even laid an **interdict** upon France. The interdict was a potent weapon: all the sacraments except baptism were suspended throughout the country, so that all the king's subjects suffered for his sin and urged him to change his ways. Philip finally submitted and acknowledged Ingeborg as wife and queen. France learned the important lesson that not even powerful kings were above the law of the Gospel as taught by the Church.

Interdict—deprives the faithful of certain spiritual benefits but permits them to remain in the communion of the Church. An interdict may be either personal or local.

Interdict was the weapon that Innocent employed to humble England's King John, too. John attempted to fill the archbishopric of Canterbury with a man of his own choice, but Innocent stood by Stephen Langton, the candidate who (in keeping with canon law) had been freely elected by the clergy. When John insisted upon upholding his own candidate, Innocent imposed an interdict upon England that brought normal Christian life to a halt for six years. To the people of England, the disruption of public worship was a terrible loss. When Philip II of France (in an alliance with Innocent) threatened to invade England, John could not even count upon his own people's support. He not only submitted on the question of the archbishopric of Canterbury, but in effect gave England to Innocent. The pope returned England to John as a feudal fief, and John did homage to Innocent.

On the other hand, even this most powerful of popes faced severe limitations. When a Gnostic group rose up in southern France, for instance, Innocent found that he could not uproot the heresy by persuasion. He appealed to the nobility of northern France to put down the heresy by force, and found the northern nobles all too eager. They slaughtered heretics, drove out the local nobles of the region, and seized the lands of southern France for themselves. Innocent was unable to stop this perversion of his plans.[1] Likewise, in his dealings with the emperors of Germany, Innocent supported a noble named Otto as a candidate to the imperial throne, only to have Otto turn against him and invade Italy. To oppose Otto, Innocent supported Frederick II of the Hohenstaufen family. Once Otto was eliminated, however, the pope found Frederick to be a greater threat to Italy than Otto or any other German emperor before or since.

Contributions

Thus, dramatic though Innocent III's victories may have been, his defeats also stood out. While it is nearly impossible to judge whether the medieval popes' reform program can be called a success, it is possible to point to some of their positive contributions that have had lasting effect. Canon law, which they helped to create and to organize, has been an important tool of the Church for many centuries. Further, nearly all Catholic moral teaching since the year 1100 has been

1. This heretical movement is discussed in more detail in chapter twenty-two.

influenced by the concept of natural law, which the medieval popes promoted. Finally, the medieval pontiffs established the papacy as a moral force to be dealt with. The modern papacy has gradually ceased to be a "political" power with lands and interests of its own, and has effectively asserted its role as interpreter of the natural law and critic of new developments in secular society. The popes of the twelfth and thirteenth centuries were the originators of this tendency. The medieval popes, then, in spite of the limitations of their power, have made their mark upon the Church.

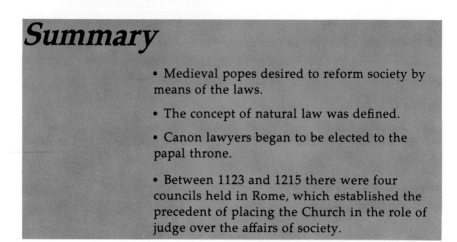

Summary

- Medieval popes desired to reform society by means of the laws.

- The concept of natural law was defined.

- Canon lawyers began to be elected to the papal throne.

- Between 1123 and 1215 there were four councils held in Rome, which established the precedent of placing the Church in the role of judge over the affairs of society.

Prayer

O most merciful Friend, my Brother and Redeemer,
may I know you more clearly, love you more
dearly, and follow you more nearly, day by day,
day by day. Amen.

St. Richard of Chichester

Discussion Questions

1. According to Gratian and others, what conditions must be fulfilled if an actual, written law is to be considered a true law that is morally binding upon us?

2. What two types of decrees came out of the four Lateran Councils? Which of these two represented a new tendency?

3. Give one example of how Innocent III held supreme power in Christendom, and one example of the limits of his power.

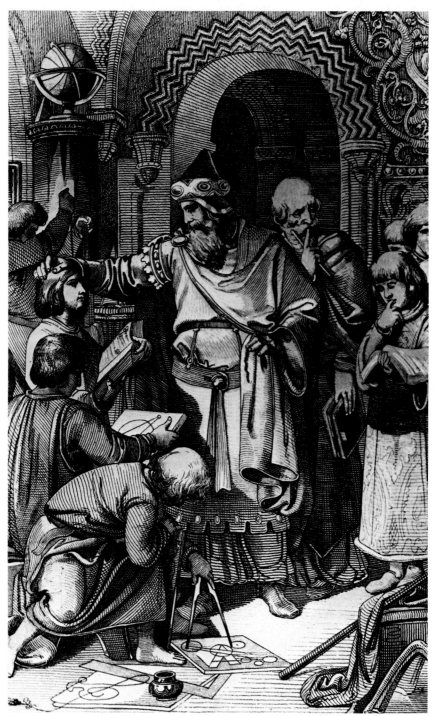

Charlemagne enters the schoolroom of his palace-school in Aachen to examine the pupils.

Chapter Nineteen

The Intellectual Flowering of Medieval Christianity

Revival

The work of Gratian and others in the field of law was not an isolated effort. Late in the eleventh century, there was a modest revival of learning that came to full flower in the twelfth century and yielded fruit in the thirteenth century and later.

The efforts during the twelfth century are termed a "revival," because they represent the first major advance in learning since the time of Augustine. Throughout the early Middle Ages, there were signs of intellectual activity, but for the most part the efforts were limited to copying and the study of Latin grammar. The Churchmen, usually monks, only hoped to master the Latin language so that they could read the sacred Scriptures, the Fathers of the Church, and the pagan classics.

During the early Middle Ages, intellectual life had been all but impossible because of the sad state of the economy. Agricultural methods were so primitive that nearly every person had to contribute to food production. But by about the year 1000, with the use of better harnesses, horseshoes, plows, crop rotation, and other innovations, there began to be food surpluses, a growth of trade, and the beginnings of town life in northern Europe.

Intellectual Life

With the towns came a significant shift in intellectual life: the monastic monopoly in education ended. Cathedral schools rose up in the larger towns, and they were the new centers of learning. The students were clerics, young men usually destined for careers within the Church, often being supported by their bishops. The youngsters studied the **Trivium,** the group of three subjects that formed the basis of the Seven Liberal Arts. The Trivium included grammar (basic skills in Latin language), rhetoric (the art of persuasive expression), and dialectic—logic (the art of thinking in an orderly way). The study of the Trivium was complemented by the "Quadrivium," namely music (music theory), arithmetic, geometry, and astronomy.

The more gifted students advanced from the Seven Liberal Arts to one of the three higher disciplines: law, medicine or theology. **Theology,** the study of God and doctrine, was called the "Queen of Sciences" because it treated the most important of all the subjects discussed by man. Knowledge of these three subjects was so valuable in the new city-culture of Christendom that the demand for teachers outstripped the supply. Young men, barely enrolled in school, left to become masters, and often commanded sizeable fees for their teaching. The intervention by many bishops and particularly by the popes in the matter of licensing masters proved essential. Standards of quality had to be maintained, but there had to be a large number of teachers to fulfill society's need for educated persons. The popes, especially Alexander III, also took the lead in founding new schools.

Trivium—group of three subjects— grammar, rhetoric, and dialectic (logic)—that formed the basis of the Seven Liberal Arts.

The more gifted students advanced from the Seven Liberal Arts to one of the three higher disciplines: law, medicine or theology.

Theology—the study of God and doctrine.

By the end of the twelfth century, students were congregated in great numbers, especially in major cities such as Paris. Master teachers were banding together into guilds, and the meeting of students with groups of masters gave birth to the world's first universities. A set pattern of degrees emerged, which provides the basis for today's university degrees: Baccalaureate for students who took the basic courses in liberal arts; Master of Arts (M.A.) for one who mastered an advanced field such as theology; and for the teachers who advanced to the highest level of learning, Doctor of Philosophy (Ph.D.).

The meeting of students with groups of master teachers gave birth to the world's first universities.

It has been said of university life in the Middle Ages that no other society has ever sacrificed so much for the education of its young people. They were given clerical status, which meant that they could be tried for crimes only in the Church's courts. Their personal security while traveling was guaranteed by the pope and often also by kings. They were protected by rent control so that they could afford inexpensive housing, and their books could not be confiscated if they failed to pay their bills. Most of them were sponsored either by bishops or by their parishes. It is typical of the value placed upon education that at the end of the thirteenth century Pope Boniface VIII called for five years of study for anyone seeking to become a priest.

The greatest thinkers of this period in Western history were all Christians and, in general, they were committed to the same goal: to gain deeper insight into their faith by examining their beliefs in a logical way. **Scholasticism** is the label given to the ideas produced by this method. St. Anselm, in the eleventh century, borrowed a slogan from Augustine that summed up the aim of most great thinkers of this period: "faith seeking understanding." If people had faith, they would naturally seek to

The greatest thinkers of this period in Western history were all Christians.

Scholasticism—"faith seeking understanding"; the use of logic to gain insight into faith.

During the early
Middle Ages, grammar
had been considered
the most important
subject of the Trivium,
but by the eleventh
century, logic was
taking first place.

understand their beliefs better, and in the
opinion of most scholastic thinkers, logic was
the best tool for improving one's
understanding. During the early Middle Ages,
grammar had been considered the most
important subject of the Trivium, but by the
eleventh century, logic was taking first place.

Logic

Anselm, the abbot of a monastic community,
made use of logic in a most extraordinary way.
At the request of his fellow monks, he
composed several proofs for the existence of
God. One of his proofs used no evidence at all;
Anselm just showed that if the very term
"God" had any meaning at all, then logically,
God must exist. Most of the later scholastics
were not satisfied with Anselm's proof, and
preferred to try demonstrating God's existence
in other ways. They picked up St. Paul's idea
that God can be known from the works of His
creation.[1] In the words of one medieval writer,
"The entire sense-perceptible world is like a
book written by the finger of God.[2]

Others employed logic to solve other
problems. Peter Abelard, for example,
composed a book called *Yes and No*, in which
he put together all the statements that the
Bible had made about a number of selected
subjects. In most instances, one biblical
statement would contradict, or at least seem to
contradict, another; Abelard then applied logic
to resolve the contradiction. Not everyone
agreed that what Abelard was doing was

1. Romans 1:20—"Since the creation of the world,
invisible realities, God's eternal power and divinity,
have become visible, recognized through the things
He has made."

2. Hugh of St. Victor, *Concerning the Three Days*,
cited in M. D. Chenu, *Nature, Man and Society in the
Twelfth Century* (University of Chicago Press, 1968),
p. 117.

proper, however. St. Bernard of Clairvaux felt that Abelard was trying to make logic a higher authority than the sacred Scriptures. Feeling that Abelard was a dangerous influence upon young students, Bernard hounded him until Abelard's ideas were condemned by a regional Church council in 1140. It is typical of the spirit of the age, though, that while Bernard did everything in his power to prevent his opponent from teaching, he did not deprive Abelard of a peaceful retirement at the monastery of Cluny. There was a tremendous respect for the power of ideas, and there were impassioned battles over the truth or falsity of some ideas. But the passions did not extend to personal animosity.

There was a tremendous respect for the power of ideas, and there were impassioned battles over the truth or falsity of some ideas.

Hugh of St. Victor

Another twelfth-century controversy centered around the interpretation of the book of Genesis. One group of men who lectured in Paris and at Chartres (southwest of Paris) followed one type of interpretation, and were opposed by the school of St. Victor in Paris, which was led by Master Hugh of St. Victor. The men from Chartres were interested in interpreting Genesis in terms of scientific categories, so that the story of the Creation of the World could be understood in purely logical terms. Master Thierry of Chartres, for example, said that "God created the heaven and earth, that is to say, the four elements: earth, air, fire, and water." Similarly, another thinker proposed that in the beginning (at the time of Creation) there was a "world-soul," which had three aspects: animal, vegetable, and mineral.

Hugh of St. Victor contended that while such theories might serve a purpose, they did little to inspire faith, and they could be applied to

Genesis only by twisting the meaning of the sacred texts to suit the theories. He unleashed a harsh criticism of the school of Chartres:

> *Seeming to tell the truth about Creation, they fall into countless lies about the subsistence of things. They invent essences and forms and atoms and "ideas of the principal constitutions" and numerous elements and infinite births and invisible motions and procreative agencies. And in all these things they multiply mere shadows of thought . . . and the truth is in none of them.*[3]

His complaint was that his contemporaries were inventing all sorts of theories which had little to do with the real Genesis, God's revelation to humanity. His belief was that any analysis had to start with the literal meaning of the Scriptures, before any other meanings could be discovered. Realizing that it was not always easy to understand the literal meaning, Hugh recommended extensive study of geography and chronology, because they could affect the meaning of a passage. He may even have made contact with Jewish scholars to talk to them about the ancient languages in which the Bible was written. Hugh aimed to consider all factors that might bear upon the meaning of a passage.

Theology in the eleventh and twelfth centuries was the "new frontier" in intellectual life.

It was only natural that controversy was a major factor in the intellectual activities at this time. Theology in the eleventh and twelfth centuries was the "new frontier" in intellectual life, where intelligent people experimented with new methods and principles. By the thirteenth century, controversy was so much a part of the normal course of school life that it was built into the educational program. At the universities, the great masters regularly made public defenses

3. Hugh of St. Victor, *Homilies on the Church*, PL 175, 238AB.

198

of their beliefs and attempted to answer any objections that might be raised against their theories. In writing books, the great thinkers listed all of the possible objections to their beliefs, then answered all the objections before proceeding to another point.

St. Thomas Aquinas

In this atmosphere of challenge, one rather unlikely man, studying at Paris, rose to become the greatest thinker of the thirteenth century. He seemed ill-suited to the circumstances: of the great universities of Christendom, the University of Bologna was famous for specialists in law, the University of Salerno was well known for medicine, and Paris and Oxford were the foremost centers for the study of theology. Out of the field of quick-witted experts in disputation, specializing in theology, most important of subjects, at Paris, most famous of all universities, appeared a slow-moving, four hundred-pound man whom the students jeeringly called "the Dumb Ox." "The Dumb Ox" was Thomas Aquinas, and the Middle Ages produced no one who could equal his intellectual accomplishments. Like most scholastic theologians, he used logic as a tool for advancing theology. But he employed that tool with greater refinement than others, on a wider variety of subjects than anyone else.

The Middle Ages produced no one who could equal the intellectual accomplishments of Thomas Aquinas.

Like most medieval intellectuals, Thomas believed that people, who are made in God's image, are essentially good, even though weakened by sin. He believed, for example, that people can understand the workings of the world. God gave people reason, and the purpose of reason is to allow them to understand things. Aquinas concluded that unless God is perverse, the world that God created can be understood by human reason; for the heavenly Father would not give people an ability only to frustrate it.

Furthermore, if people can understand the world, then to a limited degree they can have knowledge about God Himself. St. Thomas drew upon the passage in the third chapter of Exodus in which God called Himself I AM. If that is how God names Himself, then the single most important thing that people know about God is that "God is being"—God "is." By understanding all of the beings in the world that God created, people can gain limited knowledge about the perfect Being that is God.

In his most famous work, *Summa Theologica (The Theological Summary),* Aquinas was able to make numerous statements that have deepened human's understanding of God. By reading the works of Aristotle critically, Aquinas also was able to use many of Aristotle's ideas to build an entire system of Christian philosophy, covering a broad range of subjects.

Unfortunately, not all of Thomas' contemporaries were as successful as he in adapting Aristotle for Christian thought. Since about 1100, the great Greek philosopher's works had been finding their way from the East to Europe, accompanied by a large number of commentaries on Aristotle's ideas. Many of the scholars at Paris were so excited by the philosophy of Aristotle that they even accepted some of his pagan beliefs that contradicted Christian doctrine. They agreed with the Greek master, for example, that the world was eternal, even though by subscribing to this idea they were denying belief in God's creation of the world. Faced with possible condemnation by the Church, they argued that they could believe in creation as a matter of faith, while at the same time believing in the eternity of the world as a conclusion of human reason.

Thomas, meanwhile, was quick to argue that there can never be two truths, the truth of faith and the truth of reason. There are simply many things that humans believe, and some of them can be proved by reason—for example, the existence of God—while other beliefs are beyond the powers of reason and have to be accepted as a matter of faith—for example, the doctrine of the Trinity.

The Aristotelians at Paris were considered a threat to Christian belief, and in 1277 their ideas were officially condemned by the Bishop of Paris. In the heat of the controversy about the misuse of Aristotle by theologians, few people paid attention to the careful distinctions made by Thomas Aquinas. St. Thomas' works fell out of favor, and were scarcely studied for the next two hundred years. (They made a "comeback" much later, as will be seen in a later chapter.)

With the fall of the Aristotelian scholars at Paris came the end of an era. The brash confidence of the twelfth and thirteenth centuries gave way to a strong sense of human limitations. With the writings of Cardinal Nicholas Cusanus, for example, foremost theologian of the fifteenth century, came the concept of "learned ignorance." Nicholas believed that growth in wisdom consisted in learning how little people could say about God. The Christian thinkers of the Middle Ages have left the Church a mixed legacy: a wealth of new terms and concepts that have been in use for the past eight centuries, and a broad selection of theories ranging from bold speculations to modest meditations.

Thomas Aquinas argued that there can never be two truths, the truth of faith and the truth of reason.

The Christian thinkers of the Middle Ages left the Church a mixed legacy.

Summary

• Cathedral schools rose up in larger towns and became the new centers of learning.

• The meeting of students with groups of master teachers gave birth to the world's first universities.

• The greatest thinkers of this period in Western history were all Christians.

• Logic was becoming the most important means of gaining insight into theology, the "Queen of the Sciences."

• There were impassioned battles over the truth or falsity of some ideas. Controversy was a major factor in the intellectual activities at this time.

• The Middle Ages produced no one who could equal the intellectual accomplishments of Thomas Aquinas.

Prayer

*Grant me grace, O merciful God, to desire ardently
all that is pleasing to you, to examine it prudently,
to acknowledge it truthfully, and to accomplish it
perfectly for the praise and glory of your name.
Amen.*

Thomas Aquinas

Discussion Questions

1. What had been the focus of education in
   the early medieval monasteries? What
   made up the curriculum of the cathedral
   schools?

2. Show how Anselm, Abelard, or Aquinas
   was typical of the ideal of scholasticism.

3. How do the ideas of Nicholas Cusanus
   represent a departure from the scholastic
   ideals?

Roland, the French hero of medieval legend, nephew of Charlemagne

Chapter Twenty

Expression of the Popular Faith during the Middle Ages

The Middle Ages present several prominent examples of faith at work: popes who wrote laws for all of Christendom, great thinkers who speculated about God, monks who dedicated their lives to prayer. While these are commonly considered to be the "peaks" of medieval Church history, the "valleys" also are important. The faith of the great majority of people in Christendom gave rise to a rich variety of expression.

Community

In the medieval world, as in the ancient, a sense of community was very important to Christians. It is well known that the chief expression of the drive toward community was the monastery, and that the monastery had intimate ties with society. Primarily, the monastery had close contact with the noble families that supplied most of the monks and provided material support in the form of donations.

By about the twelfth century, however, many little groups came into being that were similar to monastic communities. They followed a much looser "rule" and had their closest ties with the common people rather than with the nobles. Men following a simple rule were called **canons** and they attached themselves to local churches. Usually they lived in groups of

In the medieval world, a sense of community was very important to Christians.

Canons—small groups, similar to monastic communities, assigned to service a cathedral church who live off of the modest income provided by the Church.

just three or four, eking out an existence with the modest income provided to them by the Churches and the common folk. Three men, for example, might commit themselves to the upkeep of a church building or a cemetery, obtaining a small salary that kept them fed only because their style of living was simple. Meanwhile, the common people would give them a coin or two in exchange for services, such as prayers for the departed members of their families. Because they needed so little and their rule was so flexible, these canons increased in number and fulfilled a wide variety of undramatic, but still important, functions within the Church.

Another form of Christian community was the confraternities of the Holy Spirit. These gatherings of people from each village and surrounding area focused upon festive meals together, and might best be described as the forerunners to the parish potluck dinners that are so common in the American Church today. Despite the fact that medieval agriculture was not very productive, the villagers did their best to set a full table. These "parish dinners" were far from slow-paced or dull:

> They fight, they have a bout,
> They drink, the more they drink the more
> they shout,
> And by the time they finish eating
> They talk without anyone agreeing.[1]

On the other hand, the confraternities also had a serious purpose. Since the modern welfare state did not exist during the Middle Ages, the people took it upon themselves to aid the needy. The confraternities elected new leaders each year to collect and distribute food

1. The poem, which actually was written later than the Middle Ages, is cited by Pierre Duparc in "Confraternities of the Holy Spirit and Village Communities in the Middle Ages," in Frederick Cheyette, ed., *Lordship and Community in Medieval Europe* (New York: Holt, Rinehart and Winston, 1967), p. 344.

and money for the poor of the area. Sometimes they worked together to repair the local church. It is likely that at the beginning, the confraternities existed only for the entertainment of the members; the social welfare functions were added when Church officials began to be critical of what seemed to be purposeless partying. The Church fulfilled social needs in other ways, too: after the fifth century, the bishop of each diocese was expected to support a hospital for the needy.

Sacraments

By the Middle Ages, the people of God had come to engage in seven vital activities known as sacraments: baptism, confirmation, Eucharist, penance, holy orders, marriage, and extreme unction (which today is called anointing of the sick). There was also some debate about whether the coronation of kings constituted an eighth sacrament. In spite of fundamental similarity, in some details the medieval view of the sacraments was clearly different from the present view. Extreme unction, for example, was less a sacrament of physical and spiritual healing and more a preparation for death. "Extreme unction" itself was the sick person's final confession of sins and expression of sorrow for having offended God. After confession the person received the viaticum, that is, the final Eucharist which was intended as food for the soul's final journey to God.

Marriage, too, was understood differently during the medieval centuries. Holy matrimony was officially recognized as a sacrament by the Church, but in the popular view it represented a "second-best" road to salvation. The Fourth Lateran Council even had to issue an official statement to the effect that married people, like virgins, could attain eternal happiness. So convinced were the people that the priestly or monastic ways of life were surer paths to heaven that it was not

By the Middle Ages, the people of God had come to engage in seven vital activities known as sacraments.

uncommon for a married couple to take vows of celibacy when they reached old age. The husband would commit himself to a monastery, and the wife would commit herself to a convent. There were even several kings who retired to a monastery late in life.

The Eucharist was increasingly remote from the people, as was mentioned in an earlier chapter. It became necessary to make a canon law requiring people to receive Communion one time per year. As a general practice, only priests partook of the Chalice (Blood of Christ) at Mass, and the common people's interest focused upon the Body of Christ, which they associated with miraculous powers. By the middle of the thirteenth century, there arose the new feast of Corpus Christi (Body of Christ) that came to be associated with a Corpus Christi procession: the priests and the faithful would leave the church and parade through town, following the Body of Christ that was being carried in a display-case called a **monstrance.** The Middle Ages also saw the beginning of exposition of the sacred Host (Body of Christ) in a tabernacle or special chapel. Thomas Aquinas and others composed little poems and songs in honor of the sacred Host, a few of which are still sung today.

Monstrance—an ornate display-case for carrying the sacred Host in Corpus Christi processions.

Perhaps the strongest of the devotions at this time was that to the Blessed Virgin Mary. Medieval society was clearly male-dominated, and veneration of Mary represents one of the few exceptions to that trend. The thirteenth century witnessed the first use of the cycle of Marian prayers known as the rosary.

Perhaps the strongest of the devotions at this time was that to the Blessed Virgin Mary. Medieval society was clearly male-dominated, and veneration of Mary represents one of the few exceptions to that trend.

Relics

The strong affection for St. Mary fit into a widespread tendency toward veneration of all the saints. The power of holy men and women against the forces of evil captured the imagination of the people. Popular enthusiasm focused upon **relics**—sacred objects that were believed to have supernatural powers. Wood

Relics—sacred objects that were believed to have supernatural powers.

from the Cross on which Jesus died, and the Holy Lance which pierced Jesus' side, were typical of relics which aroused people's interest, but the most common relics were saints' bodies. Fierce competition arose over which town had best claim to a holy person's body. Should the saint come to rest, for example, in the town in which he or she was born, or the town in which he or she established a famous monastery? It was not uncommon for one town to win possession of a saint's body for veneration, only to have the corpse arrive without one of its arms or fingers or toes; the faithful in the town where the saint had died had decided to keep part of the body for their own benefit. The power of relics was part of the pervasive belief that all physical things were signs of the presence of God. At one point, enthusiasm for relics became so great that the Fourth Lateran Council insisted that all holy objects had to be authenticated by the Holy See; merchants had been taking advantage of the superstitious common folk by selling fake relics.

Pilgrimages

Veneration of relics also furthered the practice of **pilgrimage.** In terms of the symbolic mentality of medieval people, the person's physical journey to a shrine represented a spiritual journey toward God. It was very common for people to confess their sins to a priest, then be told that as an act of penance they had to travel to a nearby shrine. Every church had its relics, and many had a different relic for each altar, with as many as a dozen altars in a single church. But several shrines gained such popularity that people came from all over Christendom to visit them. One was the church of St. Denis, near Paris. It was the resting place of the body of Denis, the patron saint of France; but Denis' name was also associated (mistakenly) with that of Dionysius, who had been a follower of St. Paul after

Pilgrimage—a physical journey to a shrine which represented a spiritual journey toward God.

Every church had its relics. Several shrines gained such popularity that people came from all over Christendom to visit them.

Paul's speech at the Areopagus (Acts 17:34), and thus the shrine assumed even greater importance.

Also associated with the legends of the apostles was the popular shrine of St. James at Compostella, in northern Spain. It was believed that the apostle James had settled there while doing missionary work in Spain. The apostles Peter and Paul had, of course, died in Rome, and Rome was another of the favored shrines of Christendom. Finally, the Holy Sepulcher (tomb of Christ) in Jerusalem attracted a large number of pilgrims in spite of the difficulty of the long journey. While in Jerusalem, the pilgrim was supposed to take a ritual bath in the Jordan River, and bring home palms.

So great was the number of people traveling to various shrines that there was a demand for lodging. Hostels (today called hotels) rose up to fulfill the need. The monastic order of Cluny took the lead in providing lodging for travelers. In addition, the Church's canon law protected pilgrims, threatening excommunication to any thieves who might molest them. It is not an exaggeration to state that virtually the entire society was involved in the practice of pilgrimage, either in direct participation or in support.

Crusades

The Crusades were an important feature of medieval life, and they grew directly out of the pilgrimage tradition.

The Crusades were an important feature of medieval life, and they grew directly out of the pilgrimage tradition. There was frequent warfare between Moslems and Christians in Spain, and in 1063 Pope Alexander II decreed that Christians who killed Moslems in battle were not subject to the law against homicide. He also excused these warriors from any penances that they might have been required to do for their sins. Like pilgrims, the soldiers were journeying, and the pope wished to emphasize that they were doing God's work in their journey into enemy territory. At about the same time, pilgrims were returning from the Holy Land with tales of harassment by Moslems. When the Byzantine Emperor appealed to his fellow Christians of the West for assistance against the Moslems, Pope Urban II called the knights of Christendom together at Clermont, France, to ask their participation in holy war against the Moslems. The knights responded with an excited shout, "God wills it!" and the First Crusade came into being.

Urban was shrewd enough to recognize that the excitement would wear off, so he held them all by a sacred vow, and instructed them to sew a cross onto their garments as a sign of their commitment. He granted the warriors pilgrim status, which meant that they and their possessions had the Church's protection while they were traveling; it also meant that their debts were canceled and that their march to the Holy Land was a penance that brought them remittance of their sins.

The benefits of pilgrim status, plus the lure of glory, inspired a few bands of ill-equipped commoners to begin the march to Constantinople on their own. Apparently, they were killed along the way south and east, as they attempted to steal food to feed themselves. In late summer of 1096, a well organized army of knights set out under the direction of five of the leading nobles of Christendom, and they had far greater success. They passed through Constantinople, fought off ambushes and the arid climate in Asia Minor, and finally reached Jerusalem in June of 1099. After a thirty-nine-day siege they captured the city, and the frustration of their years of struggle boiled over as they slaughtered thousands of the Jewish and Moslem inhabitants of Jerusalem.

The Moslems could not easily forget the slaughter, and soon undertook the reconquest of the cities held by the Christians. A series of

Crusades was preached over the next century with the aim of providing relief for the threatened cities. In spite of the ease with which enthusiasm was aroused, the successive Crusades, generally, were dismal failures, largely because of dissension among the leaders, who were unable to bury their old European rivalries during their journeys to Asia. On occasion, the religious purposes of the Crusades were forgotten in the warriors' age-old desire for booty. By far, the most shameful of all the performances was the Fourth Crusade in 1204, when Crusaders became distracted from their journey farther south and chose to conquer Constantinople. Oblivious to the feeling of the Greek people, they formed a "Latin Empire of Constantinople" which was overthrown by the Greeks in 1261.

The year 1204 represents the worst moment in the history of the Crusades, but it was certainly not the strangest. About ten years after the conquest of Constantinople, there were two Crusades comprised entirely of children. One group from Germany reached Italy and were persuaded by Pope Innocent III to abandon their plans. Meanwhile, a group of French children followed a twelve-year-old boy to Marseilles (on the southern coast of France), managed to gain passage on a ship bound for the Holy Land, and then disappeared. Thirty years later, stories were circulating through Europe that the children had been sold to the Moslems as slaves.

The Crusades, clearly, captured the imagination of all the Christians of Europe, rich, poor, young, and old. The holy war was even hallowed in the literature of the age, as the popular *Song of Roland* and *El Cid* celebrated the deeds of Christians who battled the Moslems in Spain. In spite of the tremendous difficulties in waging war in foreign lands, the Crusade ideal was slow to fade away. Even as late as the fifteenth century, Pope Pius II was attempting to organize another expedition to the Holy Land when he died. After Pius, however, no one made a serious proposal for another Crusade.

The Crusades are significant as an indication of the solidarity of the Western Christian people. In spite of the difficulties created by the kings' desire to pursue independent policies during the campaigns, the soldiers of Christendom were able to unite on numerous expeditions. There was unanimity among Western Christians about the plan of seizing the Holy Land by force, which is to say that the ideal of the pilgrim-soldier was an ideal generally accepted throughout Christendom. It is noteworthy, too, that the sense of Christian unity did not include the Greeks, who indeed were "the enemy" in 1204. Christians of the Latin West had developed a distinctive culture of their own, and the Crusades were this young culture's way of "flexing its muscles." The aggressiveness and self-assurance of the Christian West was not limited to the period of the Crusades; that same spirit was carried on by the Europeans when they explored and conquered most of the world after the fifteenth century.

The Crusades are significant as an indication of the solidarity of the Western Christian people.

213

Summary

- In the medieval world, a sense of community was very important to Christians.

- By the twelfth century, many little groups came into being that were similar to monastic communities.

- The seven sacraments were being celebrated by the Middle Ages.

- Relics and pilgrimages came about as the result of a widespread tendency toward veneration of the saints.

- The Crusades were an important part of medieval life.

Prayer

*O tender Father, you gave me more, much more
than I ever thought to ask for. I realize that our
human desires can never really match what you
long to give us.*

St. Catherine of Siena

Discussion Questions

1. Give one example of how medieval
   Christians understood one of the
   sacraments differently from the way it is
   understood today.

2. Belief in relics gave birth to pilgrimage,
   and pilgrimage gave birth to the Crusades.
   Explain how this took place.

3. What are some signs of how the Crusade
   ideal dominated the imagination of
   Western Christians?

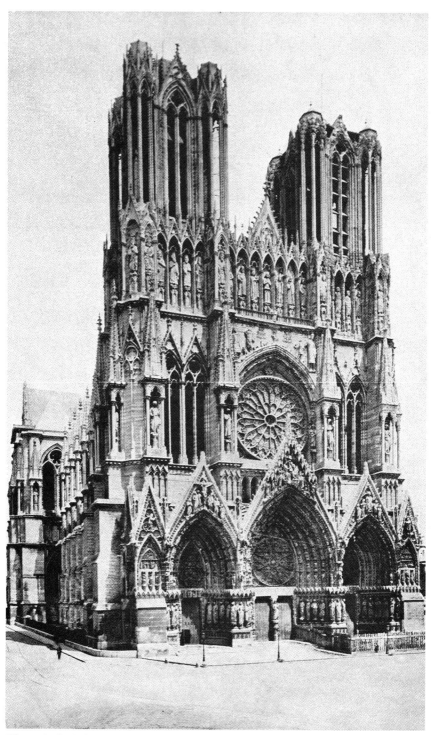

The cathedral of Notre Dame at Rheims, is one of the finest examples of Gothic architecture in the world.

Chapter Twenty-One

Gothic Cathedrals

It could be said that the Christians of the Middle Ages "spoke the language of symbolism." If that be so, then they never spoke more eloquently than in the building of Gothic[1] churches, which were at the same time models of the Heavenly Jerusalem, as well as magnificent collections of religious sculpture and stained glass pictures. The churches were built by the labor of the common people, and designed to convey messages to them; but at the same time they had an intricacy of design which displays the efforts of sophisticated intellectuals. The Gothic style of church first appeared around 1140 in the northern part of France and later became popular throughout western Europe. It is not an accident that the Abbey[2] of St. Denis, one of the first Gothic churches, was designed by Abbot Suger of St. Denis, who had been trained in the Seven Liberal Arts and was familiar with the ideas of the school of Chartres. The Gothic style represents one of the few instances in which the ideas of society's intellectuals were conveyed effectively to the common folk.

As a type of church architecture, Gothic replaced the Romanesque style that predominated during the eleventh and twelfth centuries. Earlier churches usually had

The Gothic style represents one of the few instances in which the ideas of society's intellectuals were conveyed effectively to the common folk.

1. In modern times, the people who disliked the values of the Middle Ages called the medieval churches "Gothic" to suggest that they were barbaric, like the Goths.

2. *Abbey* is another word for monastery; it often refers to the monastery's church building.

wooden roofs, which were a fire hazard; Romanesque churches, with their stone roofs, of necessity were heavy structures with massive walls to support the roof. The thick walls had small windows and usually had dark interiors as a result.

Light Shining into Darkness

Flying Buttress—a stone pillar, separate from the building, that supported the weight of the roof.

The technological advance that helped make the Gothic style possible was the **flying buttress:** a stone pillar, standing independent of the building, that connected to the building and supported much of the weight of the roof. The flying buttress and other structural features made it possible for the walls of the church to be taller, and of lighter construction. Enormous windows of multicolored stained glass became the trademark of the Gothic cathedrals; and to the symbolic mentality of medieval humans, the dark of the church's interior, like the darkness of the world, was being overcome by the divine light pouring through the windows. Considerable attention was given at this time to the Gospel according to St. John, which described Christ as the light that came into the world. In St. Jerome's translation of John, chapter one,

In the beginning was the Word, and the Word was with God; and the Word was God. He was in the beginning with God.

All things were made through Him, and without Him was made nothing that was made.

In Him was life, and the life was the light of men, and the light shines in the darkness, and the darkness understood it not. . . He was the true light, that enlightens every man coming into this world. (John 1:1–5, 9)

The symbolism went still further. The floorplan of the churches was **cruciform;** viewed from the air, in other words, the church appeared to be a cross. The main section of the church was called the nave, after the Latin *navis,* meaning ship; the ceiling had a single beam running the full length of the nave, like a ship's keel, and ribs coming out of the main beam, again like a ship. While the ribs served the function of bearing much of the weight of the roof, the entire appearance of the ceiling was calculated to resemble a ship—just as Christ's Church was sometimes called the "ship of souls." Still more symbolism: the stained glass windows on the west wall of the church, which shone most brilliantly in the evening when the sun was setting and the day was ending, portrayed scenes from another "ending," the end of the world.

Cruciform—in the shape of a cross.

The buildings had pointed arches, and these plus the tall windows, the high ceilings, and the towers on the exterior of the building impressed the viewer with a sense of verticality. Like medieval people with their bold speculations in the field of theology, the Gothic cathedral seemed to be trying to reach up to heaven itself. As more and more Gothic-style churches were built, the designers attempted to raise the ceilings of the main vault of the church even higher, until at last the ceiling of the Beauvais Cathedral, the highest ever attempted, collapsed under its own weight. The builders of Beauvais had unwittingly discovered the limit of how high people could build with stone; even so, others in other parts of Europe attempted to raise their own churches nearly as high.

Finally, there was a strong sense of geometric proportion to the buildings. One Scripture text that medieval thinkers emphasized was Wisdom 11:20: "For you (God) have disposed all things by measure and number and weight." Following the lead of St. Augustine,

219

the intellectuals of the Middle Ages believed that God created the world according to geometrical patterns, and they believed that by employing geometry, people were modeling their own artistic creation after God's Creation.

No doubt, many of the subtleties of Gothic architecture were lost on the common person, but this is not to say that there was no popular enthusiasm for the new type of cathedral.

No doubt many of the subtleties of Gothic architecture were lost on the common person, but this is not to say that there was no popular enthusiasm for the new type of cathedral. It was not simply that the cathedrals attracted pilgrims, whose presence stimulated the local economy. People of all social strata made sacrifices to bring the building projects to a successful conclusion. It is a measure of that sacrifice that during a one hundred-year period, the people of France (who numbered fewer than twenty million) helped to construct eighty large churches and five hundred abbeys.

Nobles contributed their wealth, and in token of their assistance they were allowed to hang the family banner within the church, or place the family name on one of the stained glass windows. Most generous of all was King Louis VI, who helped subsidize the magnificent Cathedral of Chartres. The people of the lower classes also contributed money and labor—which must have been a trial to their patience, since these enormous structures took up to forty years to build. It was common for all members of a guild, or trade union, to assess themselves and make a joint contribution. Many of the churches have rows of small stained glass windows depicting butchers, tanners, bakers, and others at work, in honor of each guild's contribution.

Marian Devotion

It appears that the tremendous effort expended by the common folk may have been inspired by their devotion to Mary.

It appears that the tremendous effort expended by the common folk may have been inspired by their devotion to Mary. Many of the cathedrals were dedicated to "Notre Dame,"

"Our Lady." The most famous instance of Marian devotion was the Cathedral at Chartres. In 876 the Byzantine Emperor had given France's King Charlemagne the Lady's Veil, which was believed to have belonged to the Blessed Mother herself. The Veil came to rest eventually at Chartres, and a large church was built in its honor.

But in 1194, a fire destroyed the church and nearly everything in it; the townspeople were amazed when, after a few days, several clerics tunneled their way out of the smoldering rubble and presented the Veil that they had risked their lives to save. The people of Chartres then reasoned that Mary would not have allowed her church to be destroyed unless she desired something greater in its place. Accordingly, they labored twenty-six years to construct the cathedral that is hailed today as one of the most beautiful religious monuments in the world.

Symbolism

More than simply monuments, the Gothic churches were also schools in stone, "written" in the language of symbolism to teach a mostly illiterate laity the truths of faith. In the words of one historian,

> *Since the cathedrals were the* summae *to be read by the ordinary man, we should be prepared for the blending of childlike candor and naivete with artistic proficiency and sophistication. The artists did not always teach profound theological speculation, but more often the stories of the Bible and the saints, and so helped the theologian reach the people.*[3]

3. John W. Baldwin, *The Scholastic Culture of the Middle Ages, 1000–1300* (Lexington, Mass.: D. C. Heath, 1971), p. 116.

In addition to the message in the form of the church building itself, there were numerous pictures in the stained glass, and as many as two thousand statues all around the building. The statues were grouped according to themes. At Chartres, for example, the sculpture along one of the western walls of the church depicted scenes from the life of Christ, while the northern side was dedicated to the glorification of Mary and the southern side treated the history of the Church all the way to the Last Judgment.

The education of the common people, by means of the cathedrals and other means as well, reveals a great deal about medieval society. Medieval society was hierarchial, that is, people belonged to distinct social classes, and one class of people was higher than another. The king occupied the highest position, and beneath him were the great barons, followed by lesser nobles such as the knights. Among the common people, craftsmen were differentiated as masters, journeymen (experienced workers, not so skilled as masters), and apprentices (who had no experience at all). All the common people were beneath the nobles, and within the class of commoners, peasant farmers were beneath merchants and craftsmen. The Church had a similar hierarchy: pope, archbishop, bishop, priest, lesser clerics, and then laity. The clergy were clearly above the laity, as can be seen from the fact that only priests could handle holy objects, and only priests received the Blood of Christ along with the Body of Christ.

There was no question of equality in the hierarchial society. With noble birth or with clerical status came privileges that the common people could not share. The upper classes generally enjoyed the larger share of food and material wealth, for example. But this is not to say that the society of the Middle Ages was simply exploitative. As the Gothic

> Medieval society was hierarchial; that is, people belonged to distinct social classes, and one class of people was higher than another.

> There was no question of equality in the hierarchial society. With noble birth or with common status came privileges that common people could not share.

churches' windows and statuary suggest, considerable thought and expense were devoted to the education of the people.

A similar function was fulfilled by the mystery plays that were popular during this period. They were simple plays based upon Scripture stories and the lives of the saints that aimed at teaching rudimentary doctrine or conveying a moral lesson. The plays were performed in the church buildings, or in the marketplace. Despite the fact that the people did not understand the Latin text of the Mass, then, and despite their inability to grasp the meaning of the sermon in the Mass, there still were means by which they could grow in understanding the faith.

Political theorists of this period likened the society to a body, much as St. Paul did in his Letter to the Corinthians (1 Corinthians 12:12–26). In terms of this image, some members of the body have greater dignity, but each member is necessary to the whole. Of course there was social inequality throughout the medieval centuries, and there were glaring injustices: Jews were generally mistreated on the grounds that they were heartless money-lenders and haters of Christ, for example, and the insane were locked away and often treated as subhuman. Notwithstanding such failings that grew out of inconsideration and superstition, there was a rudimentary sense of one's responsibility to another regardless of social status. In an imperfect way, Europe in the Middle Ages approximated St. Paul's ideal of community.

Summary

- The Gothic style of Church replaced the Romanesque style.

- The most basic symbolism of Gothic churches was that of light shining into darkness.

- People of all social strata made sacrifices to bring the building projects to a successful conclusion.

- The tremendous effort expended by the common folk may have been inspired by their devotion to Mary.

- The Gothic style used symbolism to teach a mostly illiterate laity the truths of faith.

- Medieval society, and the Church as well, had a hierarchial structure.

Prayer

Remember, O most gracious Virgin Mary, that never was it known that anyone who fled to your protection, implored your aid, or sought your intercession, was left unaided.

Inspired by this confidence I fly unto you, O Virgin of virgins, my Mother; to you do I come, before you I stand, sinful and sorrowful; O Mother of the Word Incarnate, despise not my petitions, but in your mercy, hear and answer me. Amen.

The Memorare
St. Bernard of
Clairvaux

Discussion Questions

1. How did a technical advance make the Gothic style of architecture possible?

2. Gothic churches reflected the importance of symbolism to medieval Christians. What was the most important symbolism in the Gothic churches?

3. How can it be said that the Gothic church buildings represented the labors or the interests of all members of society?

St. Francis of Assisi

Chapter Twenty-Two

The Quest for Salvation in the Later Middle Ages

Christians in the early Church had been perplexed by the problem of how humanity could be saved. There was clearly a sense that humanity was imperfect, inclined toward sin, and in need of salvation. But it was not so clear how salvation could be attained while living in a world full of temptation; nor did the early Christians have a consensus about how the sinner should be reconciled to God. It is not surprising, then, that so many people were attracted to the path of Anthony—the path into the desert, into the monastery.

As the years went by, the Church benefited from experience, and from the insights of men like the Fathers and the scholastic thinkers. But the tension between life in the world and the quest for salvation was not diminished during the Middle Ages. The monastic life held an enormous appeal for thousands of believers, and several signs, such as, the generally low opinion of marriage, and the practice of retiring to a monastery late in life, suggest that people living in the world were not convinced that their life could lead them to sanctity and salvation.

Even though there had been some efforts, mainly by the popes and the bishops, to remake the society in terms of Christian values, it was evident to even a casual observer that the world still was far from perfect. What is more, by about 1200, the monastic movement was losing its vigor, and even some of its appeal.

New Religious Movements

Thus to the people of the later Middle Ages, the quest for salvation once again became a source of uneasiness. That uneasiness gave birth to new religious movements, which appeared at various times in all corners of Christendom. Late medieval society had achieved an economic security far surpassing what had existed before, and it is a mark of late medieval religious movements that they generally embraced the ideal of poverty and the simple life. Only poverty and simplicity were so clearly not corrupt, not "of this world," that they held an appeal. The Church, meanwhile, was relatively wealthy and secure. Some of the late medieval groups rose in opposition to the established Church, while others strove to be a leaven within the Church.

Late medieval society had achieved an economic security far surpassing what had existed before.

There were a few strange splinter groups as early as the eleventh century but the first group of any size were the **Waldensians** of southern France. Their founder was a merchant named Peter Waldo. Upon reading Christ's call in Matthew (Matthew 19:16–26) for the rich young man to give away his wealth to the poor, Waldo gave up his own possessions and began to preach the gospel of poverty in the year 1173. Walking through the streets of Lyons in sandals and rags, he gained a large following among the lower classes. Waldensian laymen and laywomen began preaching, and in 1179 the Third Lateran Council approved their vow of poverty while insisting that they not preach in any town unless welcomed by the local priest.

Waldensians—a group founded by Peter Waldo that preached the gospel of poverty and, eventually, rejection of the authority of the Church.

But the Waldensians were not destined to stay within the bounds prescribed by the Church. Their doctrine of poverty was expanded to include rejection of the authority of the Church in favor of a free interpretation of Scripture. In fact, Waldensian preachers became notorious for jumping up to the pulpit during Masses to warn the congregation that there is no salvation in the established Church. In 1184, the Waldensians were excommunicated by the Archbishop of Lyons, but by that time they had spread into Germany and northern Italy, and they were able to survive as an underground sect. Innocent III promoted associations of poor Catholics as an alternative to the Waldensians, but he had little success.

Southern France was the homeland of another late twelfth-century group called the **Cathars.**[1] The Cathars were Gnostic dualists who, like the Gnostics of ancient times, were very numerous and offered an entire church that paralleled the established Church. It is estimated that half the population of southern France was Cathar by about 1200.

Cathars—Gnostic dualists who, like the Gnostics of ancient times, were very numerous and offered an entire church that paralleled the established Church.

Like the established Church, the Cathars had a church hierarchy, called the Perfect. The Perfect lived according to a strict moral code and were vegetarians. Like early dualists, they believed in a god of evil who was master of the material world, and they desired to escape the body to reach the realm of spirit. Having rejected the sacraments of mainstream Christianity, Cathars had their own "sacrament" called the Consolamentum, which was a ritual of self-starvation that led to death and spiritual "freedom."

Having rejected the sacraments of mainstream Christianity, Cathars had their own "sacrament" called the Consolamentum, which was a ritual of self-starvation that led to death and spiritual "freedom."

Pope Innocent III was so alarmed by the Cathar movement that he dispatched preachers to southern France on a mission of conversion. But the preachers, Cistercian

1. The word *Cathar* means "the Pure." They were also called the Albigensians.

monks who wore elegant robes and preferred the ceremonial of the established Church, got nowhere. A young canon named Dominic de Guzman, aided by a few friends, dressed himself in simple clothing and undertook his own preaching mission on behalf of Christianity in 1204.

Even though the new preachers had some success, the situation took a nasty turn in 1207. Innocent III's personal legate (representative) was murdered by the Cathars, and the pope became convinced that force was the only way of overcoming the heretics. The nobles from the northern half of France, led by one Simon de Montfort, answered the papal summons for a crusade in southern France. Many Cathars were killed, and the chief targets were the nobles of the region, whose death made it possible for the self-interested "crusaders" to seize land and call it their own.

While Innocent was unable to curb the excesses of de Montfort and his henchmen, he directed the anti-Cathar efforts along yet another new course. He sent out papal representatives with special powers to serve as inquisitors. Today, the **Inquisition** is viewed as one of the worst examples of medieval barbarity: people could be placed before the inquisitors by means of anonymous accusations, and their confessions to the charges were sometimes obtained by means of torture. Those who refused to give up their beliefs could be put to death. Such extreme measures seemed acceptable to the Church authorities because they believed that the Cathar sect was a serious threat to the Church, and they were convinced that the heretics' strange beliefs must come from the Devil himself.

Today, the medieval Inquisition is viewed as one of the worst examples of barbarity.

Inquisition—the investigation and sentencing of persons professing heresy or accused of heresy.

Preaching Orders

Even though the situation in France was far from healthy, it was evident that St. Dominic and his friends had served the Church well by their preaching. In 1215, Pope Innocent gave permission for the **Dominicans** to constitute a new order within the Church. They were to be a preaching order that adhered to a simple rule. In imitation of another new group called the **Franciscans,** the Dominicans adopted a life of voluntary poverty. Both groups aspired to live the *vita apostolica*, the "apostolic life": like the apostles they would give away their belongings and own nothing.

The life of voluntary poverty and renunciation of all worldly goods was chosen by St. Francis, founder of the Franciscans, when he was a young man. He was injured in a battle, and forced to spend a great deal of time in bed. With so much time for reflection, the bed-ridden Francis began to examine his life. His father was a wealthy merchant who expected his son to take over the family business, but Francis was becoming attracted to a simple way of living. Finally, as legend has it, Francis went to the town square of Assisi, took off all his fine clothes and recited the Our Father while standing naked. He then donned the simple tunic with a rope for a belt which was to become his order's standard garb, and he left home. After that time, he kept himself alive by begging for food.

Feeling that God had called him to rebuild the Church, Francis dwelt a short distance outside Assisi and rebuilt, stone by stone, an old abandoned church. Before long, however, he concluded that rebuilding God's Church meant winning converts to the Church, so he and his friends became preachers. Innocent III

Dominicans—preaching order that adhered to a simple rule and lived a life of voluntary poverty.

Franciscans—order that lived a life of voluntary poverty and renunciation of all worldly goods.

The life of voluntary poverty and renunciation of all worldly goods was chosen by St. Francis, founder of the Franciscans.

gave Francis authorization for a new order in 1210. One of Francis' close friends was a young woman named Clare, who was deeply influenced by the ideals of Francis. Under her leadership, in 1215 the **Poor Clares** became an order of women dedicated to prayer and the simple life.

Poor Clares—order of women dedicated to prayer and the simple life.

The Franciscans and Dominicans placed themselves at the disposal of the pope and were assigned the task of preaching Jesus' message in the cities of Christendom.

The Franciscans and Dominicans placed themselves at the disposal of the pope, and were assigned to the task of preaching Jesus' message in the cities of Christendom. In the prosperous cities, the poor preachers in their simple robes made a tremendous impression. Many city dwellers were drawn back to the Church. It is typical of St. Francis' trust in God and dedication to preaching that he accompanied the Christian warriors on the Fifth Crusade, disembarked from their ship, and attempted to convert the Moslem leader of Egypt to the Christian faith.

The one difference between Franciscans and Dominicans was that the friars (the brothers) in Dominic's order underwent extensive training in preparation for their preaching. Soon the Dominicans were rising to prominence in the universities and the Franciscans, in friendly rivalry, also began to take assignments as university masters. Nearly all the foremost theologians of the thirteenth century were Franciscans and Dominicans. By living a simple life, they could dedicate themselves single-mindedly to study.

Nearly all the foremost theologians of the thirteenth century were Franciscans and Dominicans.

The Franciscans' and the Dominicans' communities spread rapidly, especially in southern Europe. The Dominicans, for example, had sixty different houses (communities of brothers) within six years of their official recognition as an order. At the same time, another religious movement began in northern Europe. It shared the same ideals of poverty and simplicity, and was dominated by women, who were called the **Beguines.** The Beguine movement originated in the Low Countries (present-day Belgium and the

Beguines—a group that pledged themselves to a life of poverty, prayer, and simplicity.

Netherlands) around 1200, and soon spread to Germany. The Beguines pledged themselves to a simple, almost impoverished life. Generally, they dedicated themselves to prayer and vowed virginity (although many Beguines did leave open the possibility of later marriage). Unlike the friars they had no official order or rule, and maintained themselves by menial work rather than by begging. At first they did not even live in community, although later they shared houses. There may have been as many as thirty thousand Beguines by the middle of the 1300s.

The Franciscan and Dominican Orders still have thousands of members today. The Beguines, despite their almost complete lack of organization, have also had a long history. There were Beguines in northern Europe well into the nineteenth century. As early as the fourteenth century, however, the Beguines were being condemned for heretical notions.[2] The Franciscans, too, developed one faction that endorsed extreme views. They supported the strange theory of Joachim of Flora, who held that humankind was entering upon the third, and last, great age of history: the first was the age of obedience and fear, the age of the Old Testament; the second was an age of faith and obedience, the age of the New Testament; but the third age would be characterized by faith and liberty, when law and the institutional Church would no longer be needed. Once again, as had been the case with the Waldensians, a small group believed that they had reached such a high plane of spiritual perfection that the established Church could not measure up to their standards.

2. R. W. Southern, in *Western Society and the Church in the Middle Ages,* pp. 328–329, argues that the Beguines were not really heretics, but were simply victims of men who resented their independence from marriage and from the Church's leadership.

Opposition to the Church

After the mid-thirteenth century, many popular religious movements arose in opposition to the official teachings and the official leaders of the Church. In addition, the religious aspirations of the lower classes became indistinguishable from their social frustrations.

Lollard Movement— founded by John Wycliffe, who advanced the theory that all power and ownership came from God, and humans have ownership only so long as they follow God's laws.

The **Lollard movement** in England is a case in point. The founder of the Lollard movement was John Wycliffe, a master of theology who became prominent at the University of Oxford during the 1370s. Wycliffe advanced a theory that all power and ownership came from God, and humans have ownership only so long as they follow God's laws. From this principle, Wycliffe drew several revolutionary conclusions. First, the Latin Bible ought to be translated into the common people's language, so that they can learn God's laws. Second, the sacraments are unnecessary because they place the Church between humanity and God; humanity should be in direct contact with the Redeemer. Third, the Church should not own any material things, because the goods of this world distract the priests from the simple life that they should be living in imitation of Jesus and the apostles.

These and several other opinions amounted to a very scholarly criticism of the Church's practices and teachings. But at the very time that Wycliffe's scholarly opinions were being examined by Church officials who were anxious to protect orthodoxy, there was a mass uprising of peasants in southeastern England. They began looting and destroying the nobility's property, cursing the upper classes (both the laity and clerics) in the name of Wycliffe's doctrines. Even though the peasants could not understand the Oxford scholar's sophisticated theories, the association of Wycliffe with the radicals eroded his support. When his views were condemned, his old supporters from Oxford were nowhere to be seen.

The Lollard beliefs became part of a popular "underground" movement that emphasized individual interpretation of the Bible and rejection of the institutional Church. Wycliffe's theological opinions, largely misunderstood by the common people, came to be an ingredient in their long-standing resentment of society's rich and powerful people.

From the sophisticated theories of Wycliffe to the modest spirituality of the Beguines, the religious movements of the latter Middle Ages all shared a desire to rise above the standards of everyday life and seek salvation in a life of apostolic simplicity and poverty. Tied to many of the movements was a growing resentment of a rich and powerful Church. When social and political tensions were mixed in with religious sentiments, the result was potentially explosive.

Such tensions were involved in the career of Jan Huss, a Bohemian who had beliefs quite like Wycliffe's and who gained a large following. He was condemned to death by a Church council during the fifteenth century. Finally, social and political factors were involved in the career of Martin Luther, during the sixteenth century. But in the case of Luther, those factors turned out to be an aid rather than a hindrance to his attempt to challenge the beliefs and practices of the established Church.

The Lollard beliefs became part of a popular "underground" movement that emphasized individual interpretation of the Bible and rejection of the institutional Church.

The religious movements of the latter Middle Ages all shared a desire to rise above the standards of everyday life and seek salvation in a life of apostolic simplicity and poverty.

Summary

• The tension between life in the world and the quest for salvation was not diminished during the Middle Ages.

• By about 1200, the monastic movement was losing its vigor, and even some of its appeal.

• New religious movements appeared dedicated to living and preaching poverty and simplicity.

Prayer

Lord, Make me an instrument of Thy peace.
Where there is hatred, let me sow love;
Where there is injury, pardon;
Where there is doubt, faith;
Where there is despair, hope;
Where there is darkness, light;
Where there is sadness, joy.
O Divine Master, grant that I may seek
Not so much to be consoled, as to console;
To be understood, as to understand;
To be loved, as to love;
For it is in the giving that we receive;
It is in the pardoning that we are pardoned;
It is in the dying that we are born to eternal life.

Prayer of St. Francis

Discussion Questions

1. One ideal motivated virtually all of the new religious movements of the Middle Ages. What was that ideal, and why was it appealing?

2. What was the clearest difference as regards attitude toward the established Church, between the Waldensians, Cathars, Lollards and Hussites on the one hand, and the Franciscans, Dominicans, Poor Clares and Beguines, on the other hand?

St. Catherine of Sienna

Chapter Twenty-Three

The Decline of the Medieval Papacy

Loss of Spiritual Direction

The decline of the papacy's power and prestige during the later Middle Ages was both a symptom and a cause of the passing of medieval world-order. It was a symptom of the decline of respect for priests in a society dominated by priests, and of the decline of the hierarchical view of society. At the same time, the plight of the papacy hastened the end of serious efforts to remake the society by means of councils and canon law.

The humiliation of the papacy by France's King Philip IV is traditionally cited as the beginning of the decline of the medieval papacy, but actually the erosion of papal prestige began earlier. For one thing, the pontiffs had been too successful in making themselves supreme dispensers of justice in Christendom. By the middle of the thirteenth century, Rome was the home of a massive judicial bureaucracy that carried out the uninspiring work of processing thousands of complex cases. Among the lawyer-popes of this period, there was not a single saint. The popes, meanwhile, had detracted from their own reputation as spiritual leaders by their behavior in destroying the Hohenstaufen dynasty of Germany.

By the middle of the thirteenth century, Rome was the home of a massive judicial bureaucracy that carried out the uninspiring work of processing thousands of complex cases.

Historians generally agree that Hohenstaufen Emperor Frederick II was an evil, scheming man who resorted to horrible cruelty in his efforts to dominate Italy and the papacy. But many contemporaries saw the struggle between Frederick II and the successive popes who opposed him as a political struggle; the use of spiritual weapons against him—namely, three separate sentences of excommunication—was a sign that religious and political concerns were being confused.

When Pope Nicholas IV died in 1292, the cardinals were unable to agree upon a successor. Finally, perhaps in hope of restoring the spiritual vigor of the papacy, the electors chose a hermit who had a reputation as a holy man. It is perhaps a sign of what kind of office the papacy had become that Celestine V, the holy hermit, was entirely incapable of adjusting to his new role. He resigned before even one year had ended, and his successor was Benedict Gaetani, who became Pope Boniface VIII.

In 1296, the ambitious Philip IV was waging war upon the King of England. As was his custom, he squeezed as much tax money out of the French people as he possibly could, to finance his military campaign. Lateran Council IV in 1215 had forbidden the clergy of any country to pay taxes without first consulting the pope. The kings, however, habitually sidestepped this law by declaring an emergency and taxing the clergy to support a "just war." Boniface, recognizing the dishonesty of the two kings who both were taxing their Churches to subsidize "just wars" against each other, issued the decree *Clericis Laicos*. It stated that any king who seized the Church's wealth was subject to excommunication, and it instructed Church officials to resist any king who attempted to tax in this way.

Philip responded with a decree forbidding the export of precious metals from his country, which had the effect of cutting off the French Church's tax payments to the pontiff. Then a royal official traveled to Rome and stirred up opposition to Boniface. His claim was that Boniface had pressured Celestine to give up the papal throne, and that he was promoting his own family in Church offices. There were noble factions in Rome that were all too ready to believe the charges, and as a matter of fact there was some truth to the charge of nepotism. Boniface, placed in a weak position, gave in. He allowed Philip to tax the French Church whenever he felt there was an "emergency." In other words, Philip had won a victory.

Over the next few years, the king and the pontiff sparred intermittently, then in 1301 Philip provoked another major dispute. He put a French bishop on trial for blasphemy, heresy, and treason, even though ecclesiastical officials were supposed to be tried only in Church courts. Boniface responded with a series of letters and decrees against the king, culminating in the decree *Unam Sanctam* which asserted that "if the earthly power errs, it shall be judged by the spiritual power." Philip's chief minister issued a claim that Boniface was a criminal and a heretic, and Boniface was preparing a decree of excommunication against Philip when the king's men kidnapped the pontiff. They released him soon afterward, but because of the rough treatment he had received the old pope died a few weeks later.

The Avignon Papacy

It is a sign of the decline of the papacy's prestige that there was no public outcry against Philip's provocations. The king faced a few mildly uncomfortable moments in dealing with Benedict XI, Boniface's successor. But when Benedict died soon afterward, a Frenchman became the new pontiff, and he was not able to resist Philip's influence.

Clement V, the new French pope, moved the papal government to Avignon in southern France. There was a series of French popes at Avignon, who are remembered primarily for their efforts to squeeze revenues out of the Church to support an enormous bureaucracy and a splendid papal palace in Avignon.

In the meantime, a fiery woman named Catherine, from Siena, Italy, was dismayed to see the leader of Christendom removed from Rome, the traditional seat of universal leadership. As she reputedly never consumed any food other than Holy Communion, she was skinny and looked weak. But Pope Gregory XI (1370–1378) found St. Catherine to be, literally, a holy terror, and at her urging he took up residence in Rome. Gregory's hesitations about living in Rome were well founded, as political unrest had developed in the absence of the popes. Gregory's predecessor had even come to Rome and moved back to France, because he was unwilling to cope with the Roman populace. When Gregory died, the unruly Roman mob played a role in causing one of the greatest crises in the history of Western Christianity.

When Pope Gregory died, the unruly Roman mob played a role in causing one of the greatest crises in the history of Western Christianity.

The cardinals in the conclave[1] were broken into factions, unable to agree about who should be the new pope. As the debate dragged on, the people in the streets began chanting for a Roman pope, or at least an Italian. Finally, as the crowd broke into the courtyard of the Vatican Palace, the cardinals hastily elected the Italian Bartolomeo Prignano, Archbishop of Bari. Prignano was not in the palace, so one resourceful person shoved an aging cardinal out in front of the crowd, proclaiming that here, at last, was the new Italian pope. As the crowd cheered, the cardinals went into hiding.

1. *Conclave* is the term given to the cardinals' closed-door meetings in which they select a new pope.

Papal Schism

Prignano became Urban VI (1378–1389), but before long the cardinals were finding him to be an unpleasant old man with a short temper. Before the end of 1378, one group of cardinals (mostly Frenchmen appointed by the Avignon popes) were so frustrated that they left Rome, traveled to a nearby town, and elected a second pope. Their unconventional behavior was defended on the grounds that they had been pressured by the mob to elect Prignano and, therefore, the earlier election was invalid.

Regardless of what one might think about the cardinals' actions, the unmistakable fact was that now there was a Clement VII calling himself pope alongside Urban VI. Like Urban, Clement appointed his own cardinals, and maintained a papal government (in Avignon). Urban VI excommunicated Clement VII and his cardinals, just as Clement excommunicated Urban and his cardinals. Each man, upon his death, was replaced by another who called himself the one true pope, and for thirty years, until 1409, there was a **schism** (deep division) in the Church. Allegiance to one or the other was largely a matter of political inclination: the French, for example, supported the French line of popes, while the English, traditional rivals of the French, supported the Italian line.

Schism—a deep division or split.

The Conciliar Movement

The schism, following the seventy years of domination of the papacy by the French kings, brought the prestige of the See of Peter to an all-time low. It is characteristic of the condition of the entire Church, especially the papacy, that the political theorists of the period were generally anticlerical and unmistakably antipapal in their thinking. A

It is characteristic of the condition of the entire Church, especially the papacy, that the political theorists of the period were generally anticleric and unmistakably antipapal in their thinking.

theorist named Marsilius from the Italian city of Padua, for example, in the year 1324 penned a work entitled *The Defender of Peace.* In this book he argued that the state was the foremost protector of the people's interests, and that the Church ought to be, in effect, just a department of the state. Marsilius went on to argue that religious affairs ought to be governed not by the pope, but by a council consisting of all the leaders of the Church.

Conciliarism—the call for the Church to be ruled by general councils rather than by popes.

Marsilius' idea of the council was developed by other scholars, notably at the University of Paris, into a fully articulated theory of **conciliarism.** It hearkened to the ancient councils such as Nicea as the models of good procedure, and considered the successor of Peter to be primary in honor only—not in authority. Europe at this moment in history was experiencing a widespread reaction against centralized rule, as the most influential nobles were thwarting royal authority in England, France, Spain, and Germany. Thanks to the scandal of the schism, papal government was no exception to this trend.

Council of Pisa—general council in 1409 that deposed the two acting popes and elected Alexander V as pope. But because the two deposed popes refused to step down the end result was the existence of three separate popes.

The cardinals of both popes met in a single assembly and called for a general council. The **Council of Pisa,** in 1409, deposed both popes, elected its own pope (Alexander V), and issued a series of decrees which promoted an increase in the power of bishops. But as neither of the deposed popes would step down, the end result of the Council of Pisa was the existence of three separate popes. No solution was to be found until late 1414, when Emperor Sigismund engineered a new **Council at Constance.**

Council at Constance—held in 1414 the council put an end to the three popes by electing Cardinal Odo Colonna, who took the name Martin V, as the true pope, thereby, ending the schism.

The gathering at Constance was an unusual one. In addition to nearly two hundred bishops, there were about three hundred lawyers and theologians, numerous princes and nobles and town leaders, and about fifteen thousand clerics of various kinds. Because there was no overriding authority to determine which participants had the right to vote in the council, all the bishops and scholars were allowed a vote, but voting was done by blocs, or "nations"—the Italians, English, French, Spanish, and Germans each representing one vote. Besides condemning Jan Huss for heresy, the nations voted the three rival popes out of office and replaced them with Cardinal Odo Colonna, who took the name Martin V. The leaders of Constance also issued a statement proclaiming that true authority in the Church rested with the general council, and they arranged for a council to convene every five years.

The leaders of Constance also issued a statement proclaiming that true authority in the Church rested with the general council.

Somewhat surprisingly the new popes, Martin V and his successors Eugenius IV and Nicholas V, did everything in their power to undermine the conciliar movement. They were aided in this endeavor by the council members themselves, who could not overcome national jealousies to achieve a unified front. It is significant that after the experience of the long and fruitless Council of Basle (1431–1449), Cardinal Nicholas Cusanus, a leading advocate of conciliarism, became a defender of papal authority.

End of an Era

Even though enthusiasm for direction of the Church by means of councils could not be sustained during the fifteenth century, it can hardly be said that the papacy fully recovered its position of leadership in Christendom. Too many meaningless excommunications had been hurled by one successor of Peter against another; bishops and local clergymen had operated independent of the popes for too many decades; too many opportunities had arisen for kings and nobles to assume for themselves powers that had once belonged to the pope.

A great era in history, such as the Middle Ages, is made up of many factors. Each factor has a "life" of its own, and grows and fades because of its own inner strengths and weaknesses. Thus to say that the ancient world "ended" in 410 or 476, or to say that the medieval world "ended" during the fifteenth century, is to impose a false unity upon independent developments. Nevertheless, the rise of nations at the Church councils and the rise of centralized states in Europe coincides roughly with the decline of the crusade ideal, a decrease in the number of Gothic churches being built, a reaction against the doctrines of scholasticism, and a change in the nature of papal leadership. Many long-standing characteristics of medieval Christianity were still prominent during the fifteenth century, but it can be said that this century marks the end of medieval Christianity. One important feature of the century yet to come was that neither the popes nor their most severe critics fully recognized to what extent the medieval papacy had been crippled by the events of the fourteenth and fifteenth centuries.

Summary

- The power and the prestige of the papacy declined in the late Middle Ages.

- Rome became a judicial bureaucracy.

- Kings taxed the clergy to support their "just wars."

- Pope Gregory XI, at the urging of Catherine of Siena, took up residency in Rome.

- During this period the Church had two popes, and when the cardinals tried to depose them and elected a new pope, they would not step down.

- The Council of Constance was held in 1414 and put an end to the schism of the papacy.

Prayer

Eternal God, you have made the Blood of Christ so precious through his sharing in your divine nature. You are a mystery as deep as the sea; the more I search, the more I find, and the more I find, the more I search for you. I can never be satisfied; what I receive will ever leave me desiring more.

St. Catherine of Siena

Discussion Questions

1. It could be said that success helped to undermine the papacy in the later Middle Ages. What was the papacy's problem, as reflected in the election of Celestine V?

2. What circumstances explain how the schism of the papacy came about?

3. What were the aims of the conciliar movement? What frustrations caused this movement to grow? What frustrations killed the movement?

—

Section III
The Reformation

Introduction

The history of Western Christianity becomes much more difficult to follow after ca. 1520. Up to that time, there was a rich variety of religious movements springing up in various corners of Christendom, but they rose under the umbrella of a single Christian Church. Most Christians acknowledged one set of leaders, and most shared a large number of common assumptions and common beliefs.

After the Lutheran movement began to develop in opposition to Rome's influence, however, it was joined by similar independent movements: the English, the Anabaptist, and the Calvinist, each of which grew in response to its own fundamental principles, which principles were not shared by either Rome or the other independent groups. One indication of the new state of affairs is that while the original meaning of *catholic* was "universal," meaning that it was for all people, after the sixteenth century the word "catholic" was understood as a label for those Christians who still looked to the hierarchy in Rome for leadership.

A recent trend in historical scholarship has been to downplay the differences between Rome and the new branches of the Church; to urge that the basic similarities between the various kinds of Christians were more important than the differences. This trend is a healthy replacement for the earlier tendency of Protestant and Catholic historians to condemn each other's leaders and beliefs. But the desire for unity among twentieth-century Christians should not be allowed to obscure the fact that to sixteenth-century Christians, the divisions seemed insurmountable and the issues seemed more important than life and death. The hatreds generated by the controversies of the sixteenth century spelled the death of the unity known as Christendom and created a strange phenomenon that has continued even to this day: a Christian Church divided against itself.

Woodcut by Albrecht Dürer

Chapter Twenty-Four

The Condition of the Church at the Time of the Reformation

It is common for historians to list the problems that plagued the Christian Church in the fifteenth century, then portray the Protestant Reformation as an attempt to cure a sick Church. The questions often arise whether the Protestant reformers went too far in their reform, or whether the Church might have healed itself if the reformers had not pulled away from the jurisdiction of the pope and the bishops.

It is far from certain, however, that the Church at the time of the Reformation was in worse condition than it had been before or has been since. To put it another way, the Church is always in need of reform, because it is made up of people who are imperfect. Problems such as clerical concubinage, simony, ecclesiastical **pluralism,** nepotism, and clerical illiteracy were certainly not limited to the early sixteenth century.

In addition to the problems, the Church at this time showed signs of good health. Some reformers were restoring older forms of spirituality, others were taking new directions; many of them might have made a greater contribution to the development of Christianity if they had been given direction.

Pluralism—the practice of some bishops, who ruled several sees at the same time, to collect the revenues from each without giving them any pastoral attention.

If there was a crisis in
the Church at the time
of the Reformation, it
was not from lack of
spiritual life, but from
lack of direction by the
leaders of the Church.

If there was a crisis in the Church at the time of the Reformation, it was not from lack of spiritual life, but from lack of direction by the leaders of the Church.

Many of the medieval religious orders had been slipping in membership and fervor during the later Middle Ages, and the fifteenth century witnessed numerous attempts to revitalize the orders. As a general rule, one or two persons—a holy nun or a vigorous abbot—would rise out of each order and undertake a reform of discipline. While during the tenth century, the reformers had desired to make their monasteries independent of outside influences, the reformers of the fifteenth century were inclined to put their orders under the jurisdiction of bishops or the pope in the hope of imposing discipline from outside.

Just as the medieval monastic and preaching orders were showing signs of life, several forms of medieval spirituality were also thriving among the laity. The veneration of saints and relics was still quite popular, for example. During this period, there arose the belief in patron saints for specific causes. The people would pray to one saint when planning a trip, to another to help a sick mother, to another for the progress of missionary work, and so forth. It was during the 1400s, too, that nearly all Christians began giving saints' names to their children.

As had been the case during the Middle Ages, the Mass continued to be appreciated for the divine gifts that it obtained. The power of the sacred Host was still foremost in people's minds: it was at this time that the Church began the custom of ringing a bell during the elevation of the consecrated Host, for example. To "tap the power" of the Mass, people in ever greater numbers made donations to their Churches in order to have Masses said on behalf of their souls. It was common for wealthy people to request hundreds of Masses for themselves in exchange for large gifts: King Henry V of England probably holds the "record," having arranged for twenty thousand Masses after his death. But many of the newly-rich merchants of Europe's growing middle class were doing the same on a smaller scale.

The multiplication of the number of Masses, besides reflecting a debased appreciation of the Eucharist, reveals the people's powerful desire to be certain that they were saved from eternal damnation. That desire was foremost in an era characterized by religious emotionalism. The early medieval image of Christ the dignified King had disappeared, for example, in favor of a bloody, crucified Christ portrayed in realistic detail. A larger-than-life wooden carving of the crucified Lord might be carried into a village one day, causing a disruption of normal life as people wept and moaned and pledged to give up all luxury. Florence, one of the most prosperous cities of the world, was practically controlled for several years by a Dominican preacher, Girolamo Savonarola, who ranted about the coming end of the world and the horrors of divine judgment. He incited people to burn their pagan books, luxurious clothing, jewelry, pictures of women, playing cards, and dice. Throughout Europe, a common practice of the time was **flagellation:** whipping oneself as an act of self-discipline and penance.

The fifteenth century was also the time of printed collections of prayers, manuals of prayer, and manuals for Christian living. The printing press, a new invention, was turning out these little books in tremendous numbers.[1] They were designed to help Christians develop personal piety. The most famous book

---

1. Interestingly, the manuals outsold copies of the Bible. To people unaccustomed to reading the Scriptures, the manuals must have seemed easier to work with.

The multiplication of the number of Masses, besides reflecting a debased appreciation of the Eucharist, reveals the people's powerful desire to be certain that they were saved from eternal damnation.

Flagellation—whipping oneself as an act of self-discipline and penance.

The fifteenth century was the time of printed collections of prayers, manuals of prayer, and manuals for Christian living. They were designed to help Christians develop personal piety.

of this sort was the *Imitation of Christ,* which has gone through hundreds of editions in many languages, and is still read today.

Brethren of Common Life—laypeople who lived in community, prayed together, and studied the Scriptures together, and preached spiritual regeneration to their fellow lay-people.

Oratory of Divine Love—a group that began in southern Europe about 1500 and served the same purpose as the Brethren of Common Life.

The *Imitation* and other manuals were promoted by the **Brethren of the Common Life,** who got their start in the Netherlands around the year 1400. They were laypeople who preached spiritual regeneration to their fellow laypeople. Although they took no monastic vows, they lived together, prayed together and studied the Scriptures together. Many became teachers and spread the Brethren's ideals among the Germans. In southern Europe, the **Oratory of Divine Love,** which began just after 1500, served a similar function. Taking St. Jerome as their patron saint, Italian clerics and laypeople joined in small groups on a regular basis to pray and to study the Scriptures and the Fathers of the Church.

What these two groups shared was a common desire to reform the lives of individuals, and an interest in Scripture. Both these movements appear to have been a reaction against excessive interest in the externals of Christian life—rituals, fasts, pilgrimages, etc., that had become empty observances for many Christians. The scholars of Christendom took up the same emphasis upon the spirit of Christ's teachings, insisting that an inward change of heart was needed to make the external practices meaningful.

Two of these scholars, influenced by the Brethren's teaching that all Christians should study the Scriptures, studied Greek so that they could bypass Jerome's Latin translation and get to the original text of the Bible. Desiderius Erasmus and Jacques Lefevre d'Etaples managed to publish their own translations of the New Testament. But their achievements were surpassed by the scholars of the University of Alcalá, in Spain. Cardinal Ximenes, founder of the university, promoted study of the Bible in the original languages. In about 1502, he began gathering Greek and Jewish scholars around him. Within twenty years they had produced a triple dictionary for Greek, Hebrew, and Aramaic languages (the languages in which the sacred Scriptures were written), as well as a multi-language edition of the entire Bible.

The Christian Church, then, did not suffer from any lack of spiritual energies in the period before the Reformation. There were excesses, of course, but even during this period of religious emotionalism there was a decline in the number of heresy trials. The Waldensians and Hussites were either dying out or maintaining a low profile. At the same time, the reform movements showed much promise. But the promise could only be fulfilled if the various forces for reform could be given direction. In the sacerdotal society of medieval Europe, that direction traditionally had come from the clergy. At the beginning of the sixteenth century, was there any reason to expect the clergy to assume leadership and provide the necessary direction?

The Christian Church did not suffer from any lack of spiritual energies in the period before the Reformation.

The answer was, no. The clergy, far from being at the head of a reform movement, was justifiably viewed as being the reason why reform was needed. Many priests, for example, were not adequately trained. The desire to contribute money to the Church in exchange for having Masses said for the donor led some unscrupulous bishops to ordain new men to say the Masses even before they were adequately trained. Besides being relatively ignorant about the faith, many such priests were impoverished vagrants. The problem was widespread, and remedies were slow in coming. The Oratory of Divine Love gave rise to the **Theatine Order** in Italy, a group of priests who maintained normal roles as pastors while subjecting themselves to rigorous personal discipline. But while the Theatine Order ultimately produced some of the great reforming bishops of this era, until the latter

Theatine Order—a group of priests in Italy who maintained normal roles as pastors while subjecting themselves to rigorous personal discipline.

part of the sixteenth century its effects were limited primarily to the area around Rome.

Within the hierarchy of the Church, there were individual bishops who vigorously disciplined their priests and upheld the cause of reform, but they were the exception to the rule. Most men had obtained episcopal status by virtue of their noble birth, not their reputation for good faith. The scandal of the day was pluralism: bishops who ruled several sees at the same time, collecting the revenues from each one but paying scarcely any pastoral attention to any of them. One Italian noble managed to hold eight different bishoprics at once.

The leadership of the Church, then, had to come from the papacy. But the popes of the Renaissance period were subject to all the tendencies of the secularized culture in which they operated: enthusiasm for the arts, political intrigue, and nepotism were the marks of Renaissance Italy as well as the papacy. It is possible to justify each of these tendencies. Great art was completed under the popes' patronage, for example: the Vatican Library was founded, the magnificent new St. Peter's Church was begun, and Michelangelo executed some of his finest works such as the Sistine Chapel ceiling and the "Moses."

It could be said, too, that political involvement seemed necessary for the papacy's survival; and in times of political intrigue the popes naturally preferred to give power to their trusted relatives. It should also be noted that in spite of their poor reputation, the Renaissance popes never fell into heresy. But their commitment to reform was sporadic at best. And in most respects, they behaved after the fashion of Italian secular princes rather than as successors of the Prince of the Apostles.

> Most men had obtained episcopal status by virtue of their noble birth, not their reputation for good faith.

After the pontificates of Martin V and Eugenius IV, Nicholas V (1447-1451) faced several attempts at revolution and even assassination. Rather than become a victim of the political situation, Nicholas attempted to be an aggressive part of it; and from that time the popes engaged in the endless diplomatic maneuvers and military escapades that were the ruination of Italy during this period. Italy's disunity was an invitation to France and Spain, the great nation-states, to intervene and promote their own interests. The papacy's involvement in power politics reached its height with Julius II (1503-1513), the "soldier-pope" who used the French to crush his Venetian rivals, then had to rely upon diplomacy to ward off the French.

The habit of nepotism began with Paul II (1464-1471). He and his successors appointed their own relatives as cardinals. Like most of the nobles of Italy, these cardinals lived luxuriously and immorally, and they perpetuated the problem by electing men like themselves as popes. The papacy came to be the prize for powerful aristocratic families such as the della Roveres, the Borgias and the Medicis. Innocent VIII (1484-1492), elected thanks to the power and pay-offs of the della Rovere family, brought the papacy to new levels of notoriety by placing his own illegitimate children into strategic marriages to strengthen the papacy's diplomatic position.

The papacy came to be the prize for powerful aristocratic families.

It is generally conceded that the most infamous man of the times was Rodrigo Borgia, who by bribing the cardinals became Pope Alexander VI (1492-1503). His personal morals were far from admirable, and like Innocent VIII and Julius II, he fathered several children. One of his illegitimate offspring, Cesare Borgia, became a cardinal at the age of seventeen; another Borgia child, Lucretia, grew tired of her husband, and Cesare reportedly killed the poor man in a fight. By becoming Captain of the Papal Guard, Cesare took control of the Papal States for the Borgia family; then after Alexander VI's death, Pope Julius II spent ten years fighting to regain control of the Papal States.

The papacy, in other words, was in a sorry state. Perhaps the most discouraging evidence of the times was the Fifth Council of the Lateran, which began in 1512. Compared to Lateran IV under Innocent III, it seemed to promote reform of the Church in an unconvincing way. Plurality of offices was mentioned as an abuse, for example, but offenders were instructed only to resign all but *four* of their simultaneous offices. The Council ended in 1517, and one of its last two acts was a decree against the looting of cardinals' palaces. There were sincere reformers at the Council, but the problem of Rome's leadership can be seen in the very fact that cardinals owned palaces. Small wonder that Martin Luther, on pilgrimage to Rome in 1510, was dismayed by what he saw.

Summary

- People in great numbers made donations to their churches in order to have Masses said on behalf of their souls.

- Religious emotionalism was prevalent during this period, and flagellation became a common practice.

- Printed prayers, manuals of prayer, and manuals for Christian living were designed to help develop personal piety.

- Groups of laypeople lived in community and preached spiritual regeneration.

- Because of the problems of the clergy and hierarchy, there was a lack of leadership and direction in the Church.

Prayer

Do not continue to live like the heathen, whose thoughts are worthless and whose minds are in the dark. They have no part in the life that God gives for they . . . have lost all feeling of shame; they give themselves over to vice and do all sorts of indecent things without restraint.

That was not what you learned about Christ! You certainly heard about him, and as his followers you were taught the truth that was in Jesus. So get rid of your old self—the old self that was being destroyed by its deceitful desires.

Your hearts and your minds must be made completely new, and you must put on the new self, which is created in God's likeness and reveals itself in the true life that is upright and holy.

Ephesians 4:17–24

Discussion Questions

1. Looking at the entire chapter, find three examples of reform spirit, or good health, in the Church at this time.

2. Find examples of the religious emotionalism of this period.

3. What suggests that there were serious problems in the Church of this period?

Martin Luther burning the pope's bull containing his condemnation.

Chapter Twenty-Five

Martin Luther and the Beginning of Protestantism

Even though the Fifth Council of the Lateran produced little of lasting value, it had a promising beginning. The opening address was a stirring call to reform by Abbot Giles of Viterbo, who at the time was attempting to restore the discipline and spiritual vigor of the Augustinian Order of friars. The question should be asked: why did the efforts of Giles and other reformers—men of power, such as, abbots and bishops and cardinals—come to fruit so slowly and quietly over the next several decades, while the reform efforts of Martin Luther, an obscure German friar of the Augustinian Order, yielded such immediate and often violent results?

One explanation is that Luther's theological opinions were strongly anti-Roman, and they tapped the German people's explosively anti-Roman feelings. But there were other anti-Roman reformers in Germany, whose influence was neither so deep nor so long-lasting as Luther's. Martin Luther's beliefs, besides being against Rome, were born out of a common desire. For as his writings show, Luther—perhaps more than any person before him—sensed deeply the medieval Christian's desire to be certain that he was saved.

Son of a man in the mining business, Martin Luther was enrolled in law school and on his

Confessor—a priest who hears a person's confession and acts as counselor and spiritual guide.

way to a career in business when he gave it all up to be a friar. Tormented by fear of damnation, he regularly fasted, attended Mass, confessed his sins and scourged himself. Still, he did not feel free from sin; he was not assured that he was saved. His **confessor** urged him to study Scripture, and it was in this pursuit that he was struck by St. Paul's Letter to the Romans, 1:17: "The just man shall live by faith." Out of this passage Luther developed his concept of justification by faith alone. Humanity is irreversibly bound by sin, said Luther; it is part of our nature. Nothing that we can do—not Masses, pilgrimages, fasts, confessions—can ensure our salvation. We can be saved only by Christ's redemptive power.

With God's help humanity can have faith, and because of that faith do good works. But this is not to say that the good works justify a person; only faith justifies a person. On the surface this appears to be like the humanists' criticism of the over-emphasis upon external observances, but, actually, Luther went much further than Erasmus and the other humanists.[1] He was arguing for a point that became the foundation of early Protestant thought: the total depravity of humanity. Luther utterly rejected the medieval view of the essential goodness of humanity.

According to the traditional teaching, humanity even though weakened by sin could be made more whole by grace.

According to the traditional teaching, humanity even though weakened by original sin could be made more whole by grace. By receiving the sacraments and performing good works, people participated in their own salvation. The sacraments and good works

1. At first, Martin Luther's chief support came from the university students, called *humanists*, who followed the lead of men like Erasmus in their thinking about religion. But as Luther's rejection of authority and his doctrine of the depravity of humanity became more prevalent, the humanists abandoned him. At his friends' urging, Erasmus wrote an essay opposing Luther on the question of free will; Luther, in response, wrote that humanity has no freedom of will whatsoever.

were not meaningless externals, but were an essential part of a person's interior change. But Luther understood Paul's idea of faith with no reference to works whatsoever. Luther's concept would ultimately lead him, by the year 1520, to the conclusion that the Church's sacramental system was entirely superfluous.

The Indulgence Controversy

The German scholar's ideas about justification might never have been known beyond the University of Wittenberg, where he taught, except for the controversy over **indulgences.** In the late-medieval Church, there was a common belief that the soul, before entering heaven, was consigned to **purgatory** for a period of purgation or preparation. For those who confessed their sins, obtained forgiveness, and were truly sorry, it was possible to be spared some of the time in purgatory by the obtaining of an indulgence. Usually, the person would make some sort of donation to the Church, and the bishop or pope would grant the indulgence. The power of granting the indulgence was derived from the apostles' power of binding and loosing, and Luther himself had acknowledged the propriety of this common practice as late as 1516.

Indulgence—a belief that, for having performed a good work, one would be freed from time in purgatory.

Purgatory—according to tradition, upon a person's death he or she underwent purgation, or cleansing from sin, prior to being united with God.

For those who confessed their sins, obtained forgiveness, and were truly sorry, it was possible to be spared some of the time in purgatory by the obtaining of an indulgence.

But in 1517, Bishop Albert of Mainz was being pressured by the wealthy Fugger family to pay back the large loan that he had taken out to purchase his bishopric. The bishop turned to Pope Leo X for permission for the sale of an indulgence, and the two men agreed to split the proceeds; the pope's share would go toward the expenses on the new St. Peter's Church. Friar John Tetzel, assigned to preach the indulgence, went to extremes in whipping up the people's enthusiasm. He made exaggerated claims about its value, even to the point of suggesting that the indulgence (quite apart from any personal contrition for sin) had the power to release a person from sins that had not been committed yet. His favorite technique for promoting sales was to sell indulgences for people's deceased friends and relatives. Tetzel is credited with (or blamed for) inventing the little rhyme,

> *When the coin in the coffer rings,*
> *Another soul from purgatory springs.*

To Martin Luther, this was just another case of external work that did nothing to save humanity from sin. Legend has it that on All Saints' Day, 1517, Luther nailed ninety-five Theses, or arguments against indulgences, onto the door of the church at Wittenberg. It was an invitation to debate anyone who dared to defend indulgences. The *Theses* attracted attention, and were soon translated from scholarly Latin into German, and mass-produced on printing presses. The ninety-five Theses raised such a furor that they attracted Rome's attention, and Luther was ordered to explain his statements. The more he was questioned, however, the more inflammatory his assertions became. He denied papal and conciliar authority, on the grounds that both popes and councils had been guilty of doctrinal errors in the past. He questioned not only indulgences but even the sacraments. When the pope, in 1520, issued a decree threatening excommunication if he did not abandon his beliefs, Luther publicly burned both the decree and a copy of the *Corpus Iuris Canonici*.

Martin Luther was excommunicated in 1520 by Pope Leo X.

Three Essays

The excommunication in 1520 followed closely upon the appearance of three essays that clearly announced Martin Luther's break with the medieval Church. In the *Address to the Nobility of the German Nation* there was an appeal to the nobles to throw off the shackles of Rome's authority. But more importantly, Luther proclaimed the new doctrine of the priesthood of the laity: there should be no separate priestly class, because all Christians are priests. Further, the Scriptures are the common possession of all Christians, and all are free to interpret their meaning for themselves. Doctrinal authority lies not in popes or councils, but in the sacred Scriptures, freely interpreted. A second essay, *The Freedom of the Christian Man*, presented his concept of justification by faith alone, which prepared the way for rejection of medieval Christianity's popular devotions such as pilgrimages and fasts.

Luther proclaimed the new doctrine of the priesthood of the laity: there should be no separate priestly class, because all Christians are priests.

Finally, in *The Babylonian Captivity of the Church*, Luther asserted that the Christian people were being enchained by the Roman Church and its sacramental system. Using the Bible as the sole criterion[2] of what is true Christian teaching, he denied that confirmation, penance, unction, orders, and marriage were true sacraments. All that is left, he said, is "baptism and the bread." But the "bread," the Eucharist, he understood in a new way, too. Christ is present in the Eucharistic Bread, but that presence is not to be understood in the strictly literal way of the Roman tradition. He wished to downplay what he considered to be the excessive emphasis upon the sacrificial character of the Mass.

Taken together, these three writings amounted to the overthrow of medieval Christianity almost in its entirety, and the promotion of a completely new type of Christianity. In terms of doctrine, Christendom had been divided. It was only a matter of time before it was also divided in its institutions. In 1521 Emperor Charles V, quite anxious to protect the Church and maintain order in Germany, summoned

2. Luther's concept of the primacy of the Bible's authority is called *sola Scriptura*—"by the Scripture alone."

Luther to a diet (congress) of the Empire. But Luther, who remembered his history lessons, chose not to accept the fate of Jan Huss. He refused to attend, with the statement that has since become famous:

Unless I am convinced by the testimony of the Scriptures or by clear reason (for I do not trust either in the pope or in councils alone, since it is well known that they have often erred and contradicted themselves), I am bound by the Scriptures I have quoted and my conscience is captive to the Word of God. I cannot and I will not retract anything, since it is neither safe nor right to go against conscience.

Charles V declared him an outlaw, and Luther went into hiding.

While Luther hid from the authorities during the early 1520s there were three sets of developments—religious, social and political—that changed the shape of European Christianity. On the strictly religious level, Luther's doctrine of the Mass was put into effect, as he himself wrote hymns for congregational singing, the Mass was said at Wittenberg in German rather than Latin, and greater emphasis began to be placed upon the sermon rather than the sacrifice in the ceremony. Luther also condemned monasticism on the grounds that it was wholly devoted to meaningless external observances, and local nobles soon began closing monasteries and seizing the property for themselves. To reinforce his own rejection of priestly celibacy, the German leader took a former nun as his wife. Finally, Luther backed up his belief in the primacy of Scripture by undertaking a translation of the entire Bible into German. This monumental task was completed in 1534. His Bible was so widely read that it had lasting influence upon style of expression in the German language.

The social developments were related to the religious. Luther's concepts of the priesthood

Luther condemned monasticism on the grounds that it was wholly devoted to meaningless external observances.

of the laity and the primacy of Scripture gained him a large following among the German populace. But as the ideas became more widespread, they became subject to an ever wider variety of interpretations. A few Protestant leaders even inclined toward the extreme view that the individual Christian, guided by the Holy Spirit, was a law unto himself or herself, in need of no external authority whatsoever.

Luther was appalled by such ideas. But the troubles were just beginning, as Luther, like John Wycliffe before him, saw his notions of Christian freedom become the rallying-cry of a peasant rebellion against the upper class. He issued sermons which contended that the Christian ought to be obedient to the secular authority,[3] and he urged that the secular authority is ordained by God. The princes of Germany, meanwhile, approached the rebellious peasants with force rather than theory; perhaps as many as 100,000 peasants were killed during the year 1525. The uprising was thus stopped, but the lasting effect of the incident was that Luther's theory of dominance of secular authority became a common belief among most Protestants. Here, as in so many respects, Protestant Christians rejected the heritage of medieval Christianity while Catholic Christians preserved the medieval tradition.

Luther's theory of dominance of secular authority became a common belief among most Protestants.

Protestant Christians rejected the heritage of medieval Christianity while Catholic Christians preserved the medieval tradition.

Luther and the Princes

The peasant uprising also contributed to the most important political development of the 1520s: the alliance between Lutheranism and the German princes. It was a prince who protected Martin Luther from Charles V after

3. In emphasizing the need to obey the secular authorities, Luther focused upon two Scripture texts, Romans 13 and 1 Peter 2. His attitude toward the peasant uprising is seen in the title of one of his essays of 1525: "Against the Murderous, Thieving Gangs of Peasants."

the Diet at Worms, and the peasant rebellion only confirmed a natural alliance. The German princes wanted independence from Emperor Charles, who was supporting the Catholic Church. No doubt many of them sincerely believed in Luther's teachings, but many princes saw in Lutheranism a rallying-cry against a Catholic emperor and an opportunity to enrich themselves by seizing the bishoprics and monasteries.

In 1530 there was one attempt by the Lutherans, especially Luther's friend Philip Melanchthon, to reach a compromise with Emperor Charles over basic principles of the faith. The emperor, however, found the Lutherans' beliefs unacceptable.[4] After that time, the fate of Lutheran Christianity was largely determined by the rivalry between the imperial forces and those of the German princes, led by the ambitious Philip of Hesse. Open war broke out in 1534. By 1547 Charles had almost achieved total victory, but an alliance between the princes and the King of France thwarted him, and by 1552 the war was clearly a stand-off. Charles, weary after twenty years of bloodshed without success, gave up his crown to his brother Ferdinand, and retired to a monastery. Having fought the battle to save Germany, he felt it was time to fight the battle to save his own soul.

Ferdinand, faced with a stalemate, decided to negotiate. The result was the Peace of Augsburg in 1555, which did little more than make the stalemate official. The need for religious unity among a given group of people was acknowledged by the negotiators, and it was decided that lands controlled by Lutheran

4. The document that Melanchthon drew up for Charles was called the Augsburg Confession. Luther was unhappy with the Augsburg Confession because he felt that it diluted Lutheranism to appeal to the Catholics; but modern-day Lutherans look to the document as their basic statement of belief.

princes (in northern Germany, primarily) would remain Lutheran while lands controlled by Catholics would remain Catholic.[5]

After the Peace of Augsburg, Lutheranism spread to Scandinavia, but no further. The cause of Protestant expansion had passed into other hands. Martin Luther had been thoroughly alarmed by the extremists who led the peasants in 1525, and the last twenty years of his life were characterized by a conservative retreat from the excesses of their views. The result was that while Lutheranism was substantially different from Catholicism in its basic doctrines, and constituted a substantially different type of Christianity, in actual practices it remained fairly similar to Catholicism.

It was no accident that at Augsburg in 1555, the Lutheran and Catholic negotiators were careful to note that their peace and their division of lands applied to themselves only. In spite of their differences, both parties agreed that the greater enemies were the other types of Protestants, who had taken Luther's ideas of justification, priesthood of the laity, and individual interpretation of the sacred Scripture to their logical conclusion. When Luther called for a stripping away of externals and an emphasis upon the individual's faith in God, he opened up an entirely new approach to the Christian life. When he broke from the medieval tradition, denied the authority of Rome and of councils, and laid stress upon individual interpretation of the Scriptures, he opened the floodgates for a wide variety of interpretations. Protestantism was never a single type of Christianity, but from its beginning included a variety of competing religions.

> Protestantism was never a single type of Christianity, but from its beginning included a variety of competing religions.

5. The principle of division was called *cuius regio, eius religio*—whose region, his religion. If the prince was, say, a Catholic, then all his subjects had to be, also.

Summary

- The Fifth Council of the Lateran called for reform.

- Martin Luther left law school to become a friar.

- Tormented by the fear of damnation, he regularly fasted, attended Mass, confessed his sins, and even scourged himself.

- Luther developed a concept of justification by faith alone.

- Luther's excommunication from the Church followed closely upon the appearance of three essays that clearly announced his break with the Church.

- Luther's concepts of the priesthood of the laity and the primacy of Scripture gained him a large following.

- Luther's notions of Christian freedom became the rallying-cry of a peasant revolt.

- While Lutheranism was substantially different from Catholicism in its basic doctrines, in actual practices it remained fairly similar to Catholicism.

Prayer

Ah, dearest Jesus, holy Child,
Make thee a bed, soft, undefiled,
Within my heart, that it may be
A quiet chamber kept for thee.

Martin Luther

Discussion Questions

1. Why was it that of all the would-be reformers from this period, only Luther had a great impact upon history?

2. Which of Luther's ideas set him apart from traditional Christianity? Which of his new ideas were later adopted by the Roman Catholic Church?

3. How did politics affect the progress of the Lutheran movement, and lead to the new state of affairs reflected in the Peace of Augsburg?

Albrecht Dürer's Four Horsemen of the Apocalypse

Chapter Twenty-Six

The Christians Who Were Persecuted by Christians

The Christians who were condemned and even persecuted by both the Lutherans and the Catholics were called **Anabaptists.** Actually, there were many groups, representing many different beliefs, who were given this name. They were given the same label because they all rejected infant baptism in favor of adult baptism.[1] Apart from that one doctrinal similarity, they shared mostly tendencies: rejection of papal authority, denial of the value of good works, and other beliefs common to Protestant Christians.

Anabaptists —rejected infant baptism in favor of adult baptism.

That the Catholics condemned the Anabaptists is not surprising. But why was Luther their opponent, if they followed the Protestant way of thought in so many respects? The answer lies in the Anabaptists' tendency to press Protestant beliefs to extreme conclusions, with results that most Protestants considered dangerous.

Luther, for example, rejected papal authority in favor of individual interpretation of the Scriptures. He also put forward the concept of a priesthood of the laity while throwing out the priesthood as a separate order within the community. To hold these opinions, it is necessary to believe that each person's understanding of the Scriptures is being aided

1. *Anabaptism* means rebaptism.

by the Holy Spirit. But many Anabaptists placed such great emphasis upon the Spirit that even the Scriptures fell into the background. In the words of one Anabaptist, the Bible was just a "paper pope." Filled with the Spirit, many Anabaptists prophesied; and having the Spirit they believed they had no need of the law.[2] Thus while Luther and others like him saw no need for papal authority, some Anabaptists saw no need for any authority at all, even the secular authority of the state.

Again, Luther condemned many of the practices and beliefs that had grown up during the Middle Ages: pilgrimages, fasts, monasticism, papal primacy, votive Masses— all these things had grown up in the medieval Church, and to Luther they appeared to be unhealthy additions that diluted the earlier purity of the Church. But the Anabaptists were not content to eliminate individual practices or beliefs. They were determined to be rid of the entire Church as it had developed in the world over the centuries. The Catholic Church was rooted in history; that is, as the Christian faith was introduced to different peoples at different times, it assumed new forms. The Church, of course, was not the world; but it responded to the world, and thus it changed throughout its history.

Antihistorical and Antiworld

In contrast, the Anabaptists were clearly antihistorical and antiworld. One branch of the Anabaptists sought to bring about the end of all time. They attempted, by means of violence, to destroy the secular authority, vanquish the godless people of the world, and hasten the Second Coming of Christ.

2. The idea that the select few have no need of law is called *antinomianism*.

276

The other branch of the Anabaptists was also antihistorical and antiworld, but in an entirely different way. They sought to recreate a perfect community on the model of the Acts of the Apostles, and erase all of the changes that Christianity had experienced in fifteen centuries of contact with the world. According to this line of reasoning, for example, infant baptism ought to be eliminated on the grounds that the Scriptures describe only the baptism of adults, not of babies. (Martin Luther, on the other hand, accepted infant baptism on the grounds of tradition: it was acceptable because the faithful had baptized their babies for centuries.) Thus the belief about baptism that the Anabaptists had in common was actually a product of their shared attitude toward time and the world, which was more basic to their outlook.

Martin Luther accepted baptism of infants on the grounds of tradition.

The militant version of Anabaptism first made its appearance in 1520, and by 1535 it had been rooted out by a society that found its doctrines simply too dangerous to be tolerated. The nonviolent version of Anabaptism started at almost the same time, and still exists today.

The first well-known Anabaptist was Thomas Munzer, who originally was a priest and then became a Lutheran minister. In 1521 he was greatly impressed by a preacher named Nicholas Storch. Storch was a Bohemian whose religious ancestors can be traced back to the followers of Jan Huss. Following Storch's lead, Munzer emphasized the power of the Spirit at work within the believer; the special gifts of the Spirit, however, were granted only to a few, the Elect of God. These were revolutionary ideas that led him to break from Lutheranism. But the real thrust of his thinking became clear when (again following Storch) he proclaimed that mankind was entering upon the Last Days of the world: first there would be suffering, then the Elect would rise up to overpower the godless, and Christ's Second Coming would usher in a thousand-year reign.

The first well-known Anabaptist was Thomas Munzer. Munzer emphasized that the gifts of the Spirit were granted only to the Elect of God.

Munzer, a fiery preacher, presented this doctrine in town after town in Germany; and each time, as his following grew, the frightened townspeople would send him packing. Finally, when peasant unrest broke into open revolt against the nobles in 1525, Munzer and three hundred loyal followers seized leadership of a peasant revolt at Mulhausen, in northern Germany. Suddenly, the Anabaptists were in charge of an army several thousand strong. But the untrained peasants proved no match for the soldiers of the German princes, and Munzer's rebellion ended not in the Second Coming, but in torture and death for Munzer and his followers.

Actually, the Peasant Rebellion of 1525 was a social revolt, not a religious one. But Munzer's role in the revolt at Mulhausen gave both the Lutherans and the Anabaptists some idea of the explosive possibilities of Anabaptism. The Anabaptists were natural rivals of the Lutherans, as they both competed for the allegiance of the Germans who were disenchanted with Rome's brand of Christianity. But the far more numerous Lutherans drove their rivals out of town after town for a period of ten years. After a brief stay in the Netherlands, the Anabaptists finally gained a stronghold in Münster, northwestern Germany, in 1534.

The violent rejection of Anabaptism by most Christians might have been expected to bring the movement to an end, except for one quirk of Anabaptist belief. The Elect were expected to suffer greatly in their struggle. Suffering like Christ's was truly the way to salvation; in fact, their suffering was the clearest sign of their own election, and of the nearness of the End. Thus the more violent the opposition they faced, the more sure they were of their beliefs.

Anabaptists under Siege

The horrible implications of the militant Anabaptists' creed were worked out to the fullest during the siege of Münster. A preacher named Jan Matthys found willing ears among the citizens of Münster in 1534, and the Anabaptist leaders flocked to the city, led by Matthys' disciple Jan Bockelson from the town of Leyden—"Jan of Leyden," as he was called. The true believers established themselves in power, then put their principles into effect: they drove out all the unbelievers (Catholics and Lutherans), baptized all the new believers, burned all books except the Bible, and seized possession of all land and buildings. Anyone who resisted was killed. Then the leaders began to practice polygamy (there were many nuns in town who had abandoned their convents, so there was a surplus of candidates for marriage).

The Catholics and Lutherans of Germany, despite their dislike for each other, joined forces to lay siege upon the town, seeing in the Anabaptists a threat to all Christianity. Jan Matthys attacked the Catholic-Lutheran forces with just twenty men beside him, having learned in a vision that God would give him victory. Matthys' death left leadership in the hands of Jan Bockelson, who took the title "King Jan of Leyden."

Anabaptist raiders came from all over Germany to harass the besiegers and protect their brethren. At one point, King Jan's army even managed to sally forth from Münster and inflict a temporary defeat upon the Catholic-Lutheran forces. But the siege went on. Finally, the Anabaptists, weakened by starvation, could no longer resist. The Catholic and Lutheran soldiers broke through the walls of the city and then hunted down the Anabaptists of Münster, killing most of them.

The Catholics and Lutherans of Germany, despite their dislike for each other, joined forces seeing in the Anabaptists a threat to all Christianity.

The Münster episode brought about the end of the militant form of Anabaptism. Unfortunately, the reputation for violence outlived the militants, and the more moderate Anabaptists were persecuted long after 1535. The moderate Anabaptists had denounced the errors of the militants' ways as early as 1527, in a document called the *Schleitheim Confession.* The radical Anabaptists, they claimed,

> have missed the truth, and to their (own) condemnation are given over to lasciviousness and self-indulgence of the flesh. They think faith and love may do and permit everything, and nothing will harm them or condemn them since they are believers.[3]

The moderate Anabaptists had denounced the errors of the militants' ways as early as 1527.

Hutterites and Mennonites

Like the militants, the moderate Anabaptists believed that they were the few who were called by God. Under such leaders as Menno Simmons (founder of the Mennonites) and Jacob Hutter (founder of the Hutterites), they formed small communities that made a modest living from farming and remained apart from the world. Their separateness was a central tenet of their faith, not simply a matter of avoiding persecution. Motivated by a strong sense of the corruption that the Devil has brought about in the world, they sought to avoid the ways of darkness and the flesh. The *Schleitheim Confession* was very explicit about the need to shun the world in every way.

3. "The Schleitheim Confession of Faith," printed in Hans J. Hillerbrand, ed., *The Protestant Reformation* (New York: Harper & Row, 1969), p. 130.

*By this is meant all popish and antipopish
works and Church services, meetings and
Church attendance, drinking houses, civic
affairs, the commitments made in unbelief
and other things of that kind, which are
highly regarded by the world and yet are
carried on in flat contradiction to the
command of God, in accordance with all
the unrighteousness which is in the world.
From all these things, we shall be separated
and have no part with them for they are
nothing but an abomination, and they are
the cause of our being hated before Christ
Jesus, who has set us free. . . .*[4]

Like the apostles, these groups held all goods
in common. Sharing all things and supporting
each other in the radical rejection of all the
world's temptations, they have maintained
their way of life virtually unchanged for the
past four centuries. Persecution drove the
Hutterites from country to country, until today
most of them maintain community farms in
South Dakota, Montana, and the prairie lands
of central Canada. The Mennonites similarly
were driven from place to place, and today
most of the 400,000 Mennonites dwell in the
United States and Canada. The sparsely
populated farming regions of North America
have proven to be a natural home for people
who so strongly desire to keep apart from
secular influences.

Like the apostles, the
moderate Anabaptists
held all goods in
common, sharing all
things and supporting
each other in the
radical rejection of all
the world's
temptations, for the
past four centuries.

The sparsely populated
farming regions of
North America have
proven to be a natural
home for people who
so strongly desire to
keep apart from
secular influences.

4. Hillerbrand, p. 132.

Summary

- Anabaptist groups rejected infant baptism in favor of adult baptism.

- Anabaptist Christians were rejected and persecuted by both Catholics and Lutherans.

- One branch of Anabaptists sought through violence to bring about the end time.

- The moderate Anabaptists denounced the errors of the militants' ways as early as 1527 and have continued to live quietly throughout North America for the past four centuries.

Prayer

Take Lord, all my liberty. Receive my memory, my understanding, my will. Whatever I have, you have given to me; to you I return it, and to thee will I surrender. Give me only your love and grace, and I am rich enough.

St. Ignatius Loyola

Discussion Questions

1. How did the beliefs of the Anabaptists depart from the traditional Catholic idea of how the Church interacts with history and culture? Remember that there were two separate branches of Anabaptists, each of which had its own ideals.

2. How were the religious ideas of the militant Anabaptists reflected in the behavior of Thomas Munzer or the Anabaptists of Münster?

3. Where are most Anabaptists found today, and why have they chosen to settle there?

John Calvin

Chapter Twenty-Seven

Origins of the Calvinist Tradition

John Calvin

When the story of the Protestant Reformation is told, it is usually Martin Luther who occupies the central place, because his concepts and his bold action gave the movement its start. But it was John Calvin, not Luther, whose ideas ultimately dominated Protestantism, and it was Calvin's emphasis upon discipline that ensured the success of the Protestant movement. When the spread of Lutheranism had been checked by the Catholics, and when theological disagreements were dividing the Lutheran Church after Luther's death, it was Calvin's brand of Christianity that showed the greatest power of survival.

The man who founded a new, hardy strain of Protestantism was entirely unlike the man who originated the Protestant movement. While Luther was a person whose powerful emotions sometimes boiled over into crude obscenities and sometimes led him to contradict himself, Calvin was cooly logical in nearly all situations. The thoroughness and precision of his writings reflected his training in law and theology. It is said that Calvin never allowed himself a break from his work, and was plagued by severe backaches because he spent so many hours in study. During his thirty-year career he wrote over four thousand letters, usually on doctrinal subjects, and

When the story of the Protestant Reformation is told, it is Martin Luther who occupies the central place, because his concepts and his bold action gave the movement its start; but it was John Calvin, not Luther, whose ideas ultimately dominated Protestantism.

delivered more than two thousand sermons. It is true that his theological concepts created a third type of Protestantism to stand alongside Lutheranism and Anabaptism; but it is equally true that his own austere personality created it.

Luther's starting point had been a dramatic personal conversion, in which he became convinced that he was saved only by faith, not by works. Calvin, on the other hand, appears not to have experienced any dramatic conversion. After being chased out of his native France for espousing Protestant beliefs, he composed his masterpiece, *The Institute of the Christian Religion,* in 1535 while traveling from city to city. Throughout his career, he reedited this original work to accommodate new insights.

The Institute of the Christian Religion showed Calvin to be the leader of the "second generation" of Protestant reformers. His starting point was an analysis of the ideas and experience of Lutheranism, and he reasoned from that point to a new emphasis. Luther's concept of justification by faith pointed toward the sovereign power of God. But the experience of the Reformation in Germany showed that even though belief in justification by faith had been generally accepted, there clearly were many Germans who still had little faith. From this evidence, Calvin reasoned to a new conclusion: God gives faith to some (the elect) but not to others. This, the doctrine of **predestination,**[1] was the central tenet of **Calvinism.** Some persons are predestined to be saved by God.

Predestination—belief that some persons are predestined to be saved by God.

Calvinism—the doctrine of predestination was the central tenet of Calvinism.

1. Luther, commenting upon the writings of St. Paul, also upheld the concept of predestination, but it did not hold a central place in his doctrine.

St. Paul clearly testifies that, when the salvation of the remnant of the people is ascribed by the election of grace, then only is it acknowledged that God of His mere good pleasure preserves whom He will, and moreover that He pays no reward, since He can owe none.[2]

Predestination

When a group of reformers invited Calvin to take up residence in Geneva, Switzerland, he introduced his theology of predestination and put it into practice. The obvious expectation is that the concept of predestination might lead Calvinist Christians to be self-satisfied—if they are the elect, if their salvation was predestined by the will of the Lord Himself even before their birth, then what more must they do themselves?

But far from being self-satisfied, the Christians of Calvinist Geneva were renowned for being earnest, hardworking, and rigorously moral. The key to the Calvinists' behavior was the notion that people could know in their own minds that they were saved, *only if* they behaved in an upright way through all of life's trials. If they were truly predestined and aided by the power of almighty God, then they would persist in right living in spite of all trials and temptations. The disciplined, strong-willed followers of John Calvin were precisely the kind of people who could survive the persecutions and dislocations of the turbulent Reformation era.

The Christians of Calvinist Geneva were renowned for being earnest, hardworking, and rigorously moral.

Swiss Reformation

Calvin established Geneva as a training ground for the new type of earnest Christian. The cities of Switzerland had begun their own version of the Reformation in about 1521,

2. *Institute*, chapter 31, article 1 (1559 edition). In this discussion, he is referring to Paul's Letter to the Romans, 11:5–6.

under the leadership of Ulrich Zwingli. Zwingli's reform was aimed at many of the same practices to which Luther objected: fasts, the cult of the saints, indulgences, clerical celibacy, monasticism, pilgrimages. Like Luther, Zwingli found himself opposing Anabaptists, and even more than his German counterpart, the Swiss reformer became tied to a political movement. The Swiss Reformation was, in part, a reaction of great cities, Zurich, Basel, and Berne, against the jurisdiction of prince-bishops. When the bishops were deposed, the burgomasters and city councils took charge of religious affairs in the cities. Zwingli sought to protect his reformation by means of an alliance of Swiss cities in 1527, but the alliance prompted formation of a Catholic league of cities. A religious war broke out, and Zwingli himself perished in the Battle of Kappel in 1531.

Geneva had been pressured to join forces with the other cities, but its citizens, after accepting other cities' help in expelling the Bishop of Geneva, had carefully guarded their own independence. Thus when Calvin arrived in 1536, Geneva was anti-Catholic, but not clearly committed to any particular type of reform. At first, Calvin's ideas were not well received, and in 1538 he was expelled from the city. But after three years of disorder, Geneva's city fathers requested his return, and from that time his influence grew steadily.

City Life Controlled by Religion

His organization of the city was a recreation of what he understood to be the structure of the original Church, without any later additions. (In this respect, he was like the Anabaptists.) With Scripture as his guide, he created the offices of pastor, doctor, deacon, and elder: the pastors preached and administered sacraments; the doctors were the teachers for the community; the deacons took care of charity toward the poor; and the elders watched over the operations of the Church, making the most important decisions. In his only concession to the Swiss tradition of civic life, Calvin allowed the city magistrates to choose the elders. But in actual practice, the city government only became the servant of a religion that controlled all aspects of life.

Geneva had had a reputation for immoral living, but the new regime changed all that. Drunkeness and gambling were outlawed, as were adultery and blasphemy. Laws encouraged personal cleanliness, and schooling was compulsory. Citizens could be fined for not attending Sunday sermons, and they were advised that they ought to hear weekday sermons, too. With the approach of Easter Sunday, elders visited every household to inquire about the conduct of each person; not everyone was judged fit to receive Communion.

Public whippings were common, and those who resisted the teachings of the Church could be banished or even put to death.[3] Because of the success of the Calvinist message, historians have called Geneva "the Protestant Rome." In view of the harshness of discipline, it could as well be called "the Protestant Sparta." In the discipline lay the genius of Calvinism; for more than Lutheranism, Calvinism forced people to

Because of the success of the Calvinist message, historians have called Geneva "the Protestant Rome."

3. In 1552, Geneva's city government decreed that Calvin's teachings were "Holy doctrine which no man can speak against." In that same year, Calvin ordered the death of Michael Servetus, a refugee from Spain who was known for his attacks upon the doctrine of the Trinity. The Reformation produced a small number of Unitarians, who were despised by all the other branches of Christianity. In another celebrated case, Calvin banished one of the leading teachers in Geneva.

change the way they lived their lives. People could feel assured of salvation because life in Geneva was so clearly different from ordinary life.

Worship

Calvin and his followers also introduced a new type of Sunday worship. All religious images were removed from the church, and the service focused upon a lengthy sermon. The element of sacrifice was entirely eliminated from worship. Christ, Calvin taught, could not be enclosed in bread and wine, but rather was spiritually present. Bread and wine could be the means by which the believer received grace, however.

The Spread of Calvinism

Calvin's three-year exile after 1538 had allowed him to circulate among Protestant leaders and make a name for himself as one of the guiding lights of the Reformation. Not surprisingly, he sought to promote his reform outside Geneva during the 1540s and 1550s, and he met with success. The Calvinist doctrine first spread into France, where his followers came to be called **"Huguenots,"** and eventually constituted a large minority in that Catholic country.[4] Soon there were also Calvinist communities in Hungary, Bohemia, Germany, the Netherlands and Scotland. In keeping with the importance of teaching and preaching for this new brand of Christianity, John Calvin founded the College of Geneva, which quickly grew to be the University of

Huguenots —French followers of the Calvinism doctrine.

4. Geneva, Berne, and Friebourg were united, and their union was called the Eidgenossen. When Calvinism was introduced in France, the French identified the new creed by its place of origin. However, they had difficulty pronouncing "Eidgenossen," and "Huguenot" was the result.

Geneva. Approximately five thousand people settled in Geneva during the 1550s to escape Catholic and Lutheran persecution, making that city both the chief refuge and the foremost training ground of Protestantism.

In the Netherlands, Calvinists successfully established what is called today the Dutch Reformed Church. In Scotland, Calvinists led by John Knox established what presently is called the Presbyterian Church. The rise of Calvinism in Scotland was tied to a successful revolution in which the Scots rose up against French Catholics, who by means of a diplomatic marriage, had taken control of Scotland's monarchy. In 1560, after the revolution, Scotland's Reformation Parliament passed laws abolishing papal jurisdiction, repealing old ecclesiastical laws and forbidding any saying of the Mass, under penalty of death.

The second half of the sixteenth century was probably the most untolerant of all ages, as Protestants and Catholics both were eager to drive their religious enemies out of their lands. Calvinists usually constituted the minority in the countries in which they lived, and they survived the persecutions because of their discipline and determination. In Scotland and the Netherlands, where Calvinists were the majority, they established Church organizations that have endured to this day. In France, their struggles as a minority ultimately led to the drafting of Europe's first laws that granted religious toleration. The most dramatic growth of Calvinism was among the Europeans who settled and flourished in America. How they came to leave Europe for America will be one of the subjects of the following chapter.

Approximately five thousand people settled in Geneva during the 1550s to escape Catholic and Lutheran persecution, making Geneva the main refuge and the foremost training ground of Protestantism.

In Scotland, Calvinists led by John Knox established what presently is called the Presbyterian Church.

Summary

• It was John Calvin, not Luther, whose ideas ultimately dominated Protestantism.

• The doctrine of predestination was the central tenet of Calvinism.

• The Christians of Calvinist Geneva were earnest, hardworking, and rigorously moral.

• The Swiss Reformation was, in part, a reaction of great cities against the jurisdiction of prince-bishops.

• Because of the success of the Calvinist message, historians have called Geneva "The Protestant Rome."

• Many people settled in Geneva during the 1550s to escape Catholic and Protestant persecution.

Prayer

First of all, I urge that petitions, prayers,
intercessions, and thanksgivings be offered for all
men, especially for kings and those in authority,
that we may be able to lead undisturbed and
tranquil lives in perfect piety and dignity. Prayer of
this kind is good, and God our Savior is pleased
with it, for he wants all men to be saved and come
to know the truth.

1 Timothy 2:1–5

Discussion Questions

1. How can it be said that Calvin was a
   "second generation reformer," taking a
   step beyond what Luther first proposed?

2. What was new and different from
   traditional ideas of worship, in the
   proposals of Zwingli and Calvin?

3. What made Geneva the "new Rome" of
   Protestantism?

Puritans on the Road to Church by G. H. Boughton

Chapter Twenty-Eight

Anglicanism and Puritanism in England

The three main branches of Protestantism discussed in the preceding chapters have several things in common. All grew out of frustration with the practices that existed in the medieval Church, and the frustration in each instance gave birth to a new approach to the mysteries of grace and salvation. In the effort to be free of a tradition that they considered corrupt, the reformers turned to the Scriptures, and new ways of understanding the Scriptures yielded new doctrines and new practices. In the case of Luther and Calvin, there was a dominant personality who gave the movement direction.

English Reformation

England's version of the Reformation represented an altogether different process. There had long been frustration with clerical corruption in England, but no new approach to Scripture or theology developed out of it. In fact, the leading figure of the English Reformation, King Henry VIII, had in 1521 written a treatise against Luther's teachings on the sacraments, and for his efforts had been declared a "Defender of the Faith" by the pope.

Henry's break with the Roman Church had its origins in political expediency. Convinced that

Henry VIII's break with the Catholic Church had its origin in political expediency.

295

his wife, Catherine of Aragon, would never bear him a son, Henry became interested in a young lady named Anne Boleyn. But Pope Clement VII refused to annul his original marriage. During this period in history, the royalty of Europe had often sought to make and unmake marriages, and the Renaissance popes, generally, had been willing to oblige. No one can say for certain why Clement was uncooperative this time. Catherine's nephew, Charles V, had sacked Rome in 1527, and it is likely that the pope was under considerable pressure to protect Catherine's interests.

Whatever the reason, Henry, impatient for a son, was in no mood for papal delays. He began his move toward control of the English Church in 1529 when he dismissed Thomas Cardinal Wolsey, his chief minister. He felt that Wolsey had not applied sufficient pressure in Rome for the divorce, so he replaced him with Sir Thomas More, one of the greatest scholars of the realm and an avid advocate of Church reform. Henry's intentions became clear in 1532, when the Archbishop of Canterbury passed away and the king gave this most important see to Thomas Cranmer. Cranmer was an unlikely choice for Henry; besides being secretly married, he was sympathetic with Martin Luther's ideas. But he suited Henry's purposes because he could expound biblical reasons to justify the king's annulment. One of his first acts as Archbishop of Canterbury was to review His Majesty's request and declare the marriage to Catherine invalid. The king's own secret marriage to Anne Boleyn was then validated and Anne, though she never bore a son, did give birth to Elizabeth, who was later to be one of England's greatest rulers.[1]

> One of Thomas Cranmer's first acts as Archbishop of Canterbury was to review His Majesty's request and declare his marriage to Catherine invalid.

1. In one of the many little twists of English history, Elizabeth was declared illegitimate by Parliament in 1536, at the same time that her mother was executed on a trumped-up charge of adultery. Henry's next wife, Jane Seymour, finally gave him a son (Edward VI), but she also fell from favor; altogether, Henry had six wives.

The anti-Roman maneuvers by Henry were beginning to make Thomas More uneasy, and as his confidence in the king flagged, the way was open for another man, Thomas Cromwell, to rise as the king's chief advisor. This new advisor was committed to the concept of an all-powerful secular ruler, and under Cromwell's influence, Henry finally took the definitive step of breaking from Rome. Parliament's Act of Succession in 1534 declared Anne Boleyn to be true Queen of England, and the Act of Supremacy declared the King to be "Supreme Head of the Church in England." Soon afterward (again at the urging of Cromwell) the government began confiscating the property of England's monasteries.

Break with Rome

Here, at last, was the definite break, the beginning of what is called the Anglican Church. To guard his interests, Henry insisted that all political and religious leaders of England declare their loyalty to him. The only men who held out were Bishop John Fisher of Rochester, a vocal opponent of Protestant beliefs, and—here was the surprise—Thomas More, formerly the man closest to the king. More could have put up with the king's remarriage—such bending of the rules was not uncommon in the Church—but he was deeply concerned about Henry's decision to defy the pope and undermine the unity of Christendom. That, to More, threatened the fundamentals of the faith. More and Fisher were put to death, but their martyrdom did not inspire any widespread resistance to the new regime.

Most of the English did not see a break with Rome as a break with the faith. To them, Henry was rejecting only the power of the papacy, when the papacy was unpopular; other aspects of traditional belief and practice

Between 1536 and 1540, official decrees upheld every major tenet of the Catholic faith including the cult of the saints, veneration of images, votive Masses, clerical celebacy, and confession.

were untouched. In fact, between 1536 and 1540, official decrees upheld every major tenet of the Catholic faith, including the cult of the saints, veneration of images, votive Masses, clerical celibacy, and confession. Three Protestants were even put to death by the royal government in 1540. Anglicanism, which came into being to fit the practical needs of England's ruler, gradually emerged as a unique form of Christianity under King Henry's successors. Thanks to political circumstances some were Protestants and some were Catholics, and each one left an imprint upon England's Church.

Shaping the Anglican Church

The rulers were not alone in shaping this Church. From the beginning of the Protestant Reformation, there had been a small but strong Protestant minority in England, and when Henry died in 1547, the political ball was tossed briefly into their court. Henry was succeeded by his son Edward, who was only nine years old. The young king's two chief advisors were nobles who promoted Calvinist ideas, and under their influence the English shifted away from their anti-Roman but otherwise Catholic practices, toward a more Protestant orientation. Clerical marriage was allowed, and in a wave of iconoclasm, England's greatest pilgrimage shrines were shut down. But more important for the future was the return of Protestant refugees who had fled the country to avoid Henry's anti-Protestant laws of the late 1530s. Most of them had spent their exile in the Netherlands or Geneva, where they had drunk deeply of the ideas of John Calvin.

Important for the future was the return of Protestant refugees who had fled the country to avoid Henry's anti-Protestant laws. These reformers were to leave a mark on English religious thought that would never be erased.

These reformers were to leave a mark on English religious thought that would never be erased. But the effort to make England totally Protestant was thwarted by another change of rulers. In 1553 Edward died, leaving the throne to Mary Tudor, Catholic daughter of Catherine of Aragon. With a certain "un-English" vigor, Mary set about making her country Catholic again. She is called "Bloody Mary" because in the effort to restore Catholicism, she had Thomas Cranmer and three hundred other Protestants put to death. By the standards of the age, Mary was scarcely a headhunter; but to a nation that for twenty-five years had watched both Catholics and Protestants die for failing to agree with their rulers' religious policies, the beheadings were a sorry business and the victims were martyrs. When Mary died in 1558, Roman Catholicism in England died with her.

Anglicanism became the law of the land again under Elizabeth I, daughter of Henry by Anne Boleyn and Queen from 1558 to 1603. It was not that she was a Protestant; actually, she appears to have had no strong religious inclinations. What she did believe in was power: she desired to rule a peaceful and united country, and by this point in time, England could be peaceful and united only if the Anglican Church was free of the taints of "popery" and the more militant forms of Protestantism. She supported the Church as her father had, with only a few changes from the traditional forms to satisfy the people of the kingdom. A politician at heart, she strove above all to support a strong episcopacy, because she was convinced that strong bishops were one of the best supports for a strong monarchy. Since the time of Elizabeth, episcopal leadership has been one of the distinguishing marks of Anglican Christianity.[2]

> Elizabeth I strove to support a strong episcopacy, because she was convinced that strong bishops were one of the best supports for a strong monarchy.

2. In the United States, this branch of Christianity is called the Episcopal Church.

Puritan Minority

Puritans —English Calvinists who placed great stress on moral discipline and the primacy of Scripture.

While this solution was generally well accepted, it was far from satisfactory in the eyes of the Puritan minority. The **Puritans** were English Calvinists who placed great stress on moral discipline and the primacy of Scripture. They were split into two factions. There were the Presbyterians, who maintained ties with Scotland's Presbyterians and dreamed of a national Presbyterian Church to replace the Anglican; and there were the Separatists who, generally, took the local congregation of believers as their model of the ideal Church, and increasingly sought only to separate themselves from a corrupt society.

The label *Puritan* is given to the Separatists, whose religious views put them at odds with society, and led them into some momentous political experiments.

The label *Puritan* is usually given to the Separatists, whose religious views put them at odds with society, and led them into some momentous political experiments. Central to their creed was the depravity of humanity: humanity is so thoroughly corrupt that it cannot grow in grace, and can be saved only by being reborn—this is a dramatic personal experience, quite apart from any Church. Once a person has been reborn or regenerated by the power of God, he or she has to exercise rigorous self-discipline in following the law of God. Scripture is the one sure guide about how to live a saintly life. (*Puritanism* today usually refers to the desire to maintain moral purity by means of self-discipline.)

The Anglican Church, like the Roman Catholic, Lutheran, and original Calvinist Churches was believed to be made up of both saints and sinners.

The Anglican Church, like the Roman Catholic, the Lutheran, and the original Calvinist Churches, was believed to be made up of both saints and sinners. In the eyes of Elizabeth and other late-sixteenth-century leaders, the Anglican Church was the same thing as the populace of England, which surely included many sinners. Quite different was the Puritan view that the Church consisted only of the regenerate—the saints, the elect of God. In a country ruled by the unregenerate, where there was no tradition of religious toleration, the Puritans were bound to feel uncomfortable. How could the saints be satisfied to live under the authority of sinners?

Many of the Puritans joined forces with the Presbyterians in an effort to undermine the established Anglican Church. In the middle of the seventeenth century, the incompetence of Elizabeth's successors (the Stuart dynasty) provoked a revolt against the king in which both the Presbyterians and the Puritans played a part. But once King Charles and his armies were eliminated, there was a falling-out between the Puritans and Presbyterians. Oliver Cromwell, victorious Puritan general, finally entered the Parliament and with a truly Puritan sense of right and wrong, denounced member after member for their impure lives. Finally, he shouted, "You are no Parliament!" and made himself dictator of a Puritan regime. Cromwell's death in 1658 ended the experiment with Puritan theocracy, and another thirty years of political ups-and-downs finally resulted in an established Anglican Church that tolerated other creeds. It was becoming apparent to the English that with so many dissenters in the country, religious uniformity could never be enforced.

Many Puritans joined forces with the Presbyterians in an effort to undermine the established Anglican Church.

The Puritan Experiment in New England

The other important development by the Puritans took place in New England. Facing resistance in old England, the reborn Christians sought to avoid the pollutions of a corrupt society. The Puritan settlement in Massachusetts during the seventeenth century was the product of this hope. One of the guiding ideals for the Puritans who left England was that of the covenant community. God had entered into a covenant with them, the elect, just as he had done with Abraham; and just as the people of Abraham had

One of the guiding ideals for the Puritans who left England was that of the covenant community.

traveled to the Promised Land, so were the Puritans to do so. More than they sought to avoid religious repression back home, the saints were sailing across the Atlantic Ocean to establish a new Jerusalem in America.

The Massachusetts community was basically theocratic, as the saints followed the teaching of the Scriptures and not only lived out their creed of self-denial, but enforced the discipline upon each other. But the problem of who were going to be the saints eventually arose, as time went on. In one sense the answer was obvious, for just as God gave a promise to Abraham and his descendants so, too, the land and the faith would be handed down to the Puritans' children.

The Puritan creed was founded upon the idea that humanity, corrupt by nature, could be saved only by an experience of total conversion, or regeneration by God's overpowering grace.

But the Puritan creed was founded upon the idea that humanity, corrupt by nature, could be saved only by an experience of total conversion, or regeneration by God's overpowering grace. The rule of discipline was easily established in the Massachusetts colony, but how could deep personal conversion be built into the structure of a community? Not surprisingly, as they grew old and observed their children and grandchildren, the original Puritan settlers expressed disappointment. A constant theme in their later writings is the decline of spiritual intensity among their own people. Among the succeeding generations of Puritans, the sign of one's election by God was not so much upright living as material success—not constant vigilance in matters spiritual, but constant diligence in matters material. So was born one of the fundamental characteristics of American culture, the belief in the value of hard work, and in material success as a sign of God's approval.

Another important development took place in the settlements in Rhode Island. The Massachusetts Puritans had not believed in diversity of opinions—God intended people to know only one set of truths, so presumably all right-thinking persons would understand the Scriptures the same way and draw the same conclusions. Life in Massachusetts had become uncomfortable for a man named Roger Williams, who had not seen things the same way as the authorities until, eventually, Williams broke away and started his own Rhode Island community.

That experience, plus a typically Puritan dislike of any political authority wielded by the nonsaints, led Roger Williams to advocate a split between the Church (consisting of the regenerate saints) and the state (consisting of all people, including those who did not have the faith). According to this view, the Church should be an independent society, perhaps existing alongside other Churches, within a state that had no religious identity at all. Thus arose another fundamental concept of American culture, the separation of Church and state. It was closely related to the idea of the limitation of the power of government. Given the Puritan view of the corruptness of human nature, humanity is too sinful to be trusted with much power.

Some of these ideas, notably the separation of Church and state, also gained acceptance in Europe. But America, which had no existing religious heritage, was the most fertile ground for such ideas. Religious toleration was particularly slow in coming in Europe and, generally, was accepted only as a necessary evil in response to Catholic-Protestant bloodshed.

> Roger Williams advocated that the Church should be an independent society within a state that had no religious identity at all. Thus arose another fundamental concept of American culture, the separation of Church and state.

And bloodshed was becoming more common: as the Catholic Church reformed itself during the sixteenth century, it defined its doctrines on a wide variety of questions, and left no room for doubt about differences between Catholic and Protestant belief. The lines were clearly drawn, and a united community of Christians was a thing of the past. In such a situation Anglicanism, despite its origin in political expediency, still could not steer clear of religious controversy; and in such a situation Puritanism, clearly a religion of a minority, quite naturally gave birth to the ideas of separation and toleration.

Summary

- England's Reformation represented a process entirely different from that of Calvinism, Lutheranism, and the Anabaptism.

- Henry VIII's break with the Catholic Church had its origin in political expediency.

- Religious policies changed with each new ruler, but eventually England supported Anglicanism and yet left room for dissent.

- The Puritans tried to undermine the established Anglican Church, and when they failed left England to establish colonies in America.

- Puritan Roger Williams advocated the separation of Church and state.

Prayer

Give me the grace, good Lord:
To set the world at naught, to set the mind firmly
on you and not to hang upon the words of men's
mouths.

To know my own vileness and wretchedness; to
humble myself under the mighty hand of God; to
wail my sins, and for the purging of them, patiently
to suffer adversity.

Gladly to bear my purgatory here; to be joyful in
tribulations; to walk the narrow way that leads to
life.

> *St. Thomas More*
> *Composed in the*
> *Tower of London*
> *preceding his death*

Discussion Questions

1. Unlike the Lutheran, Anabaptist, and
   Calvinist Reformations, the English
   Reformation had its roots in politics rather
   than in theology. Explain.

2. What was new, and unlike earlier ideas, in
   the Puritan concept of salvation?

3. How does this concept of salvation help to
   explain the Puritans' move to America,
   and Roger Williams' proposal to separate
   Church and state?

Major Branches of Christianity

Churches of Ancient Origin

(roots in early Christianity)

- Roman Catholicism
- Coptic Church
- Eastern Orthodox

Protestant Churches — Four Major Traditions

(origins in sixteenth century)

Lutheranism

- Lutheran Churches

Anabaptism

- Mennonites
- Hutterites

Calvinism

- Reformed
- Presbyterian
- Disciples of Christ

Anglicanism

- Church of England
- Episcopal Churches
- Methodism
- United Church of Christ

Independent Protestant Churches of Recent Origin

(nineteenth and twentieth centuries)

- Adventists
- Latter-day Saints
- Christian Scientists

Jesuit missionaries among the Indians.

Chapter Twenty-Nine

The Catholic Reformation: The Society of Jesus

While the Protestant reformers were fashioning new Churches on the basis of their distinctive readings of holy Scripture, there were Catholic reformers trying to renew their own Church more in terms of the tradition of the preceding centuries. The renewal of discipline in the old orders of friars and monks was matched by the creation of new orders, and individual bishops strove to improve conditions in their dioceses. Like the holy men and women of the fifteenth century, the reformers each seemed destined to struggle in virtual isolation. But the isolated reforms grew to be a general reform of the entire Catholic Church in the sixteenth century, when the papacy slowly shook off the worst of its worldly habits, and resumed its aggressive leadership of the Church.

Isolated reforms grew to be a general reform of the entire Catholic Church when the papacy resumed its aggressive leadership of the Church.

A modern revitalization of medieval institutions would most likely have been short-lived, however, and scarcely suited to face the challenge posed by Protestant Christianity. As it turned out, the Catholic Church managed to win back some of the territories lost to the Protestants, and win numerous converts among the peoples of the New World. This was possible because the Church developed new forms of spirituality that addressed modern needs while remaining true to the Church's traditions. Nowhere did this combination of newness and tradition have greater results than in the Society of Jesus, which appeared during the 1530s.

Ignatius of Loyola

In an obscure battle over an unimportant fortress in northern Spain during the year 1521, a young soldier was crippled by a cannonball that shattered his leg bone. A soldier from a family of soldiers, this man, Iñigo (Ignatius) of the Palace of Loyola, soon realized that the leg was never going to heal properly and that his military career was at an end. At the same time, he found himself drawn closer to God. During his long convalescence, he became an enthusiastic reader of biographies of the saints, and he resolved to become a holy man. For a year he took up residence in the Spanish town of Manresa, where he dedicated himself to the harshest asceticism imaginable. He lived in solitude in a cave, ate very little, and devoted himself to prayer. A year of such material deprivation but spiritual enrichment brought him to the conclusion that he was not suited for the hermit's life; rather, he was called to share his new insights with others.

Ignatius' way of sharing his insights was a small, thin book called the *Spiritual Exercises*. It was not written to be read in the same way as Calvin's *Institute* was to be read. Instead, it was a manual designed to be the basis of a religious experience known as a retreat, which could last part of a day or up to thirty days, depending upon a person's needs. A spiritual advisor, using the Exercises, would lead others through a series of meditations that would eventually give the retreatants a deeper understanding of their own faith and their direction in living out that faith. People did not read the Exercises, they *experienced* the Exercises, and were changed by the experience.

This little manual was based upon principles that had long been part of the Christian tradition. It presumed, especially, that humanity was essentially good; Original Sin had weakened humanity, but in place of the Protestant concept of humanity's depravity, there was the conviction that humanity could become better by accepting divine grace.[1] Sin, in the Ignatian view, was a product of will, not of nature, and thus the people who were led through the Exercises were repeatedly asked to examine their consciences. This approach to sin shows up clearly in one portion of the Exercises, known as the Meditation on the Two Standards. The retreatant imagines two hostile armies confronting one another: that of Christ, and that of Lucifer; that of Jerusalem, and that of Babylon. Complete loyalty to Christ consists in reforming the will and utterly rejecting Satan's ways.

Alongside the traditional view of sin and human nature, there were some new elements in Ignatian spirituality. For one thing, like Protestantism, it focused upon the individual; the Exercises were originally given to individuals, in contrast to monastic prayer, which was done by the entire community. Monastic prayer also was done on a regular basis, several times a day, while the Spiritual Exercises were meant to be taken during a break from regular life, so that the soul could be renewed and the believer could return to a life of action with new vigor and a sense of direction.

Many years passed before Ignatius had much success in sharing his distinctive spirituality with his fellow Christians. After his

1. Luther would have argued that his view of depravity was every bit as traditional, having grown out of Augustine's concept of concupiscence. On the other hand, Augustine also insisted upon the essential goodness of humanity and upon sin as an act of the will, and those ideas were developed throughout the Middle Ages and adopted by Ignatius.

experience in Manresa, he traveled to the Holy Land to preach to the Moslems and Jews, but soon became discouraged. He then returned to study at the University of Barcelona, where he became distracted by various projects for reform and also had some unpleasant encounters with Church authorities, who suspected that he was a Protestant. He finally settled down to seven years' serious study of philosophy at the University of Paris. There he made friends among the students, some of whom he led through the Exercises.

New Type of Religious Order

The Jesuits, as they were called, a true reflection of the new spirit of the *Spiritual Exercises,* were an altogether new type of religious order. The candidates for the Society spent sixteen years in training, taking courses in classical studies, philosophy and theology, and submitting to various tests of their calling. All Jesuits made a vow of obedience to their superiors, and many of them vowed total obedience to the pope. But they did not wear the special clothing of monks, called the habit; they did not vow to live in one place, as monks did; and they were not required to sing the Divine Office (daily cycle of psalms and prayers) after the manner of monks. Jesuit spirituality broke from the monastic mold, as the Society eliminated any impediment to a life of active service. Jesuits were trained to serve in any place their superiors might judge they were needed: thus St. Peter Canisius worked among the Lutherans in Germany, St. Francis Xavier did missionary work in China, and others showed up in South America, England, and France—wherever the Church perceived a need.

Jesuits were trained to serve in any place their superiors might judge they were needed.

Wherever they traveled, the men of the Society of Jesus carried the *Spiritual Exercises* with them, and in this way Ignatian spirituality became part of the personal renewal that is essential in any movement of reform. Jesuit priests led some of the foremost reformers in the Church through the Exercises, and soon Ignatian retreats were being given to young men training for the priesthood, monks whose monastic orders were being renewed, priests and laypeople who desired a clearer vision of their own direction in life.

Jesuit spirituality, designed to lead a person to action, was ideally suited to a Church that insisted, against the Protestant view, that faith must be accompanied by works if humanity is to be saved. The Jesuits promoted a Catholic view of the importance of the sacraments, as well. Members of the Society recommended frequent reception of Holy Communion, for example, even to the point of daily Communion for monks and nuns who could easily attend Mass on a daily basis. The Society also promoted frequent confession, and trained its priests to be skillful confessors. As a means of encouraging complete honesty in confession, the Jesuits favored use of the **confessional,** a small, two-chambered room in which the penitent spoke to the priest through a screen, and was able to remain anonymous.

A clear sign of the Jesuits' impact upon the Church was their remarkable growth in numbers. There were only ten Jesuits in 1540, but that number had grown to one thousand by the time of Ignatius Loyola's death in 1556, and to thirteen thousand shortly after the beginning of the sixteenth century. The discipline of the Society and the new vision of

Wherever they traveled, the men of the Society of Jesus carried the *Spiritual Exercises* with them, and in this way Ignatian spirituality became part of the personal renewal that is essential to any movement of reform.

Confessional

St. Ignatius clearly were fulfilling a need in people's lives. In the meantime, the Church as a whole was struggling to reform its doctrine and its practices so that the spiritual "energies" being generated by the Society of Jesus and other religious orders would not come to nothing.

Summary

• General reform began in the Catholic Church when the papacy resumed its aggressive leadership, but personal spiritual renewal was the key to the reform of the Church.

• Ignatius wrote a manual called *Spiritual Exercises* that was designed to be the basis of a religious experience known as a retreat that would eventually give the retreatants a deeper meaning of their own faith and their direction in living out that faith.

• The Jesuits were a new type of religious order that broke away from the monastic mold and led a life of active service.

• A clear sign of the Jesuits' impact upon the Church was its remarkable growth of members.

Prayer

O saving victim, open wide
The gates of heaven to man below,
Our foes press on from every side;
Your aid supply; your strength bestow.

To your great name be endless praise,
Immortal Godhead, One in three;
Grant us for endless length of days,
In our true native land to be. Amen.

O Salutaris

Discussion Questions

1. Compare the story of the conversion of Ignatius with the stories about Augustine (chapter eight) and Francis (chapter twenty-two). Do these stories have anything in common?

2. How does Ignatius' concept of sin differ from Luther's, and how does it explain Ignatius' dedication to giving retreats?

3. In what ways was the Society of Jesus unlike earlier monastic orders?

Council of Trent

Chapter Thirty

The Catholic Reformation: The Papacy and the Council of Trent

During the early stages of the Protestant Reformation, there were Catholic leaders who, by assignment or even out of personal attachment to the Church, debated Martin Luther and others. Like most debaters during most periods in history, the defenders of Catholicism saw that their exchanges of ideas with their opponents really had little effect upon people's convictions; but the Roman Catholic spokespeople also faced another frustration, namely that it was difficult to defend the Church when its leadership was so undeniably corrupt. The Protestant Reformation grew out of a variety of circumstances, but more than anything else the debauchery of the leaders in Rome was the scandal that prompted sincere people to believe that there could be no salvation within the established Church.

Return of Spiritual Leadership

The return of the papacy to some measure of spiritual leadership after 1534 made the Holy See the natural "anchor" of the Catholic Church's attempts to recover and face the Protestant challenge, and the papal reform became in effect a model of the Catholic view of how humanity is saved: some obviously

The return of the papacy to some measure of spiritual leadership after 1534 made the Holy See the natural "anchor" of the Catholic Church's attempts to recover and face the Protestant challenge.

corrupt men, brought to power under the corrupt regime of the Renaissance Papacy, attempted to reform their personal lives and use their power for the good of the Church; they made no attempt to repudiate their past, and indeed at times they seemed trapped by it, but still attempted to work toward a better future for themselves and the Church. Further, they discovered that their own work of reform could not be carried out without some response to Protestantism, which had grown to be a powerful force in the world.

Typical in this regard was Alessandro (Alexander) Farnese, first of the reforming popes. Born of a powerful noble family, Farnese had become a cardinal while still in his teens; he was teasingly called "Cardinal Petticoat," because of the rumor that his lovely sister Giulia had secured her brother's appointment by her amorous liaison with Pope Alexander VI. No stranger to Roman excess himself, Cardinal Petticoat fathered three illegitimate children.

But he was shaken by the experiences of the Fifth Lateran Council (1512–1517), in which sincere reformers decried the behavior of popes and cardinals. He attempted to change himself, and was ordained a priest in 1519. In 1523, the reformers among the cardinals nearly managed to elect him pope, but the Medici family prevailed, and one of their sons became Pope Clement VII. When Clement died in 1534, Alessandro was unanimously elected Pope Paul III.

One of his first acts as pope was the elevation of two of his own grandsons as cardinals. He was sensitive enough to refer to the new appointees as "nephews," but to the reform-minded people in Rome it was just another case of papal nepotism. As it turned out, though, one of the new cardinals—named Alessandro Farnese like his grandfather—turned out to be a tireless advocate of reform, living proof that God works in mysterious ways.

Cardinals Dedicated to Reform

Once his family was satisfied that their kin were "taken care of," Paul III initiated his own program for reform of the Church, and somewhat ironically, his first move was to make the office of cardinal a tool of reform rather than a political plum. A cardinal's "red hat"[1] was granted to men renowned throughout Europe for their reform efforts. Among them were Bishop Jacopo Sadoleto, originator of a modest reform in the Diocese of Carpentras, southeastern France; Giovanni Pietro Carafa, cofounder of the Theatine Order of priests, outstanding for its discipline; Reginald Pole, an English humanist; Gasparo Contarini, a layman known for his personal piety; and several others. These four men were placed at the head of a special commission charged with the task of investigating all aspects of Church life so that the work of reform could begin.

Their report, drawn up at the end of 1537, exposed serious abuses, even at the highest levels of authority. Pope Paul was urged to suppress the report on the grounds that it would be used by Luther and others to embarrass the Church, and while indeed the fears were well-founded—Luther had a field day—the pope insisted that corruption was more to be feared than criticism, and he made the report public in 1538. In 1540, he again braved criticism in approving the new Society of Jesus, which had been opposed by Cardinal Carafa and others for its rejection of traditional monastic practices. Yet another effort toward reform was the creation of the Holy Office in 1542, modeled after the Inquisition of medieval times, to "unmask those suspected of heresy."

1. The red hat has long been, and still is, worn by cardinals. When a man becomes a cardinal, it is often said that "he was given the red hat."

Council of Trent

Once he had restored some of the papacy's credibility as a leader in the cause of ecclesiastical reform, Paul III directed his efforts toward the second stage of his program, the calling of an ecumenical council to address the problems of the Church.

Once he had restored some of the papacy's credibility as a leader in the cause of ecclesiastical reform, Paul III directed his efforts toward the second stage of his program, the calling of an ecumenical[2] council to address the problems of the Church. Such a council could never take place so long as the two greatest Catholic monarchs, Francis I of France and Charles V of the Holy Roman Empire, were at war—any council attended by one ruler's bishops would have been boycotted by the bishops of the other. In 1538, after considerable effort, the pope convinced the two men to sign a ten-year truce.

As a council came closer to becoming a reality, there was serious disagreement concerning the agenda. One group, representing Charles V, called for a reform of discipline to be the first item for discussion. Charles' Empire was split between warring Lutherans and Catholics, and he felt that if the two sides could only get together to discuss the one point on which they agreed—the need for renewal of discipline—then a compromise might be reached, and there could be peace in his realm. Another group, whose chief spokesman was Cardinal Carafa, had long since concluded that the Lutherans were serious in their claims of rejecting both papal and conciliar authority. With no hope for compromise, the rigorists argued that debate over doctrine should come first; once the doctrinal groundwork had been laid, it would be more clear how discipline could best be restored.

In 1541, there was a meeting of Lutheran and Catholic theologians at the town of Ratisbon, as Emperor Charles made a last, desperate attempt to bring the two sides together. The

2. *Ecumenical* means worldwide; the word is often used as a label for the Church's largest gatherings of Church leaders, such as Nicea and Vatican II.

pope sent Cardinal Contarini as his representative. They struggled to achieve a consensus on the key question of justification, and they nearly succeeded; but the Eucharist and penance were stumbling-blocks, and Philip Melanchthon on the Lutheran side refused to acknowledge the authority of a general council in matters of faith. After one month, the talks broke down, and there was no longer any hope of compromise between Catholics and Lutherans. Paul III summoned the Church's leaders to a council in the imperial city of Trent not long after the failure of the Ratisbon talks, and except for a brief appearance at one session, the Protestants played no part in the council.

A first meeting of the council had to be called off for lack of participants, and subsequent sessions were suspended for reasons ranging from a flu epidemic to war. The **Council of Trent** was dragged out over an eighteen-year period, from 1545 to 1563, but in spite of interruptions and changes of personnel over the years, its message was consistent. It passed judgment on theological disputes that had raged for decades, and left no room for doubt about the differences between Catholic and Protestant belief. While the Protestants placed authority entirely in sacred Scripture, for example, the Fathers at Trent urged that ". . . The teaching mission of the Church is to guard the perfect integrity of Scripture and tradition, the two sources of faith." Throughout its decrees the authority of the Fathers and Doctors of the Church was cited in addition to the decisions of councils and popes; Scripture was a source of authoritative texts, of course, but it was not the sole source. Catholics, it could be said, believed that the Bible is in the Church, unlike Protestants who held that the Church is in the Bible.

Other crucial points that were treated at Trent were the nature of humanity, the effects of sin

Paul III summoned the Church's leaders to a council in the imperial city of Trent not long after the failure of the Ratisbon talks, and except for a brief appearance at one session, the Protestants played no part in the council.

Council of Trent— verified the differences between Protestant and Catholic belief: Original Sin affects humanity, but humanity is perfectible in spite of Original Sin; humanity is saved by God's grace, but freely cooperates with grace; faith in God must be accompanied by good works that can sanctify.

and the doctrine of justification. The teaching that emerged was that Original Sin affects humanity, but humanity is perfectible in spite of Original Sin. Humanity is saved by God's grace, but freely cooperates with grace; faith in God must be accompanied by good works that can sanctify.

Upon this basis the council Fathers were able to reaffirm the necessity of the seven sacraments as a source of grace and a means of sanctification. Finally, the council ended with the disciplinary measures, which gave bishops power to reform their dioceses, called for a cardinal to be appointed for each nation to oversee reform efforts, and established uniformity in the Church's practices, such as, the manner of celebrating the Mass.

Uniformity

The decrees of the Council of Trent reflected a conscious attempt to be true to the Church's tradition but, at the same time, they revealed that the Church was being forced into a new posture.

There was an aura of defensiveness and combativeness about the policies of the Church during and after the Council of Trent.

Index—list of books considered to be dangerous for Catholics to read.

The decrees of the Council of Trent reflected a conscious attempt to be true to the Church's tradition but, at the same time, they revealed that the Church was being forced into a new posture. The Protestant Reformation had drawn millions away from the Catholic Church, and had leveled serious criticisms against its fundamental beliefs and practices. There was, quite understandably, an aura of defensiveness and combativeness about the policies of the Church during and after the Council of Trent. Symbolic of this change was the pontificate of Carafa, who ruled as Paul IV from 1555 to 1559. He supported the activities of the Inquisition, which came to be notorious for cruelty and intolerance,[3] and he created an **Index** of prohibited books, to make certain that Catholics would never have contact with writings considered dangerous. It was typical

3. The Inquisition gained its worst reputation in Spain during the reign of Philip II, son of Charles V. Torture and uncorroborated accusations were employed in obtaining convictions, and the people who refused to give up their errors were burned to death in a public ceremony known as the auto-da-fe.

of the mentality prevailing in Rome that at one point, even the report about corruption that Paul III's reform commission had drawn up in 1537 was placed on the Index.

Pius IV (1559–1565), who succeeded Paul IV, was a very different type of person from his predecessor, and he issued a series of decrees that carefully defined the limits of the Holy Office's powers. But the difference between the two popes was largely a difference of temperaments. Anxious to guard orthodoxy like all the Catholic leaders of his time, Pius IV defined limits but made no move to do away with the Inquisition.

Under St. Pius V (1556–1572), the defense against Protestantism took yet another form, which might be called the quest for uniformity. Four crucial books were issued during his pontificate: the **Catechism of the Council of Trent,** which succinctly summarized Catholic doctrine; the **Missal,** which contained all portions of the new, standardized, Tridentine[4] Mass; the **Breviary,** which standardized the Divine Office; and a new edition of St. Thomas' ***Summa Theologiae,*** which became the common handbook of Catholic theology.

The Catholic Church's drive toward uniformity was a natural response to the bewildering variety of Protestant beliefs that were splintering the Church. Much more surprising was the fact that this aggressive reform of doctrine and practice could be directed by such unlikely men as the popes of this period. Like Paul III, both Paul IV and Pius IV had handed out Church offices to relatives upon becoming pope, and Pius, like Paul III, had even sired three illegitimate children.

But Rome was shocked when Paul IV, renowned as the ill-tempered and inflexible

Under St. Pius V, the defense against Protestantism took another form, which might be called the quest for uniformity.

Catechism of the Council of Trent—succinctly summarized Catholic doctrine.

Missal—contained all portions of the new, standardized, Tridentine Mass.

Breviary—standardized the Divine Office, the cycle of prayers based on the Psalms, which had been developed by the medieval monks.

Summa Theologiae— common handbook of Catholic theology by St. Thomas Aquinas.

The Catholic Church's drive toward uniformity was a natural response to the bewildering variety of Protestant beliefs that were splintering the Church.

4. *Tridentine* is an adjective that is derived from "Trent."

Carafa, called a meeting of his cardinals in 1559 to announce that he had made poor judgments, and now was forced to dismiss three of his nephews from their positions. And Pius IV, for all his nepotistic inclinations, made one shrewd choice when he appointed his twenty-two-year-old nephew, Charles Borromeo, as Papal Secretary of State. In spite of his inexperience, Charles became the driving force behind the final sessions of the Council of Trent, and later in life this man who drew strength from Ignatius' *Spiritual Exercises* applied his enormous spiritual energies to the task of reforming the troublesome Diocese of Milan, Italy, according to the dictates of the Council of Trent.

For exactly opposite reasons, St. Pius V was also an unlikely leader. He followed a monastic discipline, and made barefoot pilgrimages to Rome's shrines, and was known to break into tears while reciting the rosary. Yet his eccentric and emotional piety did not prevent his being the hardnosed administrator who brought the publication of the Breviary and other books to completion in spite of obstacles.

The uniformity of Catholic doctrine and practice, then, was a fact—but it was certainly not the only important fact about the Catholic Reformation. The most diverse and seemingly unlikely personalities were being put to work for the reform of the Church.

Summary

- The return to leadership of the papacy made it the natural "anchor" of the Church's attempts to face and to recover from the Protestant challenge.

- A special commission, given the task of investigating all aspects of Church life so that the work of reform could begin, exposed serious abuses at all levels of authority.

- Pope Paul III, after restoring some of the papacy's credibility as a leader in the cause of reform, called an ecumenical council to address the problems of the Church.

- The Council of Trent addressed theological disputes that had raged for years.

- The council Fathers reaffirmed the necessity of the seven sacraments as a source of grace and a means of sanctity.

- There was an aura of defensiveness and combativeness about the policies of the Church during and after the Council of Trent.

- The Church strove for uniformity in response to the variety of Protestant beliefs that were splintering the Church.

Prayer

O Holy Mother of God, pray for the priests your Son has chosen to serve the Church. Help them by your intercession to be holy, zealous, and chaste. Make them models of virtue in the service of God's people. . . . Help them administer the sacraments with joy. Amen.

St. Charles of Borromeo

Discussion Questions

1. In what sense was Alessandro Farnese's personal story like that of the entire Church during this period?

2. What practical reforms were promoted by the Council of Trent?

3. How did Catholic theology as expressed at Trent differ from Protestant ideas?

4. What things did the Catholic Church do to standardize and unify Roman Catholicism after Trent?

John Wesley—Father of Methodism

Chapter Thirty-One

The Creative Tensions of the Reformation Era

The later years of the Reformation Era could be summed up by the word "tension." Christian Europe was at war with itself, and the conflict made itself felt at many levels. Some of the tension was simply destructive: there were religious wars between nations and within nations, and many lives were lost, usually, to no purpose.

In other cases, the tension took the form of fruitless struggles within each Church. The English Protestants fought among themselves over the question of how best to organize themselves, as some advocated a national Church ruled by bishops, others favored letting independent congregations rule themselves, and still others fought for a national committee of wise elders, or presbyters. On the Continent, Protestants from the Reformed (Calvinist) tradition were badly divided over Calvin's doctrine or predestination, and whether that doctrine left any room for belief in free will. Catholics, too, quarreled about the relationship of human free will to divine grace. Lutheranism, meanwhile, was spreading into the Scandinavian countries, but the Lutheran movement suffered divisions over a variety of issues during the decades following Martin Luther's death.

Creative Tensions

The Reformation conflicts also gave rise to creative tensions. Faith could not be taken for granted; each person had to choose to be committed to one creed or another.

But there was a more hopeful side, too. The Reformation conflicts also gave rise to creative tensions. It was an age when faith could not be taken for granted; each person had to choose to be committed to one creed or another, and the power of God shone through many people's choices and actions. It was an age of religious giants, both Catholic and Protestant. Protestant Christianity produced leaders such as John Wesley, the Englishman who founded the Methodist movement and who composed over two thousand hymns in fulfillment of his belief that Christians should sing fervently to express their faith. It produced writers such as John Bunyan, author of *Pilgrim's Progress,* and John Milton, author of *Paradise Lost,* and it produced great musicians, such as Johann Sebastian Bach and George Friedrich Handel. Bach's organ music and Handel's magnificent choral work, the *Messiah,* are still favorites at religious celebrations, today.

Mystics

Catholic Christianity could boast its own examples of outstanding faith. Prominent among them was St. Teresa of Ávila, also known as "Teresa of Jesus." At the age of twenty, against her father's wishes, she left home to enter a convent of the Carmelite Order. Almost immediately she became gravely ill, and nearly died as a result of the poor medical treatments that were the standard practice of the time. She never recovered completely, but during her long period of convalescence she devoted herself to prayer. It was at this point that she first had what are called mystical experiences in prayer: visions, ecstasies, and the sense of profound union with God. Teresa was quite disturbed by these experiences, as she felt that she was a sinner who could not possibly deserve to be so blessed. But with the help of Dominican and later Jesuit spiritual advisors, Teresa came to accept her own marvelous gift. She also possessed a fine gift for analysis, and so was able to reflect upon her experiences and share them with others. Her book *Interior Castle* is one of the most famous books about prayer ever written, and her account of her own life stands alongside Augustine's *Confessions* as one of the greatest spiritual autobiographies ever written.

These books offer extraordinary images from her prayer experiences, as, for example, when she described herself as being a garden, and God as being the gentle, spring rain which fell upon her, soaked through her, and gave her life. In other places, she described her relationship with God in terms of the imagery of mystical marriage. But she was also entirely honest in describing periods when God seemed distant from her, and her prayer life seemed like a dry well. Not surprisingly, then, she looked at her own sinfulness and claimed that she could pray only because God gave her courage to pray:

> *I say courage, because . . . although we are always in the presence of God, it seems to me that those who practice prayer are specially so, because they can see all the time that He is looking at them; whereas others may be in God's presence . . . without ever remembering that He can see them. (Interior Castle, chapter 8)*

Throughout the Middle Ages and early modern times, there was a running debate about which was greater, the active life or the contemplative (prayer) life. Teresa's experience reflected her belief that while prayer was most essential, one must be active in the world as well. As often happens in the history of religious orders, Teresa's Carmelite Order had lost the original fervor of its founder, and had relaxed the discipline under which the sisters lived. With her superiors' blessings, Teresa reestablished the ascetical discipline of the Carmelite life in a large number of convents and, in fact, broke her frail health in her ceaseless travels from convent to convent.

Teresa had a friend, St. John of the Cross, who likewise was a mystic and similarly strained himself in his labors to reform his order. The Church has honored each of these people with the title of "Doctor of the Church," which means that their books about prayer have earned them distinction as two of history's greatest religious teachers.

King Philip II

Teresa and John were contemporaries of Philip II, the king who ruled Spain when the country was at the height of its power. Philip is often remembered as the monarch who sent the ill-fated fleet, the Spanish Armada, against Protestant England in 1588. Many of Philip's policies were calculated in terms of political ambition, to advance the power of his country and the Hapsburg dynasty. But unlike most modern rulers, he made no clear distinction between religious and political motives. In fact, he could be described as the last of Europe's great kings who, in the tradition of Charlemagne, saw his kingship as primarily a religious duty. The Armada was sent against England, for example, because the English were aiding the rebels in the Netherlands, which country Philip's family controlled. But in Philip's eyes the Dutch rebels and the English were to be resisted because they were attempting to overthrow Catholic leadership in the Netherlands.

Philip II, the last of Europe's great Christian kings, saw his kingship as primarily a religious duty.

Similarly, Philip sponsored projects in the New World, largely with the aim of extracting gold and silver from the Americas to enrich Spain. But at the same time, he personally labored to manage the efforts of hundreds of missionaries, because he believed that the native population of the Americas should be converted to Christianity. On top of this, he used his American gold and silver to finance a large fleet, which he sent against the Moslem Turks. Like his father, Charles V, he was instrumental in protecting Christian Europe from the threat of Turkish attacks. Also like his father—and like virtually all Christians of this age—he considered toleration of other faiths to be an evil. Philip gave his support to the Spanish Inquisition, which is remembered today for its cruelties against alleged heretics, Jews, and Moors (Spanish Moslems).

The Spanish Inquisition is remembered for its cruelties against alleged heretics, Jews, and Moors.

Philip was a devout man, but not a happy one. During his lifetime, he lost all three of his wives to illness, and his relationship with his children was not especially friendly. He was so obsessed with his duties as Christian king that he was reluctant to delegate authority, and as a result he spent up to twenty hours per day poring over the reports that came in from all over the vast Spanish Empire.

His thoroughness became the stuff of legends. According to one such story, a Spanish governor in the New World grew tired of writing out lengthy monthly reports, which he was sure were never read. Accordingly, he wrote as usual that the local mines had produced several hundred pounds of silver, and the missionaries had baptized several dozen Indians; then for a joke he wrote that a fly was resting on his desk. But Philip, who read absolutely everything, wrote back to congratulate him about the silver and the baptisms, and to suggest that he should swat the fly.

In the middle years of his career, Philip added yet another obsession to his workload when he assumed personal supervision of the construction of El Escorial. This monumental building was a combination monastery, personal residence, and administrative office

333

for the Empire. It was typical of Philip's personal vision that he would place all three types of building under the same roof; after all, he was the heart of the Empire, its administrator, and (like the monks) a man of prayer. It was indicative of the changes in the world that within a short time after Philip's death, El Escorial fell into disuse. It was a facility built specifically for an ambitious king whose worldview was essentially religious, and such people have become increasingly rare.

Missionaries

The missionaries sent to the New World at Philip's command were laying the foundation for a new Church that would eventually be not merely European, but worldwide. The same amazing capacity for work, and the same desire to bring Christ to all the world, was exemplified by St. Francis Xavier. Ignatius Loyola had roomed with him at the University of Paris, and had aided his conversion. Francis became part of the little band of men who founded the Society of Jesus.

The Jesuits had pledged their willingness to do the pope's bidding, even before they were officially approved as a religious order. While Ignatius and the others were staying in Rome awaiting approval, Pope Paul III already began sending Jesuits to various corners of Europe to work on behalf of the Church. In fact, by spring of 1540, Ignatius himself and Francis were the only Jesuits still in Rome. Most likely, Francis had been passed over for assignments because his health was poor. Like Luther, Calvin, and Philip II, who seemed obsessed to work beyond normal human limits, and even more like Teresa who ruined her health by hard labors, Francis had exhausted himself by working almost endlessly in Italian hospitals. In fact, as was again characteristic of this age, he had a powerful sense of his own sinfulness, and wore himself down with numerous fasts and penitential disciplines.

But when the ambassador from Portugal asked the pope to provide a missionary priest to work in Portuguese colonies, Xavier was the first chosen—perhaps, because he was the only available Jesuit. It is a mark of Francis' assessment of the duties that he faced that prior to leaving, he wrote his will and bade solemn farewell to Ignatius, whom he expected never to see again.

By 1542 he was in western India, winning converts to the faith. Tradition has it that little children came running whenever they saw Francis in the streets; he would ring a little bell to announce his arrival, and the children flocked to hear the Word of God. After three years in India, he shifted his sights to Portuguese settlements in western Indonesia. He left the islands several years later to coordinate the efforts of new Jesuit missionaries whom Ignatius had sent to assist Francis' labors in India.

One of Xavier's converts was a Japanese named Han-Sir, who told Francis of a faraway land called Japan. By 1549, he reached Japan; after about a year of lessons in Japanese language and customs, Francis began preaching to the Japanese. He eventually handed over his work to other Jesuit missionaries, and was newly arrived in China when he fell ill and died. Francis Xavier's exhausting ten years of traveling and preaching have earned him a reputation as the greatest Christian missionary since St. Paul.

St. Vincent de Paul

Xavier's amazing labors in faraway lands were matched by the efforts of another man who sought to heal the ills within his own country. St. Vincent de Paul labored within a France that suffered from the effects of civil wars and from the corruption of its own priests. For thirty years during the latter half of the sixteenth century, France was the scene of the most horrible religious wars of the Reformation Era. The nobility of France had long struggled to make themselves independent from the power of the king, and in the late 1500s the issue was complicated by the fact that the prominent nobles were also Huguenots. The Catholic and Calvinist armies' devastation of the country reached a peak on St. Bartholomew's Day, August 24, 1572. The Catholic king, Charles IX, became so frustrated by the struggles that he openly expressed his wish that someone would "take care of the whole lot" of Huguenots. After the Protestant leaders were assassinated, the common people became involved in the massacre, and over ten thousand Huguenots were slaughtered.

One healthy result of the St. Bartholomew's Day Massacre was that leading French thinkers became the first in Europe to propose religious toleration as the only civilized alternative to unending bloodshed. But France, meanwhile, was suffering the effects of the wars. The fighting had deflected attention away from the much-needed reforms that had been proposed at the Council of Trent: French priests were poorly trained and poorly disciplined, and their inadequacy as pastors was reflected in the common people's indifference to religion. Poverty was widespread in the war-ravaged country, and many lived under appalling conditions. One sign of the sickness of the country was that some parents even broke their children's arms and legs so that the youngsters would look more pitiful, and could raise more money begging for their families.

Vincent de Paul himself came from a peasant family, and at first he used his exceptional talents to secure for himself a good living as a priest. He succeeded: he seemed to "have it made" when he won the post as personal chaplain for the wealthy Gondi family. Then, when he was nearing the age of thirty, he began to change. He abandoned his chaplaincy to become parish priest in Chatillons, a village of poor French farmers. Moved by the desperate circumstances in which many of the villagers were living, he organized the peasants to perform charitable works for the less fortunate among them.

Vincent soon left the poor countryside to return to his position with the Gondi family, but he was a changed man. The amazing gift of Vincent de Paul was that when he changed, he had the power to change others as well. He recruited the nobles themselves to continue his work for the poor. He founded the Daughters of Charity to work among the poor and sick, for example, and inspired young women from noble families to give up their comfortable lives to carry out this work.

He was likewise dismayed by the ignorance and weak faith of France's peasantry, and recruited some friends to help him preach among the peasants on the Gondi estates. These preaching visits came to be known as "missions"—like missionaries to foreign lands, Vincent and his companions visited areas to preach and inspire faith, but among the baptized. His work became so famous that soon there were requests for missions from all over France, and Vincent's response was to recruit more priests for this work, and create the Congregation of the Mission, a religious order that still has six thousand members today.

He also held retreats for priests, organized a system of rest homes for the elderly, and started a seminary for boys interested in the priesthood. But even these do not complete the list of his many projects. Some of Vincent's programs and organizations came to an end after his death, while some endured. Much the same could be said of the works of all the outstanding persons of this era. What they all had in common was an ability to labor in this life as if everything depended on the outcome of their efforts, while believing that their relationship with God was more valuable than any of their earthly achievements.

Summary

• The Reformation conflicts gave rise to creative tensions.

• Catholic Christianity had examples of outstanding faith, such as, Teresa of Avila and St. John of the Cross.

• King Philip II was obsessed with his duties as a Christian king.

• King Philip, like all Christians of the age, believed that toleration of other faiths was evil and gave his support to the Spanish Inquisition.

• Pope Paul III began sending missionaries all over the world.

• Leading French thinkers were the first in Europe to propose religious toleration as the only civilized alternative to unending bloodshed.

• St. Vincent de Paul was instrumental in obtaining religious instruction and corporal help for the poor peasants in France.

Prayer

My soul has employed itself, and all my powers,
In the service of Him;
And now I do not guard my earthly gains,
Nor have I any other duty,
Than to exercise my love for Him.

St. John of the Cross

Discussion Questions

1. Find common themes running through the stories in this chapter. Did all these people have any opinions or outlooks in common?

2. Note one achievement for each of the persons discussed in this chapter.

Cornelis Jansen, from whom Jansenism derives its origin and name.

Chapter Thirty-Two

The Jansenists

Elitism

Because the Church is comprised of men and women who sin, the need for reform is a perennial feature of Christian life. The history of the Church is full of people who have been able to see beyond the prevailing mediocrity and corruption to a higher ideal, and persevere against an unreformed majority in pursuit of that ideal. The Leo IXs and Charles Borromeos have done the Church a great service.

There are, on the other hand, pitfalls along the road to reform. Can the reformer be sure that his or her ideal, which condemns the spirit of the times, is in tune with the true spirit of Christianity? To have the strength to persevere against the majority, the reformer has to be utterly convinced of his or her own beliefs; but this sentiment can be perverted into elitism, which is the opposite of the true spirit of reform.

Seventeenth-century France saw the rise of one such elitist group—the **Jansenists.** The movement was begun by an abbot and an obscure Dutch theologian, and at its height included only two hundred nuns and a few hermits. Still, it managed to attract the attention of several different popes, sour relations between Rome and the French hierarchy, undermine the popularity of the Jesuits in France, and influence the spirituality of the entire nation. Church officials, as they have always done with elitist groups, tried to thwart the Jansenists. But their task was a

Jansenists—believed that salvation was for the chosen few; denied humanity's ability to resist temptation; opposed frequent reception of Communion; only people with perfect contrition could receive penance.

doubly difficult one. In the first place, much of the harsh Jansenist doctrine appealed to people who were sick of the decadent French Church. Besides, the Church in France was ill prepared to fight a doctrinal controversy because it was already divided over the question of its relationship with Rome.

The French Church in which the Jansenists grew had been less receptive to Tridentine decrees than its counterparts in Spain and Italy. A few bishops, such as the great St. Francis de Sales, were attempting to establish discipline and encourage greater spiritual vigor in their dioceses. French Catholicism was also beginning to bear fruit in the form of charitable works for the needy, under the leadership of St. Vincent de Paul, a towering figure. But the Church's work was far from finished, especially in the monasteries, which had become refuges for the country's decadent noble class.

In the convents, the reform of France's women religious (nuns) had begun, and strangely enough, the leadership in this movement had fallen to teenage abbesses. One such leader was Angelique Arnauld, abbess of the convent of Port-Royal, near Paris. She became an abbess at the age of eleven, and a devoted reformer by age seventeen. Mother Angelique (an odd label for a seventeen year old) fell under the influence of another reformer, the Abbot of St. Cyran, about 1635.

Ever since he had been a college student, St. Cyran had been fast friends with a Dutchman named Cornelius Jansen. As college students sometimes do, Jansen and St. Cyran had dreamed of grand plans to reform all of God's Church—in terms of their own spiritual insights, of course. Realizing that many of those insights might be frowned upon by people less insightful than themselves, the two men even developed a secret code. There was a secret word meaning "grace," another for "sin" and another for "Jesuits" (whom they feared and disliked), and so forth. Basically, the plan was that Jansen would provide the theological principles for the great reform, while St. Cyran would take care of the practical side of things.

Jansen's theory, derived from an unusual way of interpreting St. Augustine's writings, might be described as a Catholic variation on Calvinist ideas. Original Sin, he said, had entirely corrupted human nature, to the extent that the human will was powerless to avoid sin. Only by means of divine grace could sin be avoided at all. Grace, in fact, was so powerful that humanity's will could not resist it, which is to say that humanity's free choice has no place in Jansen's theory. But grace, and the power to overcome concupiscence, were not given to all people. God did not will to save all people, and Christ did not die for all. Salvation was only for the chosen few.

In his dealings as spiritual director for Port-Royal, St. Cyran offered his own interpretation of Jansen's interpretation of Augustine's principles. The practical effects of Jansenism showed up in St. Cyran's instructions concerning Communion and penance. The Council of Trent had urged Catholics to receive Communion whenever they went to Mass, and had taught that Holy Communion purified the believer from their minor sins and helped them to avoid serious sin. But the view that prevailed at Port-Royal was that reception of Communion was a reward for a virtuous life. It was even more virtuous, however, to refuse a reward—such refusal constituted a supreme act of humility. Therefore, it was actually better to refuse Holy Communion than to accept it.

Under the leadership of St. Cyran and Mother Angelique, the desire to be more holy than the Church appeared in Port-Royal's penitential practices, as well. The Church, especially the Jesuits, called for frequent confessions, but the

Jansen's theory might be described as a Catholic variation on Calvinist ideas.

Jansenists tried to
restore the early
Church's practice of
confessing very rarely.

Jansenists tried to restore the early Church's
practice of confessing very rarely. Forgiveness
of sins was withheld until the penitent had
performed harsh penances sometimes over a
period of months. Since they believed that
there could be no forgiveness without a
perfect act of contrition, they went to great
lengths to perform penances of undeniable
severity—one famous Jansenist made a regular
habit of wearing a hairshirt that was made of
rough, scratchy material and was a torment to
the skin that it touched. More than a few of
the sisters at the convent, just as an act of
penance, would refuse to receive Holy
Communion. For the Jansenists, elitism was
not just an attitude, it was a highly refined art.

Both Jansen and St. Cyran died by 1643,
virtually unnoticed by the Church, and before
their ideas had spread to many people.
Jansen's ideas were published after his death
in a book entitled *Augustinus,* which did not
have a wide audience because it was long and
difficult to read. The movement might have
died with them had not Angelique Arnauld's
youngest brother, known as "the great
Arnauld," taken up his pen to further
Jansenist views. Upon reading a Jesuit priest's
advice in favor of frequent Communion,
Arnauld issued his own essay entitled
"Frequent Communion," that (in view of its
Jansenist sentiments) might have been better
titled "Infrequent Communion." The private
reform at Port-Royal was destined to become a
public issue.

The Jesuits and the
Jansenists were natural
enemies.

The Jesuits and Jansenists were natural
enemies. For the sons of Ignatius, schooled in
the *Spiritual Exercises,* humanity was essentially
good and grew through grace freely accepted;
for the hermits and sisters of Port-Royal,
humanity was essentially evil and the will was
enchained either by sin or by grace. The one
group would perfect the good by means of
frequent confession and Communion, the
other would chastise the elect with penances

and abstention from Communion. One enterprising Jesuit, disgusted with the Jansenists' attacks on his order, finally analyzed the *Augustinus*, reduced all the Jansenist teachings to five propositions, and submitted the five propositions to Pope Innocent X for his disapproval. Innocent obliged by condeming the five Jansenist propositions in an official decree in 1650.

Pope Innocent X condemned the five Jansenist propositions in an official decree in 1650.

Not to be outdone, the Jansenists accepted the condemnation but resorted to the tactic of denying that the five propositions had anything to do with Jansen's *real* doctrines, which they still upheld. After three more years of over-zealous lobbying, the Jesuits managed to get Pope Innocent's successor to issue yet another decree insisting that the condemned propositions were one and the same as Jansen's doctrine.

But by this time, Jansenist principles had spread to the society, and four bishops resisted the pope's decree. Further negotiations ensued during which nineteen other bishops backed their colleagues' actions. Finally, in 1665, a compromise was reached between the pope and the bishops. There followed a period of thirty years during which the Jansenists of Port-Royal enjoyed relative peace and prosperity, while the French Church fought another battle—a battle of Church and state.

It is significant that when the nineteen bishops supported the Jansenists, they gave the reason that resisting the papal decree was "for the good of the state." The French clergy had a long history of resentment of papal authority. And during these thirty years, their natural tendencies were augmented by the fact that the king, Louis XIV, was also struggling to confine papal influence.

It is significant that when the nineteen bishops supported the Jansenists, they gave the reason that resisting the papal decree was "for the good of the state."

Louis was an effective king. During his reign France prospered economically, and the king was able to extend the territory over which he ruled. Unfortunately, he then tried to take something that was not his—the pope's revenues. France had long enjoyed the right to collect revenues from sees where there was no bishop, until such time as the pope appointed one. Louis tried to extend his right to his newly conquered territories, but the pope balked. The king responded by convincing the French clergy to accept four propositions limiting papal authority in France. The pope then refused to appoint to a bishopric any candidate who accepted these four points, and when the controversy reached its height, more than thirty sees were vacant.

The king, at heart a loyal Catholic, stopped just short of schism, and in 1693, he withdrew his four propositions. But the resistance to papal intervention had become a fact of history—**Gallicanism** was born. The Gallicans, in France and elsewhere,[1] denied the personal infallibility of the pope, insisting that all questions should be decided by general councils or the consensus of all bishops. They tried to limit papal authority over temporal rulers, and insisted upon the independence of national Churches and bishops. Their attempt to make the Church a department of the state carried on into the eighteenth century.

Fortunately for France at this time, the king cast his final lot with the pope. Louis' personal life had been far from a model of moral purity, but late in life, as he tried to settle his accounts with God, he took very seriously his role as defender of the faith in France. Those shifty Jansenist heretics suddenly seemed all too prominent among the French nobility, and

1. Promotion of royal power to the detriment of papal power was common all over Europe, and the movement took different names in different countries. In Austria, there was a movement parallel to French Gallicanism, called "Josephism." Emperor Joseph passed six thousand decrees concerning religious life in the Empire, regulating every detail down to the number of candles to be lit during each Mass.

they could not be tolerated by Europe's most powerful monarch. It was time to act.

In 1710, Louis ordered every building at Port-Royal to be burned to the ground, and instructed the families of the deceased Jansenists to remove their relatives' bodies from the Port-Royal cemetery. The half-hearted followers of Jansenism quietly changed their views; they had no desire to become martyrs. The tiny remnant of the sect, made up mostly of elderly sisters by this time, limped away to the Netherlands to become a schismatic Church, one of the footnotes of the history books. A few remained to become a small persecuted sect in France, associated with the lower clergy. At Louis' urging, Pope Clement XI issued one last condemnation of the movement, and in the process the pontiff managed to add a few criticisms of the French Church's excessive independence for good measure.

Although the Jansenists were readily dismissed for their rather strange practices, and easily condemned for their dishonesty, they were, nevertheless, an important phenomenon in the history of the Church. For one thing, traces of their belief—especially their focus on humanity's sinfulness—lingered on as an undercurrent in Catholic thought, well into the twentieth century. On the other hand, the Jansenists were the last group within the Catholic Church to propose formally that humanity is fundamentally inclined toward sin. The Reformation era came to a close with Jansenism; after the seventeenth century, the focus was not upon humanity's sinful nature and the effects of divine grace, but upon humanity's natural powers, powers praised by people who denied the existence of grace altogether.

Although the Jansenists were readily dismissed for their strange practices, and easily condemned for their dishonesty, they were, nevertheless, an important phenomenon in the history of the Church.

Summary

- Seventeenth-century France saw the rise of an elitist group, the Jansenists.

- In the convents, the reform of France's women religious began under the leadership of teenage abbesses.

- Jansen's theory was a Catholic variation of Calvinism.

- Jansenism held that Communion and penance should not be used often.

- During this time, the French Church was struggling with the positions of Church and state.

- The Reformation Era came to a close with Jansenism.

Prayer

Let nothing disturb you,
Let nothing frighten you.
All things pass
God does not change.
Patience achieves everything.
Whoever has God lacks nothing.
God alone suffices.

Teresa of Avila

Discussion Questions

1. The chapter refers to the Jansenists as "elitist." Using your own knowledge or a dictionary, explain what elitism is. According to the chapter, what are the dangers that face an elitist group when it presses for reform?

2. What distinctive practices were developed at Port-Royal?

3. What differences of outlook explain why the Jansenists and Jesuits were natural enemies?

Section IV

The Church in the
Modern World

Introduction

After 1600 the Calvinists in Germany, who had been ignored by the Lutheran-Catholic settlement at the Peace of Augsburg in 1555, were growing in number and establishing control in some regions of Germany even though their religion was not legally recognized in the German Empire. War broke out in 1618, and the Calvinists banded together to resist the Catholic Emperor. There were thirty years of intermittent warfare from 1618 to 1648, with Luthern states and even the powers outside Germany becoming involved from time-to-time.

Although the Thirty Years' War began as a religious struggle, it became a matter of power politics. When the Catholic Emperor was triumphing in Germany in 1629, for example, Catholic France subsidized a Lutheran army in the attempt to thwart the Emperor. France's chief minister, a Catholic cardinal named Richelieu, was quite willing to aid the Lutherans if they could help him weaken a political rival who might threaten France's national interests. Religious considerations were being replaced by purely political motivations as the chief factor shaping policies in Europe.

Shortly after this war, a British mathematician named Isaac Newton broke new ground in the science of physics by explaining the movement of physical objects in terms of such concepts as gravity and inertia. In writing about his theories, Newton—a very pious man—resorted to an image to explain how God was related to the physical universe. God, he said, was like a watchmaker: He created the watch (the world), wound it up, and let it operate according to its own laws. Later students of Newton's theories could not fail to see the implications of the image, namely, that the workings of the physical world could be understood quite adequately without any reference to God at all.

The Thirty Years' War and the writings of Isaac Newton were symbolic of a fundamental shift in Western culture. Both in the realm of politics and in the realm of knowledge, religion was losing its central position. A new age was dawning which was at least indifferent to religion and, at times, openly hostile to it. Even more than Protestantism, Catholicism—still tied to the centuries-old tradition of a fully integrated Christian culture—was deeply threatened. The succeeding chapters will discuss the various ways in which the Church struggled to deal with the new situation.

VOLTAIRE.

Chapter Thirty-Three

The Rise of Secularism

The eighteenth century witnessed the beginning of a new era, characterized by a new set of values. These values have been given the label **secularism**—the tendency to reason about the world, about humanity, even about God with no reference to Christian revelation. The powers of human reason were greatly praised by the secular thinkers, and their movement came to be called the **Enlightenment** to distinguish the people who followed the "light" of reason out of the darkness of superstition and faith. In France, the proponents of the new view called themselves **philosophes,** that is, "the philosophers," with the clear implication that anyone who did not subscribe to their values did not deserve to be called a philosopher.

Secular thought pervaded all of Europe, but was centered in France, the cultural leader of the West. Its natural enemy was the Catholic Church, which had been a dominant force in French thought and culture since the time of Charlemagne and had long been the defender of traditional Christian values. But by the eighteenth century, French Catholicism was in poor health, an easy target for philosophe satirists, such as Voltaire. Its monasteries were havens for the nobility, its bishops were chosen by the king, usually for their noble blood rather than for nobility of spirit, and many of its intellectual leaders seemed content to repeat old formulas with little understanding of new developments.

Secularism—the tendency to reason about the world, about humanity, even about God with no reference to Christian revelation.

Enlightenment—secular thinkers who followed the "light" of reason out of the darkness of superstition and faith.

Philosophes—secular thinkers who believed that anyone who did not subscribe to their values did not deserve to be called true philosophers.

Events in seventeenth-century France had already shown how easily the Church's affairs could be complicated by a monarchical government that was convinced it should control the religious life of the country. Even the Jansenists, who had little popular support, were able to sidestep the condemnations of their doctrines by Rome, simply because the French Church and king were eager to thwart papal power no matter what the cost. The situation could only deteriorate when the French government came to be influenced by the ideas of the Enlightenment, which were not only anti-Roman but were even anti-Christian. The new state of affairs came to fruit in the expulsion of the Society of Jesus from France in 1764, and worked to its logical conclusion in 1793 during the French Revolution, when a revolutionary government guided by secular ideas first tried to control the Church, and finally set out to destroy the Church altogether.

The Enlightenment was in some respects a development of recent trends in Catholic thought.

Ironically, the Enlightenment was in some respects a development of recent trends in Catholic thought. Jansenism's bleak view of the corrupted nature of humanity was the only exception to the general tendency to believe that humanity's nature is basically good. The Jesuits, especially, spoke at great length to emphasize the good that humanity could achieve through humanity's own good nature. Some Jesuits even held that people could live the good life entirely on the strength of that nature, and needed divine grace only to be perfected in holiness.

The philosophes' tendency was to praise human powers and to discuss human nature with no reference to divine grace whatsoever.

The philosophes' tendency was to praise human powers, and to discuss human nature with no reference to divine grace whatsoever. They developed their secular view of humanity by portraying God as an impersonal force that had no clear relationship with humanity; by arguing for a natural law that had no basis in divine law; and by describing human beings "in themselves" as they could be understood through their actions, with no concern about their relationship to God.

Deism

The philosophes' view of God, sometimes called **Deism**, was utterly rationalistic. They would believe nothing that could not be established by human reason. Because there is order in the world, and there must be some kind of creative source of all beings that exist, they acknowledged the existence of a Supreme Being. But the Supreme Being, the *Deity*, was not a personal God, since the Christian concept of a loving God was drawn from revelation rather than from reason.

Also rejected was the Christian belief in divine providence,[1] which was based upon the idea of a personal God. **Voltaire's** book *Candide*, the most famous of the philosophes' satires against Christianity, poked fun at the idea of providence: a fool wanders through the rubble of deadly earthquakes, bloody battlegrounds, and so forth, muttering that "surely this is the best of all possible worlds." Near the end of the book, the fool asks a Moslem wise man about the state of the world; but the wise man contends that there is no point to such questions, and asks, "When His Highness sends a ship to Egypt, do you suppose he worries whether the ship's mice are comfortable or not?"[2] As far as God, "His Highness," is concerned, people have no more importance than mice on a ship.

The philosophes' view of God, sometimes called *Deism,* was utterly rationalistic.

Deism—Belief in an impersonal Supreme Being.

1. On the idea of providence, see the discussion of Augustine in chapter eight.

2. Voltaire, *Candide,* trans. John Butt (Baltimore: Penguin Books, 1967).

A New View of Human Law

The rational Supreme Being who ordered the universe could be the source of divine laws—such was acknowledged by the philosophe Baron de Montesquieu, author of the influential book *The Spirit of Laws*—but human laws exist alongside the divine, while conditions in the world varied greatly, and for this reason humanity needed to make their own individual laws to suit each set of circumstances. In the words of Montesquieu,

> *Law in general is human reason, inasmuch as it governs all the inhabitants of the earth: the political laws of each nation ought to be only the particular cases in which human reason is applied.*[3]

In this way, the secular thinkers created a theory that was nearly parallel to the medieval view of natural law. Individual written laws are specific applications of the natural law, which is grounded in human reason. But there was this one difference, that the medieval thinkers believed that natural law had to correspond to the divine law found in revelation, while the philosophes placed their confidence in reason by itself.

The other innovation of the philosophes was the idea that law exists to give order to society, not to make humanity better. In Catholic Christian thought, law was related to personal morality. Law was needed to encourage humanity to be morally good, so that humanity then could be perfected by grace and brought to eternal salvation. But to the philosophes, who were not concerned about salvation, society's progress was the highest value, and law existed to perfect the society.

In Catholic Christian thought, law was related to personal morality.

3. Montesquieu, *Spirit of Laws: Great Books of the Western World, vol. 38*, Robert M. Hutchens, ed. (Chicago: Encyclopedia Britannica, 1952), p. 3.

There was a variety of beliefs about how a lawful society might affect the individual person; but the idea of moral perfection was absent. The secular thinkers' rejection of the Christian view of morality can be seen in **Jean-Jacques Rousseau's** treatment of the greatest Christian rule of living. Speaking of humanity's natural instinct for self-preservation, he said,

> *Instead of that sublime maxim of reasoned justice, "Do unto others what you would have them do unto you," it inspires all men with this other maxim of natural goodness, much less perfect but perhaps more useful than the preceding one: "Do what is good for you with the least possible harm to others."[4]*

Law was a matter of crucial importance to the secular writers because it provided the means to curb humanity's most dangerous tendencies and allow society to move ever forward, toward a more perfect world on earth. The advance of humanity's knowledge and the improvement of living conditions in the Western world was unmistakable to any observer. The philosophes were so passionately devoted to furthering that progress that one historian has likened Enlightenment thought to a secular religion, which strove to create a heaven on earth.[5]

Jean-Jacques Rousseau— the forefather of modern people who, not satisfied with the Christian message of hope, look to political power as the one means of reaching a better future for all of humanity.

Law was a matter of crucial importance to the secular writers because it provided the means to curb humanity's most dangerous tendencies and allow society to move ever forward, toward a more perfect world on earth.

Human Nature

But the philosophes, having abandoned belief in Original Sin, so fundamental to Christian faith, were left to ponder the nature of humanity in new terms: what is humanity's

4. Jean-Jacques Rousseau, *The First and Second Discourses*, trans. Roger D. and Judith R. Masters (New York: St. Martin's Press, 1964), p. 133.

5. Carl L. Becker, *The Heavenly City of the Eighteenth-Century Philosophers* (New Haven: Yale University Press, 1932).

Not satisfied with the belief that had shaped Christian thought for seventeen hundred years, the philosophes could achieve no consensus on their own doctrine of humanity.

basic nature? The answer to this question was the key to determining just how perfectible human society might be. Not satisfied with the belief that had shaped Christian thought for seventeen hundred years, the philosophes could achieve no consensus on their own doctrine of humanity. They contradicted each other and were inconsistent within their own writings, as their views developed through the years.

The Protestant concept of human depravity was accepted by none of them. European explorers had returned from the Americas with tales of Indian tribes that lived happily and harmoniously with no apparent laws to guide them. This led to the idea of the "noble savage," uncorrupted by civilization, who lived in primitive purity; Indians were brought back to France so that French nobles and intellectuals could gawk at them during their parties, and wonder at the fine creatures which were humanity.[6] One leading philosophe, Denis Diderot, advanced the theory that human passions, the product of human's good nature, are basically good. A person can never do wrong by following his or her passions; evil arises only when a person reasons wrongly about the situations that are faced; teach people to reason better, give them sound laws as a guide, and evil can be all but eliminated.

Diderot's opinions had a large following, but ultimately were judged unsatisfactory by Voltaire and others, who were more impressed by the unending tale of "ravages and disasters" that they encountered in the history books. In his more optimistic moments,

6. It is a sign of the uncertainty about their own conclusions that the philosophes looked on the one hand to the unending progress of civilization, and at the same time saw civilization as a corrupting influence. Their belief in the "primitive harmony" within Indian society arose from their inability to recognize the unwritten laws that were shaping the Indians' social organizations.

Voltaire speculated that a person is born neither good nor bad, and is pushed toward either virtue or vice by the conditions of the world. But in the end, the conditions of the world seemed too overwhelmingly evil for the individual to overcome; the hero of *Candide*, after traveling all over the world, sees no better solution than to drop out of society and retire to an isolated garden-farm.

Having rejected the Christian message of hope based upon God's grace, Voltaire became the spiritual forefather of all modern people who have despaired of society and have chosen just to "tend their own garden." Jean-Jacques Rousseau, on the other hand, was the forefather of the other brand of modern people who, not satisfied with the Christian message of hope, look to political power as the one means of reaching a better future for humanity.

Like Diderot, Rousseau held that "natural man," man in himself is fundamentally good. Like Voltaire, he believed that social conditions have the power to incline a person toward good or evil. In his influential work of political theory, entitled *The Social Contract*, he built upon those two beliefs and drove to a radical, new conclusion: if throughout history an essentially good person has been corrupted by society, then society, by means of political power, has to make that person good again. The individual's personal will has to be subjected to the general will of the people, so that all humanity can be united in pursuing the common welfare of all.

Rousseau has been called one of the fathers of democratic political theory, because of his emphasis upon the people's will in government. Yet he has also been called the father of modern totalitarian political theory, because of his belief that the individual person must be subjected to the will of the powerful state. In Rousseau's *Social Contract*,

Voltaire—the spiritual forefather of all modern people who have despaired of society and have chosen just to "tend their own garden."

Rousseau has been called one of the fathers of democratic political theory because of his emphasis upon the people's will in government; yet he has also been called the father of modern totalitarian political theory because of his belief that the individual person must be subjected to the will of the powerful state.

the ideas of the philosophes ceased to be mere theories discussed by a few intellectuals, and came into the mainstream of history: for *The Social Contract* with its emphases upon the people's will and the state's power became the "bible" of the leaders of the violent French Revolution that turned Western politics upside down and nearly destroyed the Catholic Church.

Expulsion of the Jesuits

The philosophes had not gone unchallenged during their rise to prominence. Opposition came primarily from the Jesuits, whose years of university training in philosophy and theology made them virtually the only Catholics qualified to criticize Enlightenment thought.

The philosophes had not gone unchallenged during their rise to prominence. Opposition came primarily from the Jesuits, whose years of university training in philosophy and theology made them virtually the only Catholics qualified to criticize Enlightenment thought. The Jesuits tried to accommodate themselves to the latest theories, but of course they refused to reject Christian beliefs based upon revelation. They even managed to embarrass the philosophes in one instance. Denis Diderot edited a multivolume *Encyclopedia*, which included contributions from all the great representatives of the Enlightenment; the *Encyclopedia* was intended to be a monument to the broad scope of the philosophes' thought. But a Jesuit scholar named Berthier revealed that Diderot had stolen more than one hundred of his *Encyclopedia* articles from a Jesuit publication.

The philosophes were the darlings of French society.

This incident soured relations between the Society of Jesus and the philosophes, who were the darlings of French high society. The Jesuits were, generally, disliked in France, primarily because their strong loyalty to Rome ran against the current of Gallicanism. When a Jesuit mission in a French colony went broke and the Society refused to pay off the debts from the venture, a government inquiry was called, and every conceivable grievance that Frenchmen had against the Society was aired in public. It also did not help that the Jesuit confessor for King Louis refused to sanction the king's sexual liaison with Madame Pompadour, his mistress; the French monarch officially banned the Society in his country in 1764.

The Jesuits had already been suppressed in Portugal for similarly petty reasons, and after the French joined the movement there was increasing pressure upon Pope Clement XIII to disband the Society of Jesus completely. Clement resisted, but his successor (Clement XIV) who was not nearly as strong a pope, in 1773, without even attempting much by way of explanation, put the Society of Jesus out of existence. (They went underground, and were reconstituted as an order in 1814.)

The French Revolution

Thus after 1764, there was no one left in France to speak against the French habit of tying the Church to the state. When government mismanagement led to the calling of the Estates-General in 1789, the French priests (mostly commoners) joined the spokespeople of the middle class in calling for a new representative government, and with this act, the French Revolution began. The new government, however, was financially unstable, and there was hardly a murmur when the government voted to seize the Church's rich lands to pay off the nation's debts—the vote was, so to speak, an expression of the "general will," and the clergy were no less patriotic than other French people.

The revolutionary government reorganized the Church, closed some underpopulated parishes, and put the priests on government salary, and still there was no opposition. But there was furious resistance when the national assembly voted to deny all papal authority and make the bishops and priests elected civil officials. The government required clergymen to show acceptance of the new arrangement by

The revolutionary French government reorganized the Church, closed some underpopulated parishes, and put the priests on government salary.

taking an oath of loyalty, and nearly all the bishops and half the country's one hundred thousand priests became outlaws rather than give in.

While their fellow priests were going into hiding or fleeing the country, some priests still were willing to take the oath and work under the new regime; but there was hardly a clergyman in France who could agree to the government's most radical step, the execution of King Louis XVI in January of 1793. Leadership of the Revolution was now in the hands of radicals who were irrevocably committed to the secular ideals of the Enlightenment. There was really no place for the Church in the France of 1793.

The radicals' commitment to their cause was indeed irrevocable, as Austria and Prussia declared war on France to crush the democratic government that dared to execute a king. As the Austrians and Prussians drove closer to France, the revolutionaries resorted to desperate measures: church bells were melted down to make cannons, chalices that had held the consecrated Blood were melted down for their gold, and all conceivable enemies of the Revolution (including many priests) were sent to the guillotine. But in addition to desperation, the logic of secular thought was at work in the government's policies. The Year of Our Lord 1792 was renamed the Year One of the Revolution, and the Cult of Reason and the Cult of Nature were promoted, complete with ceremonies equivalent to a Mass, as well as a secular prayer equivalent to the Our Father.

The Year of Our Lord 1792 was renamed the Year One of the Revolution.

The Cult of Reason soon died out for lack of popular support, and Christianity was reestablished as the Revolution worked to its conclusion. The Church, however, was slow to recover in France, as so many of its leaders had fled or had been put to death, and seminaries had been closed for so long. The Church had learned some hard lessons in dealing with the children of the new secular philosophy, and for several generations, Catholic leaders were inflexibly opposed to the new ideas and the new governments that embodied those ideas. Secularism, in the meantime, did not die with the French Revolution, but rather assumed many new forms.

The Church in France was slow to recover, as so many of its leaders had fled or had been put to death, and seminaries had been closed for so long.

Summary

• Secular thought pervaded all of Europe, but was centered in France.

• French Catholicism was in poor health, an easy target for philosophe satirists, such as Voltaire.

• Secular thinkers created a theory that was nearly parallel to the medieval view of natural law.

• Opposition to the philosophes came primarily from the Jesuits.

• The French revolutionary government reorganized the Church, meeting with little resistance until the national assembly voted to deny papal authority and make bishops and priests elected officials.

Prayer

Jesus, I adore you and give you thanks for all the graces you have bestowed on me today. I offer you all the moments of this night and ask you to keep me without sin.

I place myself within your Sacred Heart and under the mantle of Mary, my Mother. Let your angels ever be at my side and keep me in peace.

St. Alphonsus Liguori

Discussion Questions

1. Explain what idea the leaders of the Enlightenment were promoting, and show how that idea led to an entirely new idea of what God is.

2. In your own words, explain what the difference is between Rousseau's teaching and Jesus' teaching about the basic rule for living.

3. What sorts of things were done to the Catholic Church during the period 1789–1794, by the revolutionary government?

PIVS IX

PONTIFEX MAXIMVS

Chapter Thirty-Four

Pius IX and the Struggle with the Liberals

The proclamation of the values of the Enlightenment in the French Revolution was not an isolated event. The call for equality, for representative institutions, and for freedom of expression became a widespread movement throughout Europe. In some countries, especially Great Britain, such values underlay the writings of learned men and eventually were adopted by nearly all branches of society, thanks largely to the power of newspapers (a relatively new phenomenon) to shape public opinion. The British were able to transform revolutionary values into law with scarcely any violence.

The call for equality, for representative institutions, and for freedom of expression became a widespread movement throughout Europe.

In other countries where monarchy was entrenched, however, the ideas that had arisen in France became the basis of a revolutionary creed. In the words of one historian, "France sneezed, and Europe caught cold," which is to say that the secular values and revolutionary creed of France spread throughout the Continent, reaching a crescendo in 1848 when every monarchy in Europe was threatened by a revolution.

Liberalism

The new values that were becoming the common secular religion of Europe were given the name **liberalism.** It was a coherent body of opinions built upon the fundamental notion that individuals should have the right to believe and behave as they choose so long as they harmed no one. The most important of the freedoms defended by liberalism was the freedom of religion—for the other freedoms (press, speech, etc.) meant little if there was not the freedom to believe whatever one chose about the most fundamental questions of human experience. Political liberalism, then, logically implied religious toleration.

Liberalism—belief that individuals should have the right to believe and behave as they choose, so long as they harm no one.

Political liberalism implied religious toleration.

As this creed increased in influence, the Christian Churches were on the defensive, and none more so than the Catholic Church. Partly it was a matter of historical circumstances; the Catholic Church naturally allied with the monarchies, because the kings traditionally had been protectors of the Church, and they represented order and stability where the revolutionaries all too often resorted to violence. But the Catholic Church was also a natural enemy of liberalism because Catholicism, more than other branches of Christianity, stood for orthodoxy upheld by authority.

In country after country, the fall of the monarchy and the rise of liberal government resulted in the closing of Catholic schools, convents, and even hospitals; the expulsion of the Jesuits as a symbolic act of defiance; and the adoption of liberal divorce laws over the protests of the Church, which had long prohibited divorce.

Europe's liberals were willing to tolerate anything except intolerance; thus the political creed that proclaimed religious freedom as the highest value gave birth to a most illiberal policy toward the Catholic Church. In country after country, the fall of the monarchy and the rise of liberal government resulted in the closing of Catholic schools, convents, and even hospitals; the expulsion of the Jesuits as a symbolic act of defiance; and the adoption of liberal divorce laws over the protests of the Church, which had long prohibited divorce.

All Europe was taken by surprise, then, when the Italian bishop who was elected as Pope Pius IX in 1846 had a reputation for having allowed liberal reforms in his diocese before becoming pope. The new pontiff lived up to his reputation by encouraging laymen to participate as consultants in the government of the Papal States, by creating an elective assembly to run the city government in Rome, and by devoting money to public works, such as, installation of gas lamps along the streets of Rome. Pius IX was an enormously popular pope, loved by the Italians and congratulated for his policies by the liberal governments of even the Protestant nations of Europe.

When all of the Continent erupted in revolution in 1848, many Italians dreamed of an uprising that would drive out foreigners and unite Italy as a nation. Italy was divided into little states, some of which were controlled by the Austrians. But the pope refused to lend his support to any violent overthrow, and the cooling of enthusiasm for Pius was exploited by radical revolutionaries, who flocked to Rome to create a political crisis. They incited mobs in the streets of the city, and finally murdered Pius' chief minister in an attempt to topple the papal government. Pius fled the city in November of 1848, and managed to return in 1850 only after Europe's governments, alarmed by the violence, had driven out the revolutionary forces.[1]

1. All the governments of Europe expressed alarm over the events in Rome, but it was France that sent an army to disperse the rebels. The French, the originators of liberal revolution, considered Italy's revolutionary leaders too extreme to be tolerated. The Italian radicals had brought soldiers from as far away as South America to bolster their forces against the pope.

Papal Domination within the Church

After 1848, Pius IX did not take an official stance in favor of either monarchy or liberalism. But not surprisingly he was the unbending foe of Italy's liberals and nationalists who, he realized, would stop at nothing in their drive to create a secular, liberal nation-state in Italy. At the same time, his governance of the Church promoted tendencies that seemed opposed to liberal values. He encouraged the world's bishops to visit Rome regularly; he chose theologians from all over the world to serve in the papal government, which had been dominated previously by Italians; and he directed the Church's widespread missionary activities. Pius was solidifying one-man leadership of a universal Church at the same time that democratic governments were prevailing in individual nations.

Ultramontanism—the pope is supreme head of the universal Church, with even more authority than the general council.

While the pope was establishing his primacy in the day-to-day workings of the Church, theorists in various countries were expounding the concept of **ultramontanism,**[2] which held that the pope is supreme head of the universal Church, with authority above that of even a general council; according to this reasoning, the pope could recognize no judge above himself. The triumph of this school of thought showed up in Pius' promulgation of the dogma[3] of the Immaculate Conception in 1854. At the urging of many bishops, the pope declared as orthodox Catholic teaching the belief that Mary was

2. The theory that says, in effect, that countries should look "across the mountain" to the authority of the pope, was first formulated by the Jesuit Cardinal Robert Bellarmine during the seventeenth century, and was consistently promoted by the Society of Jesus.

3. *Dogma* is any orthodox teaching.

conceived immaculate, that is, without the stain of sin. The belief itself was nothing new and, in fact, had been generally accepted by most Catholics before 1854; but the declaration was important because it was made solely by the pontiff without recourse to a general council.

Pius IX was also successful in overcoming the long-standing tendency for some countries' Churches to be almost independent of Rome's authority. Gallicanism in France and similar movements is Austria and Germany were a thing of the past. Further, the uniform rite of the Mass that had been established after the Council of Trent had been ignored for two centuries in favor of local practices; but under Pius IX, this resistance was finally overcome, and the Roman rite of the Mass was accepted throughout the world.

All these developments encouraged the ultramontanists, who called for a general council to proclaim the pope's infallibility as supreme teacher of Christian doctrine. Few Catholics resisted the idea that the pope is an infallible or unerring teacher in matters of faith and morals, but some theologians argued that an official declaration ought to be avoided at that time, because it would be inopportune, in light of European liberal governments' fears about extreme ultramontanism.

The ultramontanists called for a general council to proclaim the pope's infallibility as supreme teacher of Christian doctrine.

The Syllabus of Errors

While there was division of opinion within the Church, Pius was issuing a long series of official letters, called **encyclicals,** to combat the enemies outside the Church. Italy's liberal politicians were the chief targets of these letters. The opening lines of *Qui Pluribus*, one of the first of these encyclicals, typified the militant tone of the pope's attacks upon secular liberal thought: the enemies of

Encyclical—official letter to the faithful written by the pope.

Christian truth, he said, were "seized up by a certain blind force of mad impiety"; they were "blasphemers," characterized by a "rashness of thought."[4] In many cases, the substance of his documents were given little attention, as Pius' reputation for conservatism grew. Throughout Europe, he was jeeringly labeled "Giant Pope," the enemy of liberal reform.

Syllabus of Errors—
summary of the ideas
in the encyclical letters
of Pope Pius IX.

In 1864 the pontiff, at the request of the bishops of Italy, issued the **Syllabus of Errors,** a summary of ideas in the encyclical letters. In a note that accompanied the document, the Papal Secretary of State pointed out that the *Syllabus* was intended for bishops who desired a catalogue of Pius' previous condemnatory writings. But in spite of the technical nature of this catalogue, it was read by many Catholic and non-Catholic laypeople, and judged to be a sweeping condemnation of modern society.

Particularly dismaying to the general public was the eightieth condemned proposition, namely that "The Roman pontiff can and should reconcile himself to progress, liberalism, and the modern civilization." As it was worded, it seemed to reflect the pope's personal rejection of everything good in society. Further, by virtue of its position at the end of the document, proposition eighty appeared to be a summary of the entire series of condemnations.

In actuality, proposition eighty of the *Syllabus* was drawn from the letter to the government of Piedmont, in northern Italy. Piedmont's prime minister, a cold-blooded practitioner of power politics, had shut down Catholic convents and seminaries, claiming to do so *in the name of* "progress and modern civilization." Pius judged that relations between himself and this anticlerical prime

4. Pius IX, *Qui Pluribus* (November 9, 1846), in *The Sources of Catholic Dogma*, ed. by Henry Denzinger and trans. by Roy J. Deferrari (St. Louis: Herder, 1954), p. 410, no. 1634.

minister were ruined beyond repair, and thus had said in his letter that if this government's policies were true examples of modern progress and civilization, then the Roman pontiff could never be reconciled to such "progress." The outrage over this proposition in the *Syllabus* typified the popular misunderstanding of an essentially technical document. Several governments went so far as to disallow publication of the *Syllabus* in their countries.

The First Vatican Council

The First Vatican Council, the Church's first general council since Trent, convened just five years after the appearance of the *Syllabus*, and all of Europe held its breath in anxious anticipation of the result: the agenda called for a review of the Church's posture toward modern beliefs. In the light of recent developments, many observers were displeased by the prospect of a council, largely because the papacy seemed bent upon securing an official condemnation of the errors of the modern world.

The First Vatican Council convened just five years after the appearance of the *Syllabus,* and all of Europe held its breath in anticipation of the result.

As it turned out, the bishops at the council focused first upon the proposal for proclaiming the dogma of papal infallibility. Supporters of infallibility were in the majority, but the minority pursued its argument that a proclamation of the dogma was not appropriate at that time. Pius IX supported the proclamation, but was dismayed to see that the debates within the Vatican chambers were paralleled by pamphleteering and diplomatic maneuvering outside the council. There actually were Catholic opponents of infallibility who were sending messages from Rome to their governments, urging their leaders to send troops to disrupt the council before a vote on infallibility could take place.

But the vote did take place, and the new dogma was proclaimed: a pope, speaking *ex cathedra* (from the Chair of Peter), was infallible in making pronouncements concerning faith and morals. Most Catholics' loyalty to the pope was so strong that virtually everything that the pope had said before the Council's proclamation in 1870 had been accepted as absolutely true, and in light of this tendency the promulgation (announcement) of the dogma at Vatican I could be interpreted as limiting, not increasing, the pope's authority as a teacher; for now his pronouncements had to be accepted as true only when certain special conditions are fulfilled. Indeed, Pius IX himself wrote to assure the leaders of Europe that the new dogma was not a threat to the established order in Europe, but to no avail.[5] To a society that upheld the liberal ideals of religious toleration and representative government, the belief in an infallible successor of Peter was simply too foreign to accept.

> Vatican I could be interpreted as limiting, not increasing, the pope's authority because now his pronouncements only have to be accepted as true when certain special conditions are fulfilled.

Once the discussion of infallibility had ended, the council turned to other questions. But before much more could be discussed, Vatican I was brought to an abrupt halt by unforeseen developments. The armies of the new German Empire were inflicting heavy losses upon the French in the Franco-Prussian War. The French had so great a need for reinforcements that they withdrew their forces that had been in Rome, protecting the papacy since 1850.

5. Pius stated that "It is a pernicious error to represent infallibility as containing the right to depose sovereigns and to free people from their oath of allegiance." This has been done by previous popes, but "Only bad faith can confuse facts that are so different and epochs that are so little alike." The only infallible pronouncement by a pope since 1870 was Pius XII's promulgation, in 1950, of the dogma of the Assumption of the Blessed Virgin Mary.

King Victor Emmanuel of Piedmont had, during the previous decade, united under his leadership all of Italy except for the Papal States. Now that the French were gone, Victor Emmanuel saw that his hour had come. He issued an ultimatum to the pope, which Pius rejected. The pontiff gave a quiet farewell benediction to his small army, and Victor Emmanuel's forces began bombarding Rome. The First Vatican Council ended with its work unfinished, as the bishops fled the city to save their lives.

The First Vatican Council ended with its work unfinished, as the bishops fled the city to save their lives.

Prisoner of the Vatican

The last eight years of Pius IX's pontificate can be summed up in two symbolic acts. Europe's reaction to Vatican I was expressed in the "Kulturkampf," the "culture struggle," proclaimed by Germany's Chancellor Otto von Bismarck in 1872. Catholic monasteries and educational institutions were closed down throughout Germany, as Bismarck issued an oft-quoted statement:

> *After the dogmas of the Roman Catholic Church which have been recently promulgated, it will not be possible for a secular government to conclude a concordat (treaty) with the papacy, unless that government effaces itself to the last degree and in a way to which the German Empire at least will not consent. Do not be apprehensive. We will not go to Canossa, either bodily or spiritually!*[6]

6. Bismarck's statement is quoted in J. B. Bury, *The History of the Papacy in the Nineteenth Century* (New York: Schocken, 1964 [1908]), p. 160. Bismarck in his famous speech refers to Canossa, where Germany's King Henry IV was humiliated by Pope Gregory VII in 1077; see chapter sixteen of this text for details.

Pius, meanwhile, became the self-proclaimed "prisoner of the Vatican," from 1870 to his death in 1878. To the end, he refused to acknowledge the authority of his conqueror, Victor Emmanuel. To demonstrate his resistance he never budged from the Vatican for eight years. Pius IX's thirty-two year pontificate, the longest in the Church's history, had raised the papacy to greater spiritual authority than had been achieved by even the great Innocent III at the height of the Middle Ages. But Innocent had ruled a single Church, in a society that was entirely Catholic, at least in its avowed beliefs. For all its powers, the modern papacy was still struggling to deal with a world that was non-Catholic and even anti-Catholic in some respects. It was left up to Pius IX's successor, Leo XIII, to lead the Church into a new approach to a world that was becoming at best indifferent, and at worst hostile, to Catholic Christianity.

Summary

• Liberalism was the new secular religion of Europe.

• The Church was a natural enemy of liberalism.

• Pope Pius IX solidified the one-man leadership of the universal Church at the same time that democratic governments prevailed in individual nations.

• The First Vatican Council declared that the pope, when speaking *ex cathedra* (from the chair of Peter), was infallible when teaching about faith and morals.

• The First Vatican Council ended with its work unfinished.

Prayer

O Jesus, who came into this world to bring your grace to all souls, we beseech you to pour your Spirit on all souls so that those in the state of mortal sin may, in returning to you, find the life of grace they lost.

St. Pius X

Discussion Questions

1. What are the values associated with liberalism? Why did the Catholic Church oppose liberalism at first?

2. What event helped to make Pius IX an opponent of liberalism?

3. Why did Vatican I define the powers of the pope, but accomplish very little else?

Woman working in a coal mine.

Chapter Thirty-Five

Leo XIII: The Church's Witness to the Modern World

When Pius IX died in 1878, all Europe waited to see what kind of man would succeed him at the Vatican. The cardinals' conclaves are generally kept secret, but it appears that after several ballots, there was a deadlock between those who desired a pope on the model of Pius, and those who sought a leader who was more sympathetic to the modern culture. At last a compromise candidate came into view: Bishop Joachim Pecci, who was known to be loyal to Pius IX, but was not a dyed-in-the-wool opponent of modern trends. Pecci was the ideal candidate, since he was sixty-eight years old, rather frail, and likely to die within several years. Each side could support him, hoping that by the time the old fellow passed away, their own faction would be strengthened enough to dominate the next papal election.

But God, it would seem, had a sense of humor. For frail old Bishop Pecci, who became Pope Leo XIII, lived to be ninety-three years old; and by his letters on papal teachings—the most famous of which was issued when he was eighty-one years old—he brought about a revolution in the Catholic Church's position in the modern world.

Leo XIII preserved
Pius IX's policy of
speaking out against
the worst tendencies
in modern thought
and action.

Leo XIII preserved Pius IX's policy of speaking out against the worst tendencies in modern thought and action, but Pius' successor recognized that the Catholic Church had to be an eloquent witness to Christian values in the secular world that had come into being during the past one hundred years. While not a supporter of the liberal faith in a "free marketplace of ideas," Leo still was convinced that if the Church carefully explained its teachings, which seemed so strange in a non-Catholic world, honest people would have to acknowledge the reasonableness of Catholic beliefs.

> *For as is often said, with the greatest truth, there is nothing so hurtful to Christian wisdom as that it should not be known, since it possesses, when loyally received, inherent power to drive away error. So soon as Catholic truth is apprehended by a simple and unprejudiced soul, reason yields assent.*[1]

On the other hand, scarcely anyone was in a mood to hear what a pope had to say, and Leo perceived the need to extend a hand of friendship to the world. Many of the new pope's policies contributed to the feeling that he sought a warming of relations between the Church and the nations of Europe, such as his practice of having papal documents translated from Latin into vernacular languages, so that they could more readily be read. In 1881, to the surprise of all, Leo overrode opposition within the papal government and ordered the opening of the secret archives (records) of the Vatican, with the comment that "We have

1. Leo XIII, the encyclical letter *Sapientiae Christianae*, art. 15. Underlying this statement is the traditional Catholic belief in the inherent goodness of humanity, as well as the conviction that Catholic doctrine is based upon the natural law, which can be comprehended by any reasonable person.

nothing to fear from the publication of documents." At the pope's invitation, most of the nations of Europe began supporting scholars who took up residence in Rome so that they could use the Vatican's rich treasure of historical documents.

Most notably it was the pope's diplomatic efforts that drew attention, particularly in his dealings with the German government. Leo's diplomacy complemented the growing power of Germany's Catholic political party in bringing about the end of the Kulturkampf. After seeking to reestablish communications with the German government in 1880, Leo received Ambassador Kurd von Schlozer at the Vatican in 1882, after a lapse of ten years.

Papal Encyclicals

But the hallmark of Leo XIII's twenty-five-year pontificate was not his success as a diplomat or his promotion of learning; it was his writing of the encyclical letters, which brought Christian principles to bear upon the social and political concerns of his times. Earlier popes generally had written encyclical letters to individual bishops who sought their advice on contemporary problems in their own countries. Leo addressed his encyclicals to all bishops, and by publishing the letters in all languages demonstrated that he was writing for all people of good will. The encyclicals emerged as a new type of papal publication: reflections upon social questions, in which Christian teachings were applied to the specific problems of a specific time in history. Following Leo XIII's lead, the popes of the twentieth century have issued many such letters and, in some instances, they have modified their predecessors' teachings to meet ever-changing social conditions.

At the pope's invitation, most of the nations of Europe began supporting scholars who took up residence in Rome so that they could use the Vatican's rich treasure of historical documents.

The hallmark of Leo XIII's pontificate was his encyclical letters, which brought Christian principles to bear upon the social and political concerns of his times.

Pope Leo XIII's writings touched a wide variety of subjects, such as the Christian view of marriage, the value of praying the rosary, and the usefulness of St. Thomas Aquinas' philosophy.

Diuturnum—Pope Leo XIII's encyclical contending that all political authority comes from God and, therefore, revolution against a legitimate ruler could not be condoned by the Church, but at the same time acknowledging that the people have the right to choose their own leaders.

The Church was not officially in favor of monarchy, but rather was indifferent to the forms that governments assumed, so long as political authority was respected.

Immortale Dei— encyclical by Leo XIII that addressed the proper relationship between Church and state.

Pope Leo's writings touched a wide variety of subjects, such as the Christian view of married life, the value of praying the rosary, and the usefulness of St. Thomas Aquinas' philosophy. But best remembered are his encyclicals that offered a Catholic response to liberalism.

In the encyclical **Diuturnum,** in 1881, he contended that Catholics could not accept the common theory that all political authority comes from the people; on the contrary, all political authority comes from God and, therefore, revolution against a legitimate ruler could not be condoned by the Church. At the same time, he acknowledged that the people have the right to choose their own leaders.[2] The Church was not officially in favor of monarchy, but rather was indifferent to the forms that governments assumed, so long as political authority was respected.

In 1885, the letter **Immortale Dei** addressed the question of the proper relation between Church and state. Like *Diuturnum, Immortale Dei* was intended to do away with fears that the Catholic Church aimed to dominate Western society as it had done during the Middle Ages, or support Catholic monarchies that would deny religious freedom. Church and state, Leo insisted, were separate spheres, each created by God and each natural to humanity; neither sphere should dominate the other, but ideally each should support the other.

The pope held that in the ideal state, the government would protect the people's best interests by supporting the Catholic Church, but he recognized that this was all but impossible in most countries. For this reason, in *Immortale Dei* Leo did not condemn religious toleration, but he warned that the

---

2. In other words, the people can select their leaders democratically, but it does not follow from the act of choosing that authority comes from the people.

pitfall of a truly secular state was that it promoted indifference toward all religion, which was harmful to both the spiritual and the political welfare of the people. Catholics, then, had a duty as citizens to be actively involved in political affairs, to support laws that were compatible with the natural law and the divine law.

The effect of these and similar writings was to initiate a change in the Church's image. Catholic intellectuals and political leaders, in particular, were recognizing that even though the Church was independent of recent intellectual trends, it was not the inflexible ally of monarchy nor the foe of liberalism in all respects. Leo's most famous encyclical letter, **Rerum Novarum** of 1891, carried the process further, by establishing the Church as the protector of the poor and powerless in society. *Rerum Novarum* was also unique in being widely read and even praised by all Western peoples, even non-Catholics. It had such tremendous impact because it offered a thoughtful response to the greatest social problem of the century.

Rerum Novarum— encyclical by Pope Leo XIII establishing the Church as the protector of the poor and powerless in society.

Capitalism vs. Socialism

The Industrial Revolution had dramatically increased the wealth and productive capacity of the Western nations. But it had also been a source of misery for millions of people, as the wealth was concentrated in the hands of relatively few businessmen. The great mass of workers labored for low wages in factories where working conditions were appallingly bad, and hours were long. Fourteen- and sixteen-hour days were common, six- and seven-day work weeks were typical. Families could not survive on the father's wages, and women and young children had to toil alongside the men. The ingenious machines, which increased productive capacity, also maimed many fatigued laborers, and there was no provision for relief for these victims of the all-consuming drive toward ever-higher levels of production.

Living in cities that had not expanded quickly enough to meet an increase in population, the workers were driven to desperate measures. Some members of the working class resorted to strikes to force their employers to grant higher wages, but these efforts were forbidden by law, since the governments of Europe were dominated by the wealthy people of the upper class. The owners denied responsibility for the workers' plight, on the grounds that the existing conditions were the product of "iron laws of nature."

The owners' viewpoint was summed up in the principles of economic liberalism (sometimes called "capitalism" or "free enterprise"), which paralleled political liberalism. Economic liberalism was founded upon the belief in the value of private property and private interest. Thanks to a competitive free market, individuals' pursuit of their private interests results in the common good: the producers self-interestedly produce the best possible goods at the lowest possible price, as self-interested consumers buy the best products on the market for the lowest possible price; thus, according to the theory, competition favors all.

In competition for jobs, laborers had to work for the lowest possible price.

But in the competition for jobs, the laborers have to work for the lowest possible price, and it is only natural that wages should be low. Some liberal thinkers even theorized that in a competitive world that has limited resources, some people would naturally starve. The capitalist businessman could not overrule nature: if he tried to give his employees better wages, he would have to raise the price of his products, and could not sell those products in a competitive market. According to the theory of economic liberalism, then, the workers' plight was "natural," and there was little reason to hope that conditions would improve.

Faced with this line of reasoning, the workers lent a willing ear to anyone who offered them the prospect of bettering their conditions. Not surprisingly, in the second half of the nineteenth century the working class was attracted by the new theory of socialism, best expressed by the German intellectual, Karl Marx. Marx's theory was in most respects the exact opposite of economic liberalism, of which it was a harsh critique. But like economic liberalism, socialism described the crisis of Western society in terms of iron laws of nature.

Marx rejected private property in favor of collective ownership of all goods by all people. Private interest and private property had to be rejected, said Marx, because they make possible the owners' exploitation of the workers. In fact, the capitalist owners are using the existing power structures in society to exploit the workers: laws hold the workers down, and religion, the "opium of the masses," deceives the working class by convincing them to accept their suffering and look forward to heaven. The only possible solution is to reject political authority, reject religion, and overturn the power structures by means of violent revolution. Revolution can create a classless society, in which the working people can have their just share of the world's goods—a virtual heaven on earth.

The confrontation between workers and owners in Europe, thus, was expressed in terms of two conflicting views of "iron laws of nature": one group asserted that inequality and suffering were inevitable, while the other contended that all history was the history of class struggle. The theoretical opposition was, in fact, leading to open conflict within Western society during the 1880s, as mass strikes and spontaneous outbursts of violence by the workers were becoming more common, and the socialist parties that advocated class warfare were rapidly gaining in numbers.

Groups of Catholic workers made pilgrimages to Rome, to ask the pope for advice in resolving the great social issue of the day. In his first efforts, Leo made blunders; but by 1891 he had developed his own distinctive approach to social problems. By the pope's own design *Rerum Novarum* was released to the public at about the same time that Europe's socialists were beginning an international congress to discuss their revolutionary doctrine.

The Encyclical, *Rerum Novarum*

Rerum Novarum was a landmark in the history of Catholic thought because it developed a coherent social theory out of the Christian tradition of natural and divine law, without being limited by the secular presuppositions of liberal individualism or Marxist collectivism. With a solid base in Christian principles, the pope was able to reject collectivism on the grounds that it ignored individual dignity and rights, but also reject individualism on the grounds that it ignored social responsibility. At the same time, he felt free to borrow insights from both schools of thought.

The pope rejected collectivism on the grounds that it ignored individual dignity and rights, but also rejected individualism on the grounds that it ignored social responsibility.

Marxism—collective ownership of all goods by all people.

The opening paragraphs of the encyclical, for example, criticized **Marxism** on the grounds that it denied the basic human right to private property. Humanity is free, said Leo—not bound by "iron laws"—but cannot exercise free will unless the means are available to carry out individual decisions. Private ownership allows greater freedom of choice to the individual, by allowing the individual to plan independently for the future. Further, it is natural to raise a family, but a family cannot be provided for unless the head of the family has control over his or her own property.

Socialism stands condemned on other grounds, too—it misrepresents the true nature of religion, and advocates class warfare that is contrary to God's commandment that people should love one another.

Having employed the liberal belief in private property against the socialists, Leo XIII then turned that same belief against economic liberalism. All people have a right to private property; it is not the exclusive right of the rich. The workers' individual rights are violated when employers pay such low wages that the workers cannot support themselves or their families. When competition drives wages down, the workers "freely" agree to accept low wages, but (just as the socialists claimed) this arrangement amounts to exploitation of the laborers. Justice calls for a wage high enough to allow each worker to survive, because self-preservation is a natural human right. Free competition can be good, but justice is a higher good.

Upon this theoretical framework, the pope offered several practical suggestions that surprised his readers. Business owners should confer with their employees about wages, in the spirit of human community, and workers should band together in associations, such as unions, to protect their fundamental rights. Strikes are to be avoided, but if owners refuse to act justly, strikes are an acceptable last resort for the workers. The state, which represents the common good, has a responsibility to intervene in labor disputes if necessary, to protect the rights of the weak.

Public reaction to *Rerum Novarum* was immediate, and generally favorable. Over the twenty years following publication of the encyclical, Leo's teachings were incorporated into the laws of many Western nations. Catholics, meanwhile, began to create workers' organizations and mutual-aid societies for workers, and Catholic political parties adopted

Socialism misrepresents the true nature of religion, and advocates class warfare that is contrary to God's commandment that people should love one another.

All people have a right to private property; it is not the exclusive right of the rich.

Free competition can be good, but justice is a higher good.

Public reaction to *Rerum Novarum* was immediate, and generally favorable.

the pontiff's ideas for their own political platforms. Members of the Church became so caught up with experiments in social and political action that Leo had to write a second encyclical ten years after *Rerum Novarum*, to offer more guidelines to his flock. Catholic political parties have, with varying degrees of success, been a factor in European politics right up to the present.

Catholic political parties have, with varying degrees of success, been a factor in European politics right up to the present.

The implications of *Rerum Novarum* and the encyclicals on politics were enormous. With a distinct social message and a call for Christians to become involved in political affairs, the Catholic Church was reaffirming the value of life in the secular world, presenting in new terms the old belief that Christians have a responsibility to remake the City of Man in the image of the City of God.

Furthermore, the secular world is the proper sphere of action for the layperson, rather than the priest; thus the inherent value of the lay Christian's life was being promoted against the persistent feeling that the priestly or religious life was superior. The increasing value attributed to the layperson's calling was ultimately to bring about a fundamental shift in the very idea of what constitutes "the Church," but this change was not fully recognized until the Second Vatican Council of the 1960s.

Summary

• Pope Leo XIII spoke out on issues, believing that the Catholic Church had to be a witness to Christian values in the secular world.

• Many of Pope Leo's policies sought a warming of relations between the Church and the nations of Europe.

• The pope addressed the issue of proper relations between Church and state in the encyclical *Immortale Dei*.

• The Industrial Revolution, while dramatically increasing the wealth and productive capacity of the Western nations, also contributed to poor working conditions and low wages for the working class.

• Many of the poor working class were a willing audience for Karl Marx's theory of collective ownership of all goods by all people.

• Pope Leo's encyclical, *Rerum Novarum*, was a landmark in the history of Catholic thought.

Prayer

Certainly, the well-being which is so longed for is chiefly to be expected from an abundant outpouring of charity; of Christian charity, we mean, which is in epitome the law of the Gospel, and which, always ready to sacrifice itself for the benefit of others, is humanity's surest antidote against the insolence of the world and immoderate love of self; the divine office and features of this virtue being described by the apostle Paul in these words: "Charity is patient, is kind . . . is not self-seeking . . . bears with all things . . . endures all things."

Pope Leo XIII
Rerum Novarum

Discussion Questions

1. Explain briefly what an encyclical is, and what kinds of problems Pope Leo XIII addressed in the encyclicals.

2. Why could it be said that economic liberalism (capitalism) was good for business, but not so good for workers?

3. What practical steps did Leo XIII propose to protect the interests of workers?

POPE LEO XIII.

Chapter Thirty-Six

The New Approach to Biblical Scholarship

Changing Times

It was unmistakably clear that life in Europe and the United States during the nineteenth century was vastly different from that of the seventeenth century or even the eighteenth. Technology was changing life in the Western nations: telegraphs, railroads, canals, steamships, street lamps, printing presses, and other devices were changing the way people lived and the way they perceived their world. Accordingly, intellectuals were caught up with the phenomenon of change, and with the changes in their own culture. This new concern was taking widely differing forms, such as Darwin's and Mendel's examinations of the transformation in species of animals, and historians' bold interpretations of the rise and fall of races and nations throughout history.

The foremost thinkers within the Church were no exception to the trend. In England, for example, the leading scholar at Oxford University, John Henry Newman, converted from Anglicanism to Catholicism shortly after writing a monumental treatise entitled, *An Essay on the Development of Christian Doctrine.* Newman analyzed the changes in Christian teachings over the centuries, and concluded that the Catholic Church's development of

Life in Europe and the United States during the nineteenth century was vastly different from that of the seventeenth and eighteenth centuries.

doctrine was consistent with the sayings of Jesus and the beliefs of the first apostles in all respects.

But, in general, the very idea of a historical examination of Christianity was viewed with suspicion. The infallibility of the Church, and the truths of sacred Scripture, were guaranteed by the Holy Spirit; to suggest that ancient teachings or biblical passages had been affected by historical circumstances seemed dangerous.

Further, while it was true that the Church had carried on a dialogue between its own beliefs and non-Christian beliefs through the centuries, the situation in the nineteenth century seemed quite different. The early Christians, for example, had challenged the Greek and Roman pagans, and critically borrowed their ideas. But the pagans were an essentially religious people whose ideas shared at least some assumptions in common with the Christian religion. But the anti-Christian thought of modern times was even anti-religious—secular, worldly in its fundamental outlook. How could there be any basis for dialogue between radically different understandings of reality?

What were Christians to say, for instance, about the theories of Darwin, which seemed to offer an explanation of the development of humanity and the beasts that was not compatible with the Genesis story?[1] Indeed, the non-Christian thinkers themselves saw the

1. Since the time that Charles Darwin first presented his theory of natural selection in 1859, the theory of evolution has risen to be a kind of scientific "orthodoxy." During the twentieth century, the French Catholic scholar, Pierre Teilhard de Chardin, put together a Christian theology that incorporated the concept of evolution. Although not well received by Church officials, Teilhard's writings have been widely read in Catholic universities.

conflict in precisely the same way. The writings of Auguste Comte, the father of modern sociology, provide just one example of many secular views of Christian thought. This mid-nineteenth-century writer categorized historical time according to three stages: the age of religion, followed by the age of philosophy, that finally gave way to the age of science. Primitive, ignorant people had relied upon religion to explain what they saw in the world. As people became more sophisticated, they relied upon philosophy to explain reality, and now that they had the benefits of science and could develop their rational abilities to the fullest, there was no more need for religion or philosophy.

The writings of Auguste Comte, the father of modern sociology, provide just one example of many secular views of Christian thought.

It was inevitable that Christians would eventually undertake the task of critical borrowing from the thought of the times, for it has always been the Church's mission to "restore all things in Christ." The Church could not allow the secular culture to develop entirely apart from the Church, but rather had to "baptize" the healthy insights from the thought of the age, just as Leo XIII had done with socialism and liberalism in *Rerum Novarum*. But in some fields of study this task could be undertaken only with great pain and understandable hesitation.

The Church could not allow the secular culture to develop entirely apart from the Church.

Interpretation of Scripture

The issue came to a head in the study of the Bible. The Protestant intellectuals, who had not been the chief target of secular thinkers in the past and thus were less suspicious of contemporary thought, began to interpret Scripture by means of modern methods of historical analysis. Many branches of Protestantism rejected (and today still reject) this approach in favor of **fundamentalism,** a belief in the literal, factual accuracy of every line of Scripture; this school of thought

Fundamentalism—belief in the literal, factual accuracy of Scripture on every single point, regardless of historical and scientific evidence.

insisted, among other things, that creation of the world took place when God labored for six days, regardless of what scientists might contend. But during the 1800s, a number of Protestant scholars began treating the Bible as a book whose authors were influenced by the cultural and historical circumstances in which they wrote. They also employed literary evidence to draw new conclusions about the sacred texts, and a small number of Catholics followed suit.

Questions were raised, for example, about the traditional belief that the first five books of the Old Testament were written by Moses. The language used, as well as the questions which Genesis, Exodus and the other books seemed designed to answer, pointed to the possibility that the five books were composed several centuries after the death of Moses.

Similarly, new conclusions were drawn from the study of the Gospels. Before the nineteenth century, the Gospels had been considered to be parallel accounts of Jesus' life and work. But students of Scripture were struck by the difficulty of reconciling John's account with the other three, and John came to be seen as a later work that recast the events of Jesus' life in an attempt to emphasize certain truths of the faith. In the effort to sort out the parallels between Matthew, Mark and Luke, Karl Lachmann advanced the opinion in 1835 that Mark was the oldest Gospel; Lachmann was challenging St. Augustine's long-respected opinion that Matthew was written first.

More startling were the assertions in David Friedrich Strauss' *Life of Jesus*, which also appeared in 1835. Most of the scholars like Lachmann were faithful men who were attempting to unravel the mysteries of the texts that were the source of their beliefs, but the same cannot be said for Strauss. His work attracted great attention because he rejected all that was supernatural in the Gospel narratives—Strauss dismissed John's Gospel completely, as having no historical value—and portrayed Christ as a clever Jewish leader.

The views of Strauss and others like him prompted a condemnation by Pope Pius IX, but rationalist interpretations of the Bible continued to appear alongside more solid efforts. Ernst Renan's *Life of Jesus*, for instance, a work quite similar to Strauss' *Life of Jesus*, was published in 1863, and 50,000 copies of the book were sold within six months. It appeared that rationalist views were creeping into the very heart of Christian belief, and were gaining a large audience.

The views of Strauss and others like him prompted a condemnation by Pope Pius IX.

Rationalist views were creeping into the very heart of Christian belief.

What had been done with the Scriptures was soon attempted with the teachings of the Church, too. Louis Duchesne of the University of Paris and his outspoken student, Alfred Firmin Loisy, argued that Catholic teachings reflect the historical circumstances in which they arise; far from being infallible, they had to be reinterpreted for each age in history, to be brought into line with contemporary philosophical and scientific insights. Duchesne bowed to authority and retracted his views, but Loisy simply shifted his emphasis and argued for a rationalist reinterpretation of Scripture. Loisy continued his work at a Catholic institute of studies in France, and had the support of his colleagues as well as his superiors.

Pope Leo XIII decided that it was necessary to respond to Loisy with the encyclical letter *Providentissimus Deus*, issued in 1893. Not content simply to condemn Loisy's approach, Leo offered guidelines for the study of the sacred texts. The words of the Bible, he said, "are wrapped in a certain religious obscurity," so that no one can enter them without a guide. While affirming the belief that traditional Catholic teaching was the best guide for proper understanding of the Bible, he gave a

Pope Leo XIII responded to Loisy with the encyclical, *Providentissimus Deus*, issued in 1893.

cautious endorsement to the scholarly methods developed by the Protestant interpreters. Study of Greek and the Semitic languages, he said, is essential; attention should be paid to the use of figurative language in Scripture, and scholars should always remember that the human authors of the Bible were writing in the language of the common people of their times, not in the language of a modern scientist or historian.

Loisy and about half a dozen other men from various parts of Europe were not daunted by a warning from the pope, however. They continued to publish their ultrarationalist interpretations of Scripture and Church doctrines until Leo's successor, Pius X, issued a harsh and sweeping condemnation of their views in 1907.

Modernism

Modernism—heresy that claimed that the Bible and the Church teachings had to be reinterpreted for each age in history.

Pope Pius X declared modernism to be the most dangerous of all the heresies, because it struck at the very roots of all doctrine.

The new pontiff gave these teachings the label **modernism** and declared it to be the most dangerous of all the heresies that Christianity has ever faced: earlier heresies had attacked specific doctrines, but modernism struck at the very roots of all doctrine. In keeping with his desire to eliminate this threat, the pope called for the entire Church to be on guard against even a tendency toward modernism, and the instructions were carried out vigorously by bishops, directors of seminaries, and leaders of Catholic universities.

As a result, anything that resembled the methods of Scripture study developed by the Protestant scholars was viewed with disfavor by Catholic authorities. Shortly before his death in 1903, Leo XIII had announced the formation of a papal commission for the study of the Bible, and this plan was carried out by Pius X. But it is a sign of the state of Catholic biblical scholarship that during the first decade of the twentieth century, the commission took the position that Moses was the author of the **Pentateuch** (the first five books of the Old Testament), and that Genesis contained a factual account of the events of Creation.

Pentateuch—the first five books of the Old Testament.

Modern methods of Scripture study were finally given official endorsement by Pope Pius XII in 1943, and were promoted during the decades that followed by Cardinal Bea, an influential leader at the Vatican. After years of hesitation and mistrust of historical-critical methods of analysis, Catholic scholars joined their Protestant colleagues in the effort to gain new insights into sacred Scripture. Among their achievements have been *The Jerusalem Bible,* a precise translation by a team of French Catholics, and the massive *Jerome Biblical Commentary,* in which students from all over the world contributed articles about a wide variety of scriptural topics.

Modern methods of Scripture study were finally given official endorsement by Pope Pius XII in 1943.

The new approach to biblical research might be illuminated by the example of the parting of the Red Sea, in Exodus, chapter fourteen. A fundamentalist would contend that Moses actually raised his arm so that the Lord would send a wind and part the sea, allowing the Israelites to pass between two walls of water. A rationalist would argue that the entire event can be explained by means of a natural phenomenon, such as a low tide, if indeed the event really took place at all; the story is an example of a superstitious biblical tale that no rational person should accept. A modern critic would suggest that the Exodus account is based upon an actual event, and that the story was embellished over many years of retelling, before it was put into written form. But there is no harm in stripping away the miraculous elements of the story, because the person of faith can grow with the knowledge that God aids His people in nonmiraculous ways, being the Lord of nature. The methods that have been employed, at times, to undermine the very idea of revelation are now being used to promote faithful interpretation in a new way.

Summary

- During the nineteenth century, life in Europe and the United States was changing.

- Protestant intellectuals began to interpret Scripture by means of modern methods of historical analysis.

- Pope Pius X issued a harsh condemnation of modernism.

- Modern methods of Scripture study were given official endorsement by Pope Pius XII in 1943.

Prayer

God has created me to do Him some definite service.
God has committed some work to me that has not
been committed to another.
I am a link in a chain, a bond of connection between
persons. God has not created me for nothing. I shall
do His work. I shall be a messenger of peace, a
preacher of truth . . . . if I keep God's commands.

Cardinal John Newman

Discussion Questions

1. Comte's theory of history is used in the chapter as an example of the thinking of the times. What was Comte's view of the place of religion in modern society?

2. What were the methods used by Protestant and rationalist scholars in their study of Scripture? What new conclusions did people draw during the nineteenth century, as a result of their using such methods?

3. What is fundamentalism? Why can it be said that fundamentalism was a reaction against the new methods of interpretation?

St. Margaret Mary Alacoque

Chapter Thirty-Seven

Forms of Catholic Spirituality in Recent Centuries

Spiritual Development

Like Christians in all ages of history, Catholics in modern times developed their own distinctive ways of expressing their faith in God. And like spirituality in every age, modern Catholic spirituality developed in response to, at times in reaction against, tendencies within the world in which Christians lived.

The centuries that followed the Reformation were characterized by growing rationalism, which culminated in the self-conscious rationalism of the philosophes of eighteenth-century France. Catholic intellectuals were no exception to this trend, but popular spirituality reacted against rationalism by an appeal to the heart.

The centuries that followed the Reformation were characterized by growing rationalism.

Popular spirituality reacted against rationalism by an appeal to the heart.

The two new religious orders that sprang up in the eighteenth century were typical of the religious sentiments of the times. The **Passionists,** founded by St. Paul of the Cross in 1730, focused upon the Passion of Christ. Embracing both the contemplative and the active life, Passionist priests promoted reflection upon the Lord's suffering as a means of drawing the minds of people away from sin, and leading them to perfection. Members of the order gave retreats and worked within parishes on a temporary basis whenever asked.

Passionists—a religious order founded by St. Paul of the Cross, which focused upon the Passion of Christ.

Redemptorists—order of
missionary priests
founded by St.
Alphonsus Liguori.

The order of missionary priests known as the **Redemptorists** was begun by St. Alphonsus Liguori, one of the Doctors of the Church, in 1732. Their chief labors, even up to the present day, have been missionary work and retreats, and their order requires that on any retreat, they preach one sermon on prayer and another about the intercession of the Blessed Virgin Mary. In parishes run by the Redemptorists, devotion to the Holy Family also is encouraged.

Church leaders in Cincinnati appealed to Rome in 1828 for asistance in spreading the faith in America, and the Redemptorists were chosen for the task. Their original missionary efforts were among the Caucasians and Indians of Michigan and Ohio, but since that time the order has spread to all parts of the United States. John Neumanns, a Redemptorist, was the second American Catholic to be declared a saint by the Church.

Sacred Heart

Appeal "to the heart" was quite literally the case in devotion to the Sacred Heart of Jesus, which has been an important element in Catholic spirituality from the eighteenth century up to recent times. During the latter part of the seventeenth century, St. Margaret Mary Alacoque reported that the Lord himself had instructed her, in a vision, to recommend devotion to the Sacred Heart of His glorified body; the faithful could expect amazing rewards for carrying out and propagating this new devotion. During the eighteenth century, the Sacred Heart became a powerful symbol of Christ's divine and human love for humankind. A feast day in honor of the Sacred Heart was approved as early as 1765, and made part of the Church's official calendar of feasts by Pius IX in 1856. Leo XIII dedicated the entire world to the Sacred Heart, and the most recent official endorsement of this very

During the eighteenth
century, the Sacred
Heart became a
powerful symbol of
Christ's divine and
human love for
humanity.

popular devotion came from Pope Pius XII in 1956; devotion to the Sacred Heart of Jesus continues to be an important element in the faith of many Catholics.

Devotion to the Sacred Heart continues to be an important element in the faith of many Catholics.

Blessed Mother

Veneration of the Virgin Mary, so prominent during the Middle Ages, all but disappeared in most Protestant Churches, but continued to be widespread among Anglican and Catholic Christians. In the Catholic Church, the attachment to the Blessed Mother has taken many different forms. America during the twentieth century, for example, was the home of the family rosary movement, which prevailed until the time of the Second Vatican Council; families made a pledge to pray the rosary together every night for a period of one year. In Europe during the nineteenth century, an icon of Mary, called "Our Lady of Perpetual Help," was associated with the performance of miracles. Pius IX, in 1866, placed the icon of Our Lady of Perpetual Help in the Redemptorist church in Rome, and since that time the Redemptorists have furthered devotion to Our Lady.

Veneration of the Virgin Mary all but disappeared in most Protestant Churches, but continued to be widespread among Anglican and Catholic Christians.

While the intellectual leaders of the Catholic Church were debating with rationalist philosophers about the relative merits of faith and reason, the faith of the common people within the Church was being inspired by miraculous appearances of the Virgin. From all over Europe, particularly during the nineteenth century, came reports that the Blessed Mother had appeared to peasant farmers, little children, sisters in convents. Bernadette Soubirous of Lourdes, France, claimed, for example, to have been visited on eighteen different occasions during 1858. Naturally, Bernadette's story met with skepticism; but after the seventeenth visit, this humble peasant girl announced that Our Lady had promised to give a sign of her presence whereupon, in the presence of Bernadette and

While the intellectual leaders of the Catholic Church were debating with rationalist philosophers about the relative merits of faith and reason, the faith of the common people within the Church was being inspired by miraculous appearances of the Virgin.

many curious onlookers, a spring of water suddenly gushed out of the earth where there had been no water before. The pool at that spot has since become one of the most famous pilgrimage shrines in Europe, and water from the pool has been known to heal sick and crippled people in numerous documented cases.

In response to the astonishing events at Lourdes and elsewhere, Church officials have maintained a policy of caution. It was announced that the private messages given to Bernadette at Lourdes and to three other children at Fatima, Portugal contained nothing which contradicted orthodox teachings. In 1951, however, an official pronouncement from Cardinal Ottaviani of the Holy Office in Rome discouraged excessive enthusiasm for alleged apparitions of the Virgin, some of which clearly were not genuine.

Liturgical Spirituality

Liturgy—From the Greek meaning "the work of the people," it refers to the Church's communal worship, especially in the Eucharistic celebration.

In contrast to the enthusiasm for apparitions were the quiet developments in the field of liturgical spirituality. **Liturgy** (from the Greek, meaning "the work of the people") refers to the Church's communal worship, especially in the Eucharistic celebration. The rise of historical scholarship in Europe inspired a small group of monks to study the history of the Church's worship, and to restore traditional forms that had fallen into disuse. They promoted a return to the use of Gregorian chant in the monasteries, and their cause was taken up by Pope Pius X. Chant had been used in recitation of the Divine Office, and Pius not only created a Pontifical Institute of Sacred Music to further the restoration of chant, but also revised the Breviary and even recommended teaching Gregorian chant to the laity. For approximately fifty years, until the 1960s, Catholics were taught chants, such as

the beautiful "Dies Irae" ("Day of Wrath")
which traditionally was sung at the conclusion
of funeral Masses.

At the same time, there was a movement to
restore ancient forms of the Eucharistic
liturgy. Reading such sources as St. Hippolytus
of Rome and St. Justin Martyr, a small number
of people called for a return to a greater
emphasis upon congregational participation in
the Eucharist, after the model of the early
Church.

There was a movement
to restore ancient
forms of the
Eucharistic liturgy.

On this question as well, it was Pius X who
gave his blessing to the new emphasis upon
the ancient tradition; he encouraged further
study of the early practices. Pius' greatest
desire was to promote frequent reception of
Communion, which besides having been
common in ancient times had been
recommended by the Council of Trent. Along
the same lines, in 1910 he urged that the age
for first reception of Holy Communion should
be lowered from the age of twelve to
approximately seven. Legend has it that while
celebrating Mass one day, the pope held a
consecrated wafer in front of a seven-year-old
boy and asked him what he saw. "It is the
Body of Our Lord," came the response, and
upon hearing this the pontiff placed the Host
on the youngster's tongue, and initiated
change in practices soon afterward.

Pius X's greatest desire
was to promote
frequent reception of
Communion, which
had been
recommended by the
Council of Trent.

Advocates of liturgical reform grew in
numbers during the first half of the twentieth
century, and lobbied for sweeping changes in
Eucharistic worship. Virtually all their
proposals were adopted at the Second Vatican
Council, and the Roman Rite that had been
developed after the Council of Trent was
replaced by the "Novus Ordo," the New Order
of the Mass.

Advocates of liturgical
reform grew in
numbers during the
first half of the
twentieth century.

The altar now has been moved closer to the
people, and the priest says the Mass while
facing the people rather than with his back to

the congregation. Altar rails have been removed from many churches, and new guidelines in church architecture call for designs that enhance the sense of communal worship. The Mass is said in the language of the people, rather than in Latin, and the call for congregational singing in vernacular languages has forced Catholic Christians to borrow hymns from the Protestant Churches (as most traditional Catholic hymns were written to be sung in Latin) or attempt to write new liturgical music. Liturgical ministers, notably lectors and cantors, have been introduced in imitation of ancient practice, and two of the four versions of the Eucharistic Prayer are taken directly from ancient texts.

The intention behind these and other changes is to enhance the faithful's participation in the Eucharistic celebration. In the Tridentine Mass, the acolyte (altar boy) assumed the role of the congregation in making prayer-responses, while the people in the church looked on or prayed the rosary in silence. Not surprisingly, the transition to the New Order of the Mass has proved difficult for many, but as the Church grows more comfortable with the changes, liturgical prayer will most likely assume ever greater importance in twentieth-century Catholic spirituality.

Summary

• Spirituality during this period was characterized by an appeal to the heart.

• Devotion to the Sacred Heart of Jesus and to the Blessed Virgin accelerated during this time.

• Christians were being inspired by reports of appearances of the Blessed Virgin.

• Efforts were made to develop liturgical spirituality.

Prayer

O Heart of Love, I put all my trust in you; for I fear all things from my own weakness, but I hope for all things from your goodness.

St. Margaret Mary Alacoque

Discussion Questions

1. What was the common people's emphasis that differed from the intellectuals' emphasis, regarding religion?

2. Use the story of Lourdes or Fatima as an example of the Catholic enthusiasm of the times.

3. What is the basic aim of the new Mass that came out of Vatican II?

Pope John XXIII

Chapter Thirty-Eight

The Second Vatican Council

Secularism

In 1959, when Pope John XXIII first announced his intention to call a general council, he was speaking to a Church that had been at odds with the emerging secular values of the Western world for more than two hundred years. In this situation, there were both challenges and opportunities for Christianity. On the one hand, the Catholic Church was historically linked to the civilization of the West. Could Christianity free itself to become a truly global Church, not tied to a civilization that was giving away its leadership of the world?

On the other hand, the peoples of Europe and the United States were still the most highly educated and technologically advanced peoples of the world, and the Church during the past two hundred years had generally divorced itself from the intellectual experiments of Western humanity. Since the time of Leo XIII, for example, Catholic thought had been dominated by a revival of the philosophy of Thomas Aquinas; would it be possible to preserve what was sound in that tradition while reaching out to profit from the best insights of the modern arts and sciences?

When Pope John XXIII announced his intention to call a general council, he was speaking to a Church that had been at odds with the emerging secular values of the Western world for more than two hundred years.

Catholic intellectuals who surveyed the wreckage of the West during the decade following World War II were unanimous in the opinion that secularism, which had been the theory of relatively few philosophers in 1750, had become part of the very fabric of society by 1950.

The Catholic intellectuals who surveyed the wreckage of the West during the decade following World War II were virtually unanimous in the opinion that secularism, which had been the theory of relatively few philosophers in 1750, had become part of the very fabric of society by 1950. The officially sanctioned barbarism in Nazi Germany and the "win at any cost" policies of all the warring nations since 1914 were signs that the Christians would have to brace themselves for life in a world that denied their own deepest values. In the words of one German Jesuit theologian,

> *As the benefits of Revelation disappear even more from the coming world, man will truly learn what it means to be cut off from Revelation. . . .The last decades have suggested what life without Christ really is. The last decades were only the beginning.*[1]

Yet this situation might also provide new opportunity to proclaim the message of Christ. After World War I, for example, no one seriously upheld the nineteenth century's extreme confidence in inevitable progress toward an ideal future. The technological genius of humanity could as easily be turned toward destruction of human life as toward improvement of life. In other words, the limitations of a secularist view of life were becoming more evident to all. It seemed possible, then, that a reformed and renewed Christian Church could once again win converts to its gospel of love and hope, much as it had been done in early times.

1. Monsignor Romano Guardini, S. J., *The End of the Modern World*, trans. by Joseph Theman and Herbert Burke (Chicago: Henry Regnery Co., 1968 [1956], pp. 123–124). Guardini's thesis is that modern civilization is passing away, and a new era in history is just beginning. The nineteenth century, for all its anti-Christian pronouncements, was still at least habitually Christian, but the twentieth century is giving birth to the first truly secular culture in history.

A New View of Church

The three thousand bishops who assembled for the four sessions of the Second Vatican Council, between 1962 and 1965, were acutely aware of the gravity and the complexity of the questions that they faced. The very process of decision-making at the Council reflected their attitude. The First Vatican Council, in 1870, had been dominated by the personality of Pius IX; but at Vatican II, Pope John XXIII and his successor, Paul VI, made a point of encouraging all of the assembled bishops to lend their insights from their widely varying experiences in all parts of the world. The bishops, in turn, each brought a theologian to the Council as a consultant on technical points of doctrine. Protestant leaders were also invited to observe the deliberations by the bishops, and their commentaries were added to some editions of the Council's documents.

Vatican II issued sixteen documents in all, of which *Lumen Gentium* ("Light of All Peoples," on the nature of the Church) and *Gaudium et Spes* ("Joy and Hope," on the Church's reflections about the modern world) are generally considered the most important. *Gaudium et Spes* was drafted during the third session, and was given the status of a "declaration," which means that it was a reflection upon contemporary culture that might be subject to revision over the years as the culture itself underwent change. *Lumen Gentium* is a "dogmatic constitution," which is to say that it is an official statement about fundamental teachings.

Lumen Gentium was the product of lengthy deliberations over three separate sessions, and touched upon the subject matter of all the other documents that focused upon individual issues. It portrayed the Church as God's means of carrying on the redemptive work of Christ;

The First Vatican Council, in 1870, had been dominated by the personality of Pius IX, but at Vatican II, Pope John XXIII and his successor, Paul VI, made a point of encouraging all of the assembled bishops to lend their insights from their widely varying experiences in all parts of the world.

Protestant leaders were invited to observe the deliberations by the bishops, and their commentaries were added to some editions of the council's documents.

a sign of Christ, at the same time God's means of communicating with humanity, and humanity's means of communicating with God. *Lumen Gentium* expressed this mystery by identifying the Church with Christ's own Kingdom:

> *To carry out the will of the Father, Christ inaugurated the Kingdom of Heaven on earth and revealed to us the mystery of the Father. By his obedience he brought about redemption. The Church, or, in other words, the Kingdom of Christ now present in mystery, grows visibly in the world through the power of God.*[2]

The other vision of Church that was presented in the document was that of unity. **Lumen Gentium** described the Church as a "sacrament of unity and love for the world," humankind's chief means to achieving unity of all peoples. This vision was the theoretical basis for ideas found in other documents, such as that on the liturgy, that called for changes in Catholic worship that were intended to draw all the people of God together in the spirit of community.[3]

Lumen Gentium— Encyclical issued during the Second Vatican Council on the nature of the Church.

An equally momentous application of the ideal of unity was the *Decree on Ecumenism* that called for dialogue among Catholic, Protestant, and Greek Orthodox Christians.

Ecumenism—means "worldwide;" derived from the Greek word for family.

Ecumenism

An equally momentous application of the ideal of unity was the *Decree on Ecumenism* that called for dialogue among Catholic, Protestant, and Greek Orthodox Christians. The word **ecumenism,** meaning "worldwide" and derived from the Greek word for "family," had gained importance for Protestants during

2. *Lumen Gentium*, article 3, in Walter M. Abbott, S. J., ed. *The Documents of Vatican II* (New York: The American Press, 1966). All subsequent citations from Vatican II documents are taken from this edition, which is the standard English-language version of the documents of the Council.

3. *Constitution on the Sacred Liturgy,* art. 1: "It is the goal of this most sacred Council . . . to nurture whatever can contribute to the unity of all who believe in Christ, . . ."

the twentieth century. Leaders of each
Protestant Church, looking at the secular
world around them, recognized the need to
emphasize the brotherhood of all Christians,
regardless of differences of belief. This
conviction led to the formation of the World
Council of Churches at the conclusion of
World War II. Catholics, meanwhile, had not
taken part in the ecumenical movement. Every
year Catholics prayed for eight days during
the month of January on behalf of Christian
unity, but their foremost hope was that
Protestant Christians would return to the
Catholic Church.

Vatican II restated traditional Catholic belief
that the Catholic Church alone possesses the
fullness of the means of salvation, but added
many new sentiments that took the world by
surprise. The introduction to the *Decree on
Ecumenism*, for example, stated that God, with
providential wisdom, " . . . has begun to
bestow more generously upon divided
Christians remorse over their divisions and a
longing for unity." By its very nature, the
Council fathers urged, the Church ought to be
a sign of the loving unity of the Trinity; but
this essential quality of the Church was lost
during the Protestant Reformation—with
people on both sides sharing blame for the
division. The *Decree* then called for dialogue
between divided Christians, and for
recognition by Catholics that the essential
elements of Christian faith are very much
alive in the Churches outside the Roman
Catholic community. The new view presented
in the *Decree of Ecumenism* has indeed been put
into practice since Vatican II, as Catholic
representatives have been in frequent and
generally warm dialogue with Protestant and
Greek Orthodox leaders.

Endorsement of ecumenism by the Catholic
Church was material for newspaper headlines
all over the world; Vatican II's decrees were
seen as a turning-point in the history of

> Vatican II restated
> traditional Catholic
> belief that the Catholic
> Church alone
> possesses the fullness
> of the means of
> salvation.

> Endorsement of
> ecumenism by the
> Catholic Church was
> material for newspaper
> headlines all over the
> world.

417

Christianity. *Gaudium et Spes* prompted a similar reaction, as for the first time the Church officially praised many developments in modern culture. The document emerged out of heated debate between the bishops who desired to maintain the Church's sharply critical stance toward the developments of the past two hundred years, and those who sought more dialogue between the Church and the world; to a large degree, proponents of dialogue prevailed. *Gaudium et Spes* was, for example, full of praise for modern achievements in the fields of science, technology, and historical scholarship.

Gaudium et Spes

But the document was far from an endorsement of secularism; the contrary is true. Typical of the ideas in *Gaudium et Spes* was the discussion of science. By its nature, the bishops declared, science places exclusive emphasis upon observable data (such as, statistical evidence or the data from experiments), and maintains a kind of agnosticism, or habitual doubt, about everything else. This is entirely appropriate to the nature of scientific research, but should not become the rule of the thumb for all quests for the truth: " . . . The danger exists that humanity, confiding too much in modern (scientific) discoveries, may even think that they are sufficient unto themselves and no longer seek any higher realities."[4]

Vatican II advanced the view that the Church has a responsibility to oversee the results of humanity's physical and intellectual endeavors, building upon humanity's achievements and promoting the good that it sees in new developments. Its primary function is to be the chief speaker for human values, which at times are threatened by the

4. *Gaudium et Spes*, Art. 33.

changes that technology brings about. New developments in the technology of transportation and communication, for instance, have made the world a global community, and it is the responsibility of Christians to further the ideal of community among all persons, and speak against threats to that community, such as war and economic exploitation.

Most essentially, *Gaudium et Spes*[5] portrayed the Christian Church as the foremost protector of the belief in human dignity. Because each person has a spiritual and immortal soul, and a destiny beyond earthly life, it is not appropriate to treat any person as a "speck of nature or a nameless constituent of the city of man."[6] Vatican II looked to the Christian laypeople as apostles, the most effective advocates of truly human values in the world. Their commitment to eternal life with God, and their trust in a loving God, gave them a unique perspective upon human life, and this perspective motivates them to address the world's problems squarely.

> By contrast, when a divine substructure and the hope of life eternal are wanting (lacking), man's dignity is most grievously lacerated, as current events often attest. The riddles of life and death, of guilt and of grief go unresolved, with the frequent result that men succumb to despair.[7]

The Church, then, is the "light of nations" when its children serve the world while not becoming slaves to the world.

Gaudium et Spes— portrayed the Christian Church as the foremost protector of the belief in human dignity.

5. Along with *Dignitatis Humanae*, the decree on religious freedom.

6. *Gaudium et Spes*. art. 14. The statement is a clear criticism of materialist conceptions of humanity that prevail in, but are not necessarily limited to totalitarian nations. The term "city of man" is borrowed from St. Augustine.

7. *Gaudium et Spes*, art. 21.

Vatican II raised many questions in the hope that Catholic Christians would look at their own faith in a new light.

Vatican II raised many questions in the hope that Catholic Christians would look at their own faith in a new light. *Lumen Gentium* encouraged the Church to reflect upon itself, while *Gaudium et Spes* encouraged the Church to reflect upon the world. Since 1965, Catholic and Protestant intellectuals have written hundreds of articles and books in response to the Council's many teachings, and many changes—notably in modes of worship—have caused a great stir in the Church. It will be many years before the implications of the teachings of the Second Vatican Council can be assessed with confidence.

Summary

• Secularism had become part of the very fabric of society.

• Pope John XXIII called a general council to bring about renewal and reform in the Church.

• The chief work of *Lumen Gentium* was to define the Church itself.

• The Second Vatican Council called for ecumenism.

• *Gaudium et Spes* portrayed the Christian Church as the protector of the belief in human dignity.

Prayer

*O Child Jesus, grant that we may share in the
profound mystery of Christmas. Fill their hearts
with the peace they sometimes seek so desperately
and that you alone can give. Help them to know
one another better and to live as brothers and
sisters.*

*Reveal to them your beauty, holiness, and purity.
Awaken love and gratitude for your infinite
goodness. Join them together in your love.*

Pope John XXIII

Discussion Questions

1. Explain why, in the eyes of some Catholic
   thinkers, the times after World War II
   amounted to a new opportunity for the
   Church, but also a new challenge.

2. Name the most important document from
   Vatican II, the one that inspired many of
   the others. What was the subject of this
   document?

3. What is ecumenism, and what efforts have
   begun in response to the *Decree of
   Ecumenism?*

4. Look at the discussion of *On Christian
   Doctrine* in chapter eight, or the discussion
   of the Lateran Councils in chapter
   eighteen. How can it be said that *Gaudium
   et Spes* called the Church to do what it had
   done many times in the past?

Glossary

Adoptionism—Theory that Jesus had so thoroughly identified himself with God's will that God raised him up to divine status, presumably at the time of Jesus' resurrection.

Amen—Hebrew word for "so be it."

Anabaptists—Rejected infant baptism in favor of adult baptism.

Anti-popes—False claimants to the Holy See. Usually, supported by (1) dissident groups of the faithful or clergy; (2) political, schismatic, or heretical groups; or (3) the ruling barons or kings who demanded the right of investiture.

Apostasy—A Christian's denial of belief in Jesus.

Arianism—Theory that claimed that the opening words of the Gospel of John, "In the beginning was the Word," indicated that Jesus was created by God in the beginning; all other things were created after the Word, so that Jesus, in effect, was an exalted being who was neither fully divine nor fully human.

Asceticism—Abstinence from physical pleasures.

"Assembly of Jerusalem"—Leaders of the Christian movement met to discuss whether or not Gentiles should be circumcised.

Beguines—A group that pledged themselves to a life of poverty, prayer, and simplicity.

Brethren of Common Life—Although they did not take vows, these laymen lived in community and preached spiritual regeneration to their fellow laypeople; they offered low-cost education to many young persons.

Breviary—Divine Office, the cycle of prayers based on the pslams, which had been developed by the medieval monks.

Canon—The collection of books acknowledged and accepted by the Church to have been inspired.

Canons—Small groups, similar to monastic communities, assigned to service a cathedral Church, who live off of a modest income provided by the Church.

Cardinal—A special assistant to the pope.

Catechism of the Council of Trent—Succinctly summarized Catholic doctrine.

Catechumen—A person accepted into a three-year program of instruction before becoming a Christian.

Cathars—Gnostic dualists who, like the Gnostics of old times, were very numerous and offered an entire Church that paralleled the established Church.

Catholic—Means universal.

Celibacy—A life of abstention from sexual relationships.

Christendom—Christ's domain, as Europe came to be called.

Christology—The study of the nature of Christ.

Christos—The Greek equivalent to the Hebrew word *Messiah*.

Conciliarism—The call for the Church to be ruled by general councils rather than by popes.

Concupiscence—A general inclination of humans toward sin.

Confessional—A small two-chambered room in which the penitent spoke to the priest through a screen, and could remain anonymous.

Confessor—A priest who hears a person's confession and acts as counselor or spiritual guide.

Corpus Iuris Civili—Compilation of ancient Roman law, plus commentaries upon the law.

Council at Chalcedon—Council held in 451 that established the definition of the Creed that Christians have accepted up to the present.

Council at Constantinople—Council held in 381 that reaffirmed the teaching from Nicea, refined the wording of the Creed to eliminate possible Arian interpretations, and added several lines about the Holy Spirit, to advance the Christian belief in God as Trinity: one God, three Persons in God.

Council of Nicea—The first general, worldwide council in the history of Christianity. Called by
Constantine.

Council of Pisa—General council called in 1409 at which the two acting popes were deposed and
Alexander V was elected as pope. But because the two deposed popes refused to step down the end effect of the Council of Pisa was the existence of three separate popes.

Council of Trent—Verified the differences between Catholic and Protestant belief; Original Sin affects humanity, but humanity is perfectible in spite of Original Sin; humanity is saved by God's grace, but freely cooperates with grace; faith in God must be accompanied by good works that can sanctify.

Creed—Derived from the Latin word *credo,* which means "I believe."

Crozier—A bishop's pastoral staff, which is still used today during ceremonies.

Cruciform—In the shape of a cross.

Decius' Law—Called for Roman citizens to obtain a paper which certified that they had sacrificed to the gods.

Deism—Belief in an impersonal Supreme Being.

Depravity—Belief that humanity has been thoroughly corrupted by sin, and can do no good.

Diderot—Editor of the world's first encyclopedia; believed in power of education to overcome all human evil.

Diuturnum—Pope Leo XIII's encyclical contending that all political authority comes from God and, therefore, revolution against a legitimate ruler could not be condoned by the Church, at the same time acknowledging that the people have the right to choose their own leaders.

Divine Office—A cycle of prayers based on the psalms.

Docetism—Doctrine established by some of the Gnostics proposing that Jesus was God, and only appeared to be human. Like many ideas from Gnosticism, it was rejected as heresy.

Dominicans—Preaching order that adhered to a simple rule and lived a life of voluntary poverty.

Donation of Constantine—A forged document, supposedly written by Emperor Constantine, that strengthened the popes' claims to be political as well as spiritual leaders in Rome.

Easter Vigil—The night before Easter morning during which the joyous Christian catechumens were initiated into the Church.

Ecclesiastical—An English word derived from the Greek word *ecclesia* meaning Church.

Ecumenism—Means "worldwide"; derived from the Greek word for family.

Edict of Milan—Edict issued by Constantine that recognized Christianity as a religion and granted Christians the right to practice their religion.

Ekklesia—A Greek word meaning "assembly" specifically referred in Greek society to the assembly of those who had privileged status. St. Paul's borrowing of the term reflected his belief that all members of the Church community were endowed with special dignity.

Encyclical—Official letter to the faithful written by the pope.

Enlightenment—Secular thinkers who followed the "light" out of the darkness of superstition and faith.

Epicurean—Group of philosophers who believed that all good and evil in life takes the form of pleasure and pain, and that once a person dies, he or she cannot feel either pleasure or pain and, therefore, death is nothing to fear.

Epistle—Letter contained in the New Testament written by the apostles and disciples to the early Church.

Eucharist—Taken from the Greek word *Eucharistia* meaning "thanksgiving."

Evangelists—Authors of the four Gospels.

Excommunication—The act of excluding a person from the Christian community, and depriving that person of the sacraments.

Fathers—Saintly men from early times whose teachings have influenced Christian doctrine over the centuries.

Flagellation—Whipping oneself as an act of self-discipline and penance.

Flying Buttress—A stone pillar, separate from the building, that supported the weight of the roof.

Franciscans—Order that lived a life of voluntary poverty and renunciation of all worldly goods.

Fundamentalism—Belief in literal, factual accuracy of Scripture.

Gallicanism—France's version of the common European belief that each century's Church should be ruled by its bishops, with little papal influence.

Gnostics—People who claimed to have secret knowledge that would bring salvation to themselves alone.

Gospel—Means "Good News."

Grace—A gift from God, which deepens our relationship with Him.

Graeco-Roman—Anything based on Greek/Roman culture.

Gregorian Chant—A special form of music used by the monks to recite their poetic prayers.

Hagiography—A biography of saints.

Heresy—The denial or doubt by a baptized person of any truth revealed by God and proposed for belief by the Catholic Church.

Hermit—A particular type of monk, who lived in solitude.

Host—The consecrated Body of Christ.

Huguenots—French followers of the Calvinism doctrine.

Immortale Dei—Encyclical by Leo XIII that addressed the proper relationship between Church and state.

Index—List of books considered to be dangerous for Catholics to read.

Indulgence—A belief that, for having performed a good work, one would be freed from time in purgatory.

Inquisition—The investigation and sentencing of persons professing heresy or accused of heresy.

Interdict—Deprives the faithful of certain spiritual benefits but permits them to remain in the communion of the Church.

Jansenism—Belief that salvation was for the chosen few; denied humanity's ability to resist temptation; opposed frequent reception of Communion; only people with perfect contrition could receive penance.

Jean-Jacques Rousseau—The forefather of modern people who, not satisfied with the Christian meaning of hope, looked to political power as the one means of reaching a better future for all of humanity.

Jihad—The "holy war" of the Moslems, to bring new territories under Islam.

Legate—A representative sent out by the pope.

Liberalism—Belief that individuals should have the right to believe and behave as they choose, so long as they harm no one.

Liturgy—From the Greek meaning "the work of the people," it refers to the Church's communal worship, especially in the Eucharistic celebration.

Lumen Gentium—Encyclical issued during the Second Vatican Council on the nature of the Church.

Martyr—A person who accepts torture or death rather than give up his or her faith.

Marxism—Belief in collective ownership of all goods by all people.

Messiah—The anointed One whom God would send to liberate the chosen people.

Missal—Contained all portions of the new, standardized Trientine Mass.

Modernism—Heresy that claimed the Bible and the Church laws had to be reinterpreted for each age in history.

Monasticism—A way of life in community characterized by prayer and self-denial.

Monotheism—Belief that there is just one God.

Monstrance—An ornate display case for carrying the sacred Host in Corpus Christi processions.

Nepotism—The practice of giving employment to one's relatives.

Oratory of Divine Love—A group that began in southern Europe about 1500 and served as a support group for people engaged in the work of reform.

Order—A group of people living the same kind of life under the same rule.

Orthodoxy—The Church's official teaching on a fundamental belief.

Paganism—Religions characterized by idol worship, polytheism, and the offering of sacrifices to the gods.

Parousia—The second coming of Christ.

Passionists—Religious order founded by St. Paul of the Cross, which focused on the Passion of Christ.

Patriarch—The bishop, or father figure, of a great Christian city.

Pax Romana—Period of peace, 30 B.C.E. to ca. 180 C.E., during which missionaries, such as St. Paul, spread their message.

Pelagianism—Rejected the idea that Adam's Original Sin was inherited by all of humankind.

Pentateuch—First five books of the Old Testament.

Petronius—An official of the imperial government who wrote *Satyricon* to poke fun at the powerful elite in Rome.

Philosopher—One who speculated about the meaning of life.

Philosophes—Secular thinkers who believed that anyone who did not subscribe to their values did not deserve to be called a philosopher.

Pilgrimage—A physical journey to a shrine which represented a spiritual journey toward God.

Pluralism—The practice of some bishops, who ruled several sees at the same time, to collect the revenues from each without giving them any pastoral attention.

Polytheism—Belief in many gods.

Poor Clares—An order of women dedicated to prayer and the simple life.

Predestination—Some people are predetermined to be saved by God.

Providence—The idea that a loving God watches over the events of people's lives.

Purgatory—According to tradition, upon a person's death he or she undergoes purgation, or cleansing from sin, prior to being united with God.

Puritans—English Calvinists who put great stress on moral discipline and the primacy of Scripture.

Redemptorists—Order of missionary priests founded by St. Alphonsus Liguori.

Relic—Any physical object believed to have spiritual power.

Religious Syncretism—A minimizing of differences between religions.

Renaissance—Period of radical changes in the intellectual, artistic, political, social, and even
geographical structure of Christian civilization.

Rerum Novarum—Encyclical by Pope Leo XIII establishing the Church as the protector of the poor and powerless in society.

Revelation—God reveals Himself to His people especially through the words of prophets and wisemen.

Rigorists—Those who preferred to preserve the purity of the Church at all costs.

Sabellianism—Theory that Father, Son, and Spirit were just different "energies" or "modes" of one God.

Sacerdotal—Dominated by priests.

Schism—A deep division or split.

Secularism—The tendency to reason about the world, about humanity, and even about God with no reference to Christian revelation.

Simony—The buying or selling of religious offices or services.

St. Anthony—Father of monasticism.

Stoics—Group of philosophers who taught that the goal of life was to seek inner calm.

Summa Theologiae—Common handbook of Catholic theology written by St. Thomas Aquinas.

Syllabus of Errors—Summary of the ideas in the encyclical letters of Pope Pius IX.

Synod—Synonym for "council."

Theatine Order—A group of priests in Italy who maintained normal roles as pastors while subjecting themselves to rigorous personal discipline.

Trivium—Group of three subjects—grammar, rhetoric, and dialectic (logic)—that formed the basis of the Seven Liberal Arts.

Truce of God—Pope Urban II's decree that warfare was unlawful except on Mondays, Tuesdays, and Wednesdays, and fighting was forbidden everyday during Advent, Lent, and Easter.

Ultramontanism—The pope is supreme head of the Church, with even more authority than the general council.

Usary—Loaning money for a fee; this practice was condemned as a denial of Christian charity.

Voltaire—The spiritual forefather of all modern people who have despaired of society and have chosen just to "tend their garden."

Vulgate—St. Jerome's Latin translation of the Bible.

Waldensians—A group founded by Peter Waldo that preached the gospel of poverty and, eventually, rejection of the authority of the Church.

Index

G

H

I

Melanchthon, Philip, 270, 321
Mennonites, 280–81, 306
Messiah, 16, 18, 19
Methodist Church, 307, 330
Middle Ages, 123
Milton, John, 330
Missal, 323
missionary activity, 120, 121, 334–35
Mithras, 10
modernism, 400
monastic movement, 101, 105
monastic reform, 150–52
monotheism, 16
monasticism, 106–9
monophysitism, 77
monstrance, 208
Moses, 16, 179
Munzer, Thomas, 277
murder, 98

N

natural law, 181, 358
Nazarenes, 15
nepotism, 149
Nero, 63, 128
Nestorianism, 77
Newman, John Henry, 395
Neumanns, John, St., 406
Newton, Isaac, 353
New Testament, 17, 41, 50, 256
Nicene Creed, 76
Nicholas II, Pope, 155
Nicholas V, Pope, 245, 259

O

Old Testament, 17, 22, 50
Orders, 152
Original Sin, 138, 264, 322
orthodoxy, 52
Osiris, 33
Otto von Bismarck (Chancellor of Germany), 377

P

Pachomius, 107
paganism, 5, 6

rosary movement, 407
Roman law, 180
Roman Catholicism, 114

S

sacraments, 322
Sacrifice, 7, 62, 140
sacrificial meal, 7
Sabellianism, 74
Sadducees, 15
Sadoleto, Jacopo, Bishop, 319
salvation, 227, 264
scholasticism, 195
Scriptures, 50, 197
secularism, 355, 414, 418
Seymour, Jane, 296
Simeon Stylites, 107
Simmons, Menno, 280
Simon the Zealot, 33
simony, 149, 154, 162, 184
sin, 101, 311
socialism, 387–88
Solomon, 16, 137
Soubirous, Bernadette, 407
Spanish Armada, 332
Stephen, St., 21
Stephen II, Pope, 173
Stoics, 10
Strauss, David Friedrich, 398
Summa Theologica, 200, 323
synod, 153

T

tacitus, 63
Teilhard de Chardin, Pierre, 396
Temple, 15, 21
Ten Commandments, 16, 98
Teresa of Avila, St., 330
Tertullian, 86, 99
Tetzel, John, 265
Theodosius, 67
theology, 194
Thirty Years' War, 352
Thomas More, St., 296–97
Thomas, St. (apostle), 33
Thomas Aquinas, St., 199–201

Thor, 119
Titus, 21
Tudor, Mary, 299
Triduum, 194
Truce of God, 185
ultramontanism, 372–73
uniformity, 373
United Church of Christ, 307
unity of all Christians, 417
unity in Church, 416
Urban II, Pope, 185, 211
Urban VI, Pope, 243
usary, 185

V

Valentinian III, (Emperor of Rome), 130
Valerian, 64
Vandals, 117
Vatican II documents, 415, 416, 418–20
Vespasian, 21
Victor Emmanuel (King of Piedmont), 377
Vikings, 149
Vincent de Paul, St., 335–37, 342
Voltaire, 355, 361
Vulgate, 81

W

Waldensians, 229
Waldo, Peter, 228
Wesley, John, 330
western civilization, 3
Williams, Roger, 303
Wittenberg, 266
Wodin, 119
Wolsey, Thomas Cardinal, 296
World Council of Churches, 417
worship, 137, 140
Wycliffe, John 234

Z

Zacharias, Pope, 132
zealots, 15, 21
zeno, 9
Zeus, 10
Zwingli, Ulrich, 288